ABOUT FACE?

ABOUT FACE?

The United States and the United Nations

Robert W. Gregg

Lynne Rienner Publishers ■ Boulder & London

Published in the United States of America in 1993 by
Lynne Rienner Publishers, Inc.
1800 30th Street, Boulder, Colorado 80301

and in the United Kingdom by
Lynne Rienner Publishers, Inc.
3 Henrietta Street, Covent Garden, London WC2E 8LU

Library of Congress Cataloging-in-Publication Data
Gregg, Robert W.
    About face?: the United States and the United Nations / Robert W.
    Gregg.
    Includes bibliographical references and index.
    ISBN 1-55587-295-6 (cloth: alk. paper)
    ISBN 1-55587-406-1 (soft: alk. paper)
    1. United Nations—United States. 2. Intervention (International
law) 3. Iraq-Kuwait Crisis, 1990–1991. I. Title.
JX1977.2.U5G65   1993
341.23'73—dc20   93-15352
                                                          CIP

British Cataloguing in Publication Data
A Cataloguing in Publication record for this book
is available from the British Library.

Printed and bound in the United States of America

The paper used in this publication meets the requirements
of the American National Standard for Permanence of
Paper for Printed Library Materials Z39.48-1984.   ∞

For Barbara

Contents

Chapter I

Introduction

A funny thing happened on the way to the war in the Gulf in the winter of 1991: the United States rediscovered the United Nations. After many years during which it had either neglected or disparaged the United Nations and largely limited its participation to damage control, the United States could be found assiduously courting the global institution and working around the clock to build and sustain Security Council support for an international response to Iraq's invasion and annexation of Kuwait. The final balance sheet on the Gulf War has yet to be written, but it is no exaggeration to say that Operation Desert Storm, which visited such a disastrous military defeat upon Saddam Hussein, would have been a much more perilous undertaking had the UN Security Council not invoked Chapter 7 of the UN Charter in unmistakably strong language. Nor is it an exaggeration to say that the Security Council would not have embraced collective security so firmly had the United States not been prepared to assume the leadership role at the United Nations that it had all but abandoned in the 1980s.

This reassertion of US interest in and leadership of the United Nations was indeed a remarkable *volte face*, coming as it did so shortly after the United States had demonstrated its lack of confidence in the organization by systematically withholding large portions of its assessed contribution— a policy that had driven the UN to the brink of bankruptcy. Moreover, although foreign policy largely vanished as an issue during the 1992 US presidential campaign, the decision by the lame duck president, George Bush, to dispatch US troops to Somalia in support of UN humanitarian relief efforts seemed to demonstrate that the US-UN rapprochement may be more than a one-time phenomenon.

The revitalization of the United Nations in the Gulf crisis, a development that owes so much to US policy, has inspired talk that the UN may at long last be coming home to the spirit of the San Francisco conference. The Charter, it has been argued, may finally, after nearly half a century of

1

abuse and highly selective implementation, become the acceptable blueprint for world order that its framers intended. And the necessary, although arguably not the sufficient, condition for this resurgence of the United Nations is the commitment of the United States to a world order in which the UN plays a pivotal role.

But just as one swallow does not make a summer, neither does the UN response to one or two dramatic crises constitute a trend. There are, to be sure, grounds for cautious optimism. But it is possible that the pendulum of expectations may swing too far, overcorrecting for the generally negative view of the United Nations, which has been nurtured by decades of frustration and disappointment, and prematurely positing the durability of the US-UN rapprochement.

The relationship between the United States and the United Nations, now seemingly amicable and positive after reaching its nadir during the Reagan administration, has long been a stormy one.[1] And not all of the irritants that have strained that relationship over the years have been exorcised by the end of the Cold War and the success of Operation Desert Storm. Those irritants have their roots in the fact that the United States has interests and values that in the aggregate have constituted something very much like a prism through which the United States views the United Nations, the role the UN ought to play in world affairs, and how it ought to play that role. That conception of the UN has led, throughout much of the global body's existence, to expectations that have been both excessive and excessively ethnocentric. The US view of the UN—something less than an ideological position but more than a pragmatic, situationally specific one—has been the product of several assumptions. Although few of these assumptions or elements comprising the US conception of an acceptable United Nations have been truly immutable, most have changed remarkably little since the founding of the UN. Their persistence has accounted for much of US disenchantment with the global organization and for the caution voiced here regarding the second honeymoon between the United Nations and its most influential member.

The elements that comprise this more or less coherent view of the United Nations are of several kinds. Some reflect what might be termed self-image—the vision the United States has had of itself and its mission in world affairs. Others are specifically concerned with the UN itself, and with the permissible parameters of Charter interpretation. Some can best be characterized as assumptions about the way the world works or, more accurately, the way it should work. These elements overlap and interact with each other, producing a view of the UN that has been more consistent and less flexible than would be the case if they came into play separately.

In the beginning, when the United Nations was still young and largely untested, US expectations regarding the UN were relatively high and UN performance was either consistent with those expectations or not yet so far out of line with them as to foster disillusionment. But evidence that the United Nations would not function as the United States believed it should surfaced almost from the moment the global organization became operational. Although the US-UN relationship experienced its ups and downs in the years that followed, the trend line was negative. US assumptions about the United Nations—the way it should function and the results it should achieve—were contradicted with increasing frequency by events in New York and Geneva until, by the 1980s, even the pretense that the UN any longer mattered to the United States was hard to sustain.

This book is about the US conception of the United Nations, the deterioration of US support for the UN as conception and reality diverged, and the tentative restoration of US interest in and support for the UN in the early 1990s. The focus of the book involves two case studies. The first deals with the culmination of growing US frustration with the United Nations in what can only be called an orgy of UN-bashing during the 1980s, the second with the crisis in the Gulf and the attendant restoration of the UN to a position of prominence in US foreign policy. These two episodes or phases in the US-UN relationship, coming as they have one right after the other, raise the question of whether the turnabout in US policy can be attributed to fundamental changes in US assumptions and expectations regarding the UN or to the belated emergence of a UN that is more compatible with US assumptions and expectations. In either case, there is a further question: What are the prospects for the continuation and replication of the cooperation between the United States and the United Nations that was one of the distinctive features of the Gulf crisis?

Note

1. A sophisticated theoretical framework for the analysis of the changing relationships between the United States and international organizations more generally is provided in Margaret P. Karns and Karen A. Mingst, eds., *The United States and Multilateral Institutions: Patterns of Changing Instrumentality and Influence,* Boston: Unwin Hyman, 1990.

Chapter II

US Expectations Regarding
the United Nations

Like all institutions, the United Nations has been in important respects a reflection of the time when it was created. It was the product of demands made and bargains struck by those who dominated the international scene in 1945. And the one state that more than any other dominated the international scene in the closing days of World War II was, of course, the United States. No matter what the yardstick of measurement or indicator of power and influence, the United States was preeminent, and by a wide margin. Although other states played important roles in the creation of the United Nations, the Charter was very much the handiwork of the United States.

Those who represented the United States in the drafting of the Charter, those who argued the case for US ratification, and those who supported the new organization in those formative first months brought with them certain expectations—some explicit and vigorously voiced, others unstated and perhaps even unacknowledged—that constituted a rough consensus as to what the UN should be and what it should do. These people realized that the Charter was not, from the US point of view, a perfect document. But it was perceived as a reasonably accurate reflection of US interests and values, and the UN was widely viewed within the United States as an important institutional tool for the exercise of the leadership that was expected of the world's preeminent power—leadership that it was preparing to assume in a major departure from the isolationism of the prewar years.[1]

The expectations that shaped the US view of the United Nations were not only products of US predominance in a world in which all of the other would-be powers had been ravaged if not fatally weakened by the war. Nor were they merely the result of the struggle with the Axis powers, just then coming to a successful conclusion, or of troublesome differences with the Soviet Union, already looming on the horizon. Some had much deeper roots in US historical experience, although they were given a new sense of importance and urgency by the war and by an awareness of fundamental conflicts of interests and values with its communist ally. A brief survey follows, which outlines some of the more important expectations the United States had for the United Nations, together with several relevant aspects of the US national character, which would color the nation's view of the performance of the global organization.

US Hegemony

Ernst Haas has defined hegemony as "the national capability to advance long-range views of world order . . . by working with the preponderant resources available to the hegemon for the success of institutions charged with that task."[2] The United States did have long-range views of world order at the end of World War II, and it also had what must have seemed to be a preponderance of resources with which to guarantee the success of UN-system institutions created to advance those views. Whether the United States was in fact the hegemon, as opposed to a merely dominant power, is a matter social scientists have vigorously debated.[3] Most of the literature on hegemony and the theory of hegemonic stability is concerned with the dynamics of the world economy and especially with the hegemon's role in creating and supporting a free trade regime. But hegemony is more generally about governance in the international system, about power, and about leadership; if the United States was the hegemon in the period following World War II, its hegemony would presumably not be exercised selectively, but would extend to the United Nations. The creation of a stable world order required US leadership, and the United States was prepared to play that role and to assume disproportionately large costs to achieve the desired world order, at the UN as elsewhere.

The United States, of course, had very little experience with world leadership. The responsibilities of the hegemon were unfamiliar, and the burdens were unprecedented if the war effort is discounted. Although the distinction between benevolent and coercive hegemony had not been developed when the UN was launched (theorizing about hegemony was still over the horizon),[4] the United States did, however, see its leadership as benevolent. It was understood that the hegemon's task would not be an easy one, and that the United Nations could not be counted on to rubber-stamp US policies automatically. But it was assumed that US power would be fungible there as elsewhere, and that deference would be paid to a benign power and respect granted to the principal architect of the hard-won military victory and the new postwar international order. In effect, hegemony was construed to mean that the UN would be a relatively pliant instrument of US policy. It was a simple syllogism: The United States was the hegemonic power with primary responsibility for a stable world order; the United Nations was a major US-approved vehicle for achieving such a stable world order; ergo, the UN would respond to US leadership in the creation and maintenance of such a stable world order. Needless to say, such logic is badly flawed. US expectations were to be shattered early and often in the years after 1945.

The decline of the United States as hegemonic power has been the subject of much commentary. That decline has certainly had consequences for the United Nations and for other multilateral institutions, as well as for the international political economy. But what is equally important for assessment of the US view of the UN and US disaffection with the global body is the fact that, even before the beginning of that decline, the United States had realized that hegemony's costs—that is, the obligation to supply collective goods for the system disproportionately—may exceed, or be perceived to exceed, its benefits.

Congruence

During those hectic years of institution-building just prior to and immediately after the end of World War II, the United States, as principal architect, quite predictably sought institutions that would reflect US preferences and respect the realities of power in the international system. Thucydides observed more than two thousand years ago that the strong do what they can, whereas the weak do what they must. According to this logic, the United States, whether hegemon or merely the single most powerful state, could have demanded and held out for a United Nations that actually enhanced US power or, to use regime terminology, was dynamically stable. It did not do so, however, settling for what regime theorist Stephen Krasner has called congruence.[5]

According to Krasner, congruence means that "the characteristics of the regime reflect the preferences of individual states (weighted by their national power capabilities) and do not affect capabilities."[6] Desirous of legitimizing its position of dominance and confident of its capacity to control outcomes in any event, the United States constructed a UN in which power within the institution was much more equitably distributed than it was in the real world. But because its authority was so severely circumscribed, the UN could not actually diminish US power capabilities or enhance those of other states at the expense of the United States.

There are, however, two problems with congruence, or rather with the US perception of congruence. The first is that the United States expected too much of it. The UN was initially represented to the United States as "a natural organic outgrowth of America's own cherished institutions and fundamental instruments of government."[7] The United Nations, which had been tailored to US specifications, would evolve, under US guidance, in directions largely compatible with US interests and values. Congruence seemed to mean that the UN would be "our kind of place." In effect, the United States took congruence for granted as the normal and proper condition of US-UN relations.

Things did not turn out quite that way. Reflecting on his experience as US ambassador to the United Nations in the 1970s, Daniel Patrick Moynihan referred to it not as "our kind of place," but as "A Dangerous Place";[8] many others concurred. The second problem, of course, was that a UN that was congruent rather than dynamically stable was a UN that could relatively easily become incongruent if and when states began to use its egalitarian/majoritarian voting procedures to assert preferences other than those of the dominant (or hegemonic) power.

The US assumption regarding congruence subsumed a number of relatively specific expectations about the United Nations and its responsiveness to US leadership. They included support for the status quo, for the view that state consent rather than majority rule is the governing principle in UN decision-making, and for functionally specific UN system agencies, immune to politicization. It was also expected that the UN would display a preference for market as opposed to authoritative allocation and for pluralistic and democratic societies, that it would eschew radical solutions to the problems brought before it, and that it would support US efforts to contain the threat posed by international communism. Finally, the UN would be run in an efficient and frugal manner. And these expectations were intensified by certain attitudes—elements, perhaps, of the US national character.

The Status Quo

International organizations may be classified as custodians of an existing order or agents for the creation of a new order. The North Atlantic Treaty Organization (NATO), designed to protect Western Europe against possible assault from the Soviet Union, falls into the former category.[9] The European Community, with its commitment to the transformation of the economic and ultimately the political landscape of Western Europe, is the preeminent example of the second. Classifying the United Nations has posed a marginally greater challenge, but for the United States the call has not been all that difficult. In the US view, the Charter makes it quite clear that the UN was to be instrumental in preserving the new postwar status quo.

At the end of World War II, when the UN system was being created and change was in the air, the United States was not a status quo power, much less a champion of the status quo ante. But it was busily engaged in creating a world order visualized as the new (and better) status quo, and the UN was to be both an embodiment of that new order and one of its principal institutional defenders. The Charter was not, of course, so drafted as to proscribe change. That would have been both undesirable and impossible. But the UN was to operate within well-defined parameters. The contours and content of the new order were largely predetermined by the hegemonic power and its principal allies, and they wanted no part of a Charter that constituted an open-ended commitment to further change.

That Charter, for example, posed no challenge to the Westphalian system of sovereign states. Change, moreover, was channeled by Charter language which appeared to provide ample protection for the principal architects and beneficiaries of the status quo, the United States foremost among them. And even though the goals of the United Nations were essentially conservative and reformist, they were still more ambitious than the authority possessed by the UN for achieving them. The United Nations, in effect, was viewed by the United States as a forum for debating changes *within* the system, rather than changes *of* the system. In the language of regime theory, rules and procedures might be negotiable, but fundamental principles and norms are not.

The United States wanted a UN that would oil the wheels of the newly emergent world order, not one that would tear it down and build new orders. Needless to say, this view that the UN was an instrument for maintaining the status quo was not one shared by all of its members.

The Unit Veto

If the United Nations was to be a status quo organization, congruent with the preferences of the hegemon or dominant power, it followed that the decisions reached by its several organs could not be binding on the United States without its consent. Nor, for that matter, could *any* state be bound without its consent in this horizontally organized system of sovereign states. Lawrence Finkelstein has termed this a unit veto system, meaning that UN members may opt out of compliance with UN decisions, the only exceptions being those specified in the Charter, exceptions to which states have given their consent by becoming members.[10]

This was a critically important component of the US view of the United Nations. Article 27 of the Charter specifically conferred upon the United States, along with other permanent members, a veto in the Security Council on substantive matters. But in the other organs, and especially in the General Assembly, deference to the principles of egalitarianism and majoritarianism put US interests and values at risk unless a broader, more generalized veto could be asserted. So although the United States was prepared to support a Charter in which decisions were reached by voting, with each state possessing one vote and the majority prevailing, it insisted that those decisions, with a few exceptions, were to be treated merely as expressions of international sentiment unless states explicitly gave their consent to be bound by them.

As Finkelstein argued, "the norm of the international system is that the authoritative allocation of what states value . . . requires the consent of the states affected by the allocative decision."[11] The United Nations, with its exceptionally broad mandate, is concerned with the allocation of many things that states value, ranging from money to status to legitimacy, and it has from the beginning been the scene of an ongoing effort to vest more authority for the allocation of such values in the decisions of majorities. Although the United States has at times wavered in its support for the traditional norm requiring state consent (always when it has been at the vanguard of a majority on an issue about which it feels very strongly), its commitment has ultimately been to the unit veto, which constitutes both an escape hatch for the protection of interests and values it cannot persuade the majority to honor and a defense of the prerogatives of state sovereignty.

Functional Specificity

The UN system consists of the United Nations and an array of specialized agencies, another attribute of the postwar order that reflects the strong preference of the United States. A belief in functional specificity tends to be characteristic of Western societies generally. One of Talcott Parsons's pattern variables for measuring the transition from traditional to modern society is concerned with whether the society (or the polity) is functionally diffuse or functionally specific,[12] and the United States was presumably the very model of a modern society when it set about the task of organizing the postwar system. For the United States, the assumption that *specialized* agencies should be created was very nearly axiomatic.

But the US insistence that there should be a division of labor in the organization of postwar multilateral diplomacy, with various UN-system agencies each possessing responsibility for a particular policy area, can also be attributed to a much more pragmatic consideration. The United States took the view that the shape of the postwar economic and social order had already been decided; indeed, the United States itself had made most of the critical decisions, defining the principles and norms that would govern that order. Therefore there was no need for political institutions to debate these matters. What was required were specialized, technical agencies that would permit representatives with specialized competence to address essentially technical issues. Such an arrangement would help to ensure that the system worked efficiently and it would guarantee that the large questions of principle that had been answered at Bretton Woods and elsewhere would not be reopened.

The result was a crude variation on the doctrine of functionalism. Functionalists such as David Mitrany had argued that, unlike politicians and diplomats, technicians and experts were practical and task-oriented, and should be given the opportunity to pursue the work of solving common problems, regardless of nationality and free from the pressure of extraneous considerations.[13] The United States was not, of course, embracing functionalism à la Mitrany; such a doctrine, carried to its logical conclusion, is subversive of sovereignty, and the US government was not prepared to go so far. But it did signal early on that it was opposed to what it regarded as the "politicization" of the technical work of the UN system.

The United Nations itself was (and is) a multipurpose institution, the exception to the principle of functional specificity within the UN system; the generality of its mandate "was to be a standing invitation to challenge the functionalist division of labor that the United States so obviously preferred."[14] As a result, the United States has not only had to worry about politicization of the agencies, it has also had to concern itself with the impulse of the UN to engage in a form of institutional imperialism.

The Market

Among US assumptions regarding the United Nations, one of the most basic was surely that it would be supportive of the principle that economic allocations are to be made by market mechanisms. As Harold Jacobson claimed, "the debate about what international governmental organizations should do in the economic field is a debate about how much governmental intervention there should be in global economic affairs."[15] The position of the United States in this debate has, from the beginning, been clear and unequivocal: Laissez-faire is the optimal state of affairs, with laws of supply and demand determining what is produced, who produces it, and how it is distributed. The economic disaster of the 1930s and the Keynesian revolution made a compelling case for some governmental intervention at both national and international levels, but on the whole the liberal economic order that the United States was instrumental in establishing in the 1940s was committed to minimizing such intervention and giving market forces free rein.

The United Nations itself was not, of course, the focal point of US efforts to realize the objectives of the liberal international economic order. The agencies with primary responsibility for generating growth through the promotion of free trade were the International Monetary Fund (IMF), the International Bank for Reconstruction and Development (IBRD), and the General Agreement on Tariffs and Trade (GATT).[16] The trade regime established in the 1940s embraced several norms that reflected the US preference for a market-oriented system, among them nondiscrimination, trade liberalization, and reciprocity. The principal rationale for the monetary regime and the IMF, which was its institutional centerpiece, was to facilitate international trade by promoting the liberalization of exchange among currencies. Trade was also to be stimulated by World Bank policies designed to encourage international investment.

The importance to the United States of market allocation in the liberal economic order is indicated by the fact that primary responsibility for nurturing and sustaining it was given to institutions in which the US position was overwhelmingly dominant relative to the United Nations. But the provisions of the UN Charter, although more general, can also be read as an endorsement of the US preference for market allocation and of the proposition that security is in part a function of the economic well-being associated with a global free-market economy. At least that is the way the United States chose to read the Charter. In this case, as in others, the United States was to be disappointed by and frustrated with the UN, which later became the vehicle of choice for states wanting to challenge the tenets of the liberal economic order.

Pluralism

Closely related to, but considerably broader than, the US belief in the market was the US conviction that power should be dispersed rather than concentrated. The US view of the United Nations was thus shaped in part by the belief that pluralism is intrinsically desirable and that the UN should and presumably would reflect that belief in its work. That many UN member states were authoritarian, lacking a private sector, competitive political parties, and other attributes of a pluralistic system, was recognized by the United States, but that situation might be changed; the UN would certainly not treat it as a desirable norm.

Robert Packenham, in an insightful book written in the 1970s but still relevant today, argued that the United States has embraced several propositions that have their roots in a reading of its own historical experience.[17] One of these is that distributing power is more important than accumulating it. This proposition stresses the importance of limited governmental authority, separation of powers, strong local government, competitive political parties, numerous mediating structures, separation of church and state, voluntarism—all of the time-tested features of the US system, which, by extension, constitute a model to which others should aspire.

The UN Charter does not explicitly endorse pluralism any more than it does capitalism. And the presence of the Soviet Union among the principal founding members tends to undermine the argument that the United Nation was, among other things, intended to be a significant reaction against totalitarian concentration of power. But the United States nonetheless projected onto the UN its conviction that "the possibilities for a peaceful and free international order depended on the internal constitutions of the states making up the world community";[18] and the internal constitutions that provided the best defense against resort to policies of hostility and aggrandizement abroad were those that were patterned after that of the United States. This tendency to expect congruence between US practices and those accepted by the UN helped to set the stage for disaffection when the UN failed to acknowledge the superiority of US-style democracy to mobilization regimes in the Communist bloc and the Third World.

Reform, Not Revolution

Although the United States expected the United Nations to play an important role in the preservation of the new postwar status quo, it also anticipated and even welcomed a role for the UN as an agent of change in certain areas. The principle of self-determination of peoples is explicitly endorsed by the Charter, and the United States initially provided both the philosophical foundation and the political pressure for UN-based efforts on behalf of decolonization and self-determination.[19] Moreover, US support for democratization was inevitably an invitation to change in many places.

But this support for change was qualified by a deeply rooted conviction that radicalism and revolution are bad.[20] As Michael Hunt has argued, "revolution continued, as it had ever since the 1790s, to summon up visions of a reign of terror, of brutal assassinations, and of an international conspiracy against order and reason."[21] The American Revolution could be invoked to justify support for the self-determination of others, but it had not been a thoroughgoing social revolution of the kind experienced by France at the end of the eighteenth century or by Russia early in the twentieth century. On the contrary, the US experience had produced an aversion to radical politics and the violent challenges to established order that were to become so common in the post–World War II era. According to the liberal tradition, such extreme measures were not necessary for political and economic progress; indeed, the chaos and disorder that accompanied them made democracy less rather than more likely and posed a serious threat to US interests.

Thus, one of the elements in the US perception of the United Nations has been that the global body would be an agent for reform, not revolution. Change would be moderate and constructive; the UN would reject the argument that the goal of self-determination justified the use of any means to achieve that goal. As Packenham observed, the US liberal tradition disposed the United States to perceive even modest alternatives as massive changes,[22] a view that would put the United States on a collision course with the UN majority on more than one occasion.

Preemptive Imperialism

The United States does not think of itself as an imperialist power. Indeed, it sees itself as principal defender of a status quo that serves US interests and provides conditions conducive to the economic and political progress of other less fortunate states. In the postwar era it was the Soviet Union that had imperial ambitions. The United States opposed those ambitions and expected to enlist the United Nations in this mission. The result, paradoxically, was a US policy perceptively termed "preemptive imperialism" by Tony Smith.[23]

Smith has argued that the preferred US policy is what he terms "liberal anti-imperialism," in effect a policy that would protect weak states from the efforts of other powers to extend their spheres of influence as well as promote nondiscriminatory multilateral economic relations. From this perspective, the Monroe Doctrine and the Open Door Policy in China were classic expressions of liberal US anti-imperialism. Whether one accepts this rationale for US foreign policy or not, it is hard to disagree with Smith's thesis that in the postwar era the United States resorted to preemptive imperialism when more modest efforts to help economically weak and politically unstable Third World countries failed to arrest the spread of Soviet power and influence.[24]

One of the cardinal assumptions the United States brought to its relationship with the United Nations was that the global body would share its concern for protecting the weak and vulnerable against predator states such as the Soviet Union. Michael Hunt put it this way: "It was now the task of Americans, who had become great yet had renounced self-aggrandizement, 'to save the world from totalitarianism.'"[25] And the UN, committed under the Charter to the establishment of a stable and democratic world order, would be expected to cooperate in accomplishing that vital objective. For many UN members, however, imperialism was imperialism, regardless of the rationale offered in its defense, and it was often US intervention to halt the spread of communism that produced the greatest resentment. US efforts to justify such intervention and to treat it as a logical and legitimate application of Charter principles were to encounter strong and persistent opposition and to contribute to US disenchantment with the UN.

Optimism Regarding Progress

US expectations regarding the United Nations and the role it would (or should) play in the postwar international order were colored by certain characteristics of the country, its people, and its leaders. Among those that come to mind are US optimism, a certain naiveté with respect to the larger world (especially outside of Europe), impatience for results, and something akin to a premillennial view of at least some aspects of interstate relations.

To argue that one of the factors shaping the US view of the United Nations is US optimism about progress does not quite do justice to the phenomenon in question. Packenham came close to capturing this elusive trait of national character when, in discussing US attitudes toward Third World development, he argued that the United States believes that change and development are easy and that all good things go together.[26] These elements of the US liberal tradition, which have applicability well beyond the field of development, have their roots in the doctrine of American exceptionalism.[27] Although the United States may fall victim to selective amnesia—forgetting or ignoring elements of its own past that do not support the conventional wisdom—the propositions that change and development are easy and all good things go together have in some considerable measure been borne out by the US historical experience.

The applicability of these propositions to countries with very different natural endowments and political and social conditions from those of the United States is, of course, another matter. Nonetheless, the evidence is that the United States assumed that "American institutions would provide the models and American experience would serve as the inspiration," with the result that other nations could "accomplish in years what it had taken the advanced countries decades to achieve."[28]

The United States has typically taken the position that the principal limits to growth and progress are self-imposed. It has argued for the removal of these barriers, these deformed political systems and social institutions, these perverse economic nostrums. Follow the US example, and not only will economic development occur, but with it social reform and political democracy, and hence stability.

These assumptions have colored US attitudes toward the United Nations, particularly but not exclusively in the context of discussion and debate over ways to achieve development, which in the 1960s and 1970s became the dominant issue on the UN agenda. With the conviction that its experience is relevant and its assumptions tested and valid, the United States became impatient with UN discussion and debate that ignored the US message and even attacked the messenger. Ali Mazrui argued that it is the United States that is the poor listener, much more interested in telling other states what to do and how to do it than in learning about the problems that cast doubt on the validity of US assumptions.[29] Whether Mazrui is right or wrong, US-UN relations have been one of the casualties of this dialogue of the deaf.

Naiveté

The belief that change and development are easy and that all good things go together is thus both an assumption and, as a reflection of US optimism, a commentary on the national character. Another closely related characteristic of the United States that has shaped its perception of the UN would seem to be a certain naiveté about the world—about other countries, peoples, and cultures, and about the complexities of global problems.

It is by now a cliché to observe that the United States, by virtue of the protection afforded it by the Atlantic and Pacific oceans and the great national challenge of westward expansion during the first century of its existence, could and did indulge the luxury of relative indifference to the world beyond its shores. The conventional wisdom is that US foreign policy was historically isolationist, and that the United States perceived itself as the city on the hill, its role that of leader by example rather than by forceful intervention in the affairs of others. Although the isolationist label has always been exaggerated[30] and the role of city on the hill has been traded in of late for that of global policeman, attitudes developed in an earlier and simpler age have died hard. The United States has remained, if not exactly ignorant of the world beyond its shores, at least slow to understand and empathize with much of that world.

In part, this can be attributed to US ethnocentrism, which Howard Wiarda argued has produced "an inability to understand the Third World on its own terms, an insistence on viewing it through the lenses of our own Western experience, and the condescending and patronizing attitudes that such ethnocentrism implies."[31] Certainly ethnocentrism is at the root of some of the assumptions with which the United States has approached the United Nations. But naiveté, or a simple inability on the part of the United States to comprehend the circumstances and views of others, whether explained by US ethnocentrism or not, is also a problem. This naiveté extends beyond a failure to understand other peoples and cultures, as Henry Kissinger acknowledged in his observation that the United States typically seeks "to solve problems on their merits, without a sense of time or context or the seamless web of reality," whereas success requires a "sense of history, an understanding of manifold forces not within our control, and a broad view of the fabric of events."[32] Whether called naiveté or something else, this aspect of the US national character has often frustrated US efforts to work with and through the United Nations.

Impatience

Impatience is another element of the US national character that has contributed in significant measure to the US response to the way the United Nations does its work. It has been frequently argued that the US public is not greatly interested in foreign policy, or rather that it has a short attention span where foreign policy is concerned. As Philip Geyelin has argued, the natural and historic condition of the United States is "detached and wary of entanglement, content to nourish cultural ties and ancestral connections, pleased to profit from international commerce, but preoccupied with perfecting the American way of life, liberty, and the pursuit of its own economic well-being. Detachment—or, at the most, rare moments of engagement—is America's natural state."[33] This is not to say that the United States has reverted to isolationism, only that permanent exertion in foreign policy runs against the grain and requires a major challenge to US interest and values, a vigorous effort by political leaders to persuade the public of the need for such exertion, and tangible evidence that the policy is successful.

The implications of this aversion to the primacy of foreign policy for the United Nations are clear. The UN had been oversold as part of an effort to prepare the country for a more active leadership role in world affairs. If the UN could demonstrate its worth with significant accomplishments supportive of major US policy goals, especially in the context of a Cold War that increasingly justified permanent exertion in foreign policy, it would be adjudged successful. Otherwise, the country's characteristic impatience would come into play and the UN would presumably lose favor in the United States, even when it did not adopt positions that were explicitly contrary to US preferences. In the wake of the prodigious and indisputably successful effort to overwhelm the Axis powers on the far-flung battlefields of the world, a UN characterized by inconclusive diplomatic dithering, tedious bargaining over ambiguous language, and the absence of clear-cut "results" could only be expected to frustrate a nation with the proclivities of the United States. And it is but a short step from frustration to disengagement.

Premillennialism

There is a fine line between a foreign policy that supports certain values and one that treats those who disdain and reject those values as the forces of darkness and evil. US foreign policy has crossed this line often enough to suggest that "elements of premillennialist thinking . . . exist in vague and diffuse form" in the United States and help to shape the US perspective on international relations.[34] According to this view, international relations are a conflict between the forces of good and evil permitting of "no intermediate redoubts, no compromise positions; it is all or nothing and always the slippery slope."[35]

President Ronald Reagan's characterization of the Soviet Union as the evil empire and President George Bush's comparison of Saddam Hussein to Hitler are two of the most recent and more explicit manifestations of this premillennial impulse, but it is not a new phenomenon. The United States has tended to approach wars in this spirit—never more so than in the struggle against Imperial Japan and Nazi Germany, culminating with the demand for unconditional surrender. If one's enemy is evil, and one's own cause just in some transcendent sense of the term, then there can be little room for compromise or concession. This view of world politics shaped US foreign policy during the early years of the Cold War, with the Soviet Union and later China replacing the Axis powers as the forces of evil. Support for these states and nonsupport for US causes were often perceived as tantamount to making a pact with the devil.

This starkly bipolar view of the world was to be tested early and often in the United Nations, for the UN was a forum in which the issues that divided West from East were debated and states were expected to stand and be counted. When states equivocated or retreated into neutrality or, worse yet, came down on the side of the forces of evil, the UN suffered in US eyes. Premillennialism may be a minority position theologically in the United States, but in its secular form it has simplified the task of comprehending the complexities of the troubled postwar world, given us a series of politically powerful if analytically weak metaphors, and provided a yardstick for measuring the performance of the United Nations and hence the relevance of that organization for the United States.

Efficiency and Frugality

There is one final expectation the United States has had for the United Nations, although it was not initially as important as it has become in more recent years. At the time the UN was being launched, not much thought was given to the management of the global organization. The size of its bureaucracy and of its budget were not principal foci of debate. The United States had had little experience with the operation of permanent international organizations with multinational secretariats, and the extent of future growth of membership and hence of agenda and demands for more staff and more funds could not be fully appreciated in 1945.

In the beginning, as might have been expected, the UN Secretariat was staffed primarily with nationals of Western states, the United States foremost among them, and the US assessment made it by far the largest contributor, albeit to a relatively modest budget.[36] Questions as to whether the UN Secretariat was staffed and run in such a way as to guarantee efficiency and whether the size and nature of UN expenditures met US expectations regarding prudential fiscal management did not arise at the outset. But these were latent US concerns, and in time US assumptions regarding efficiency and frugality became more explicit in response to trends within the organization. A clue to these latent concerns can be found in the fact that the United States opted for what might be termed "the management portfolio" when the major powers first laid claim to UN Secretariat departments.[37] US assumptions as to what constitutes efficient and frugal management of the United Nations have, of course, always been closely tied to UN performance on substantive issues. When other US expectations are met, UN efficiency and frugality are less salient for US policymakers; when the UN fails the United States in other areas, however, they are quite likely to be invoked.

These several expectations and aspects of the US national character have come into play in various combinations when the United States has assessed the performance of the United Nations and decided whether and to what extent to give its support to the global body. Some have been generically critical, affecting the US view of the UN across the board on virtually all issues and at virtually all times. Others assume importance on certain issues and fade into relative insignificance on others. Collectively they suggest a set of questions, the answers to which provide a barometer of the willingness of the United States to take the United Nations seriously and give it a place of importance in the conduct of US foreign policy.

- Is the fact of US hegemony in evidence at the United Nations; that is, does the membership generally respect and defer to US leadership on matters that the United States deems important, and are the costs incurred by the United States in the exercise of its leadership role at the UN commensurate with the benefits it obtains there?
- Are UN decisions congruent with US preferences, and do they effectively leave US power capabilities unchanged?
- Does the United Nations support and facilitate the proper functioning of the international order created in the wake of World War II; that is, does it help to maintain the US-sanctioned status quo?
- Is the principle that sovereign states may not be bound against their will by the decisions of UN majorities accepted and honored, and not chronically contested, by the membership?
- Is the division of labor among UN-system agencies accepted, and does the United Nations eschew attempts to politicize what the United States considers technical issues?

- Does the United Nations support the market system as the optimum method of allocating resources?
- Does the United Nations support pluralism and Western-style democracy as opposed to authoritarian and mobilization regimes?
- Does the United Nations reject revolution as the path to change, and prefer instead orderly processes of reform?
- Does the United Nations recognize the threat posed by states bent on imperialistic expansion, and does it therefore support US efforts to preempt such expansion?
- Is there at the United Nations a healthy belief in progress and a willingness to accept US prescriptions for achieving it?
- Are US naiveté about other peoples and cultures and US impatience with the time-consuming and often inconclusive aspects of multinational and multicultural diplomacy not tested too severely at the United Nations?
- Is there an understanding at the United Nations that international politics may at times take on the character of a contest between good and evil, and will the members take the right (the US) side in this struggle?
- Is the United Nations an efficient and frugal organization, and does it go about the task of realizing US policy objectives without conspicuous waste and at modest cost?

The answer to all of these questions has been "no" often enough to create in the United States a sense of disenchantment with the United Nations. That has not been true at all times, or with respect to all issues, or for all US foreign policymakers, much less for the whole of the US public. But these have been the litmus tests for broad and sustained US support for the United Nations—support of a kind that does not require that the UN be at the center of all US foreign policy, but does include a willingness to exercise leadership there and to seek to invest the UN with greater moral authority and capacity for effective action in an increasingly complex world. For the most part, that support has been lacking for much of the UN's existence, and the explanation for that lack of support can be found in the fact that US policymakers have not been able to answer more of these questions positively more of the time.

In the early 1990s the United States has once again exercised leadership at the UN, and a case can be made that beginning with the Gulf crisis it has tried to invest the UN with the moral authority and capacity for action it has largely lacked for some time. This change, this about-face, may mean either that those questions are now eliciting different answers *or* that the United States has relaxed its expectations regarding the United Nations. Before turning to an analysis of this about-face in the US approach to the UN, it will be useful to examine the deterioration of US-UN relations, culminating in the crisis of the 1980s.

Notes

1. A relatively recent and very readable account of the original US view of the United Nations is Thomas M. Franck, *Nation Against Nation,* New York: Oxford University Press, 1985. Franck titles his initial chapter "Great Expectations."

2. Ernst Haas, "Regime Decay: Conflict Management and International Organizations, 1945–1981," *International Organization* 37, 2 (Spring 1983), p. 229.

3. The literature on this subject is extensive. See, for an introduction to debate, Robert O. Keohane, *After Hegemony: Cooperation and Discord in the World Political Economy,* Princeton, N.J.: Princeton University Press, 1984; Bruce Russett, "The Mysterious Case of Vanishing Hegemony; or, Is Mark Twain Really Dead?" *International Organization* 39, 2 (Spring 1985); Duncan Snidal, "The Limits of Hegemonic Stability Theory," *International Organization* 39, 4 (Autumn 1985); Isabelle Grunberg, "Exploring the 'Myth' of Hegemonic Stability," *International Organization* 44, 4 (Autumn 1990).

4. See Snidal, "The Limits of Hegemonic Stability Theory," for the distinction between benevolent and coercive hegemony. Most writers have taken the postion that hegemons are benevolent.

5. See Stephen D. Krasner, *Structural Conflict,* Berkeley: University of California Press, 1985, pp. 75–78.

6. Ibid., p. 75.

7. Franck, *Nation Against Nation,* p. 14.

8. Daniel Patrick Moynihan, *A Dangerous Place,* Boston: Little, Brown and Company, 1978.

9. At least it did throughout much of its history. With the collapse of the Soviet Union and the end of the Cold War, it is not so clear what NATO's role will be in the future.

10. See Lawrence S. Finkelstein, ed., *Politics in the United Nations System,* Durham, N.C.: Duke University Press, 1988. The argument is developed in Chapter 1.

11. Ibid., p. 3.

12. See Talcott Parsons, *The Social System,* New York: The Free Press, 1951.

13. See David Mitrany, *A Working Peace System,* London: Royal Institute for International Affairs, 1946. The best short summary of the functionalist thesis is in Inis L. Claude, Jr., *Swords into Plowshares,* 3rd ed., New York: Random House, 1964.

14. Robert W. Gregg, "The Politics of International Economic Cooperation and Development," in Finkelstein, *Politics in the United Nations System,* p. 121.

15. Harold K. Jacobson, *Networks of Interdependence,* 2nd ed., New York: Alfred A. Knopf, 1984, p. 211.

16. The GATT occupies the institutional niche in the liberal international economic order created when agreement could not be reached on the proposed International Trade Organization (ITO).

17. Robert A. Packenham, *Liberal America and the Third World,* Princeton, N.J.: Princeton University Press, 1973.

18. Michael H. Hunt, *Ideology and U.S. Foreign Policy,* New Haven, Conn.: Yale University Press, 1987, p. 152.

19. This familiar thesis is succinctly argued in Donald F. McHenry, "Confronting a Revolutionary Legacy," in Sanford J. Ungar, ed., *Estrangement: America and the World*, New York: Oxford University Press, 1985, pp. 75–99.

20. Packenham, *Liberal America and the Third World*, p. 170.

21. Hunt, *Ideology and U.S. Foreign Policy*, p. 170.

22. Packenham, *Liberal America and the Third World*, p. 149.

23. See Tony Smith, *The Pattern of Imperialism*, New York: Cambridge University Press, 1981, p. 3.

24. Ibid., Chap. 4.

25. Hunt, *Ideology and U.S. Foreign Policy*, p. 157.

26. Packenham, *Liberal America and the Third World*, pp. 112–129.

27. For an explication of this doctrine, see Louis Hartz, *The Liberal Tradition in America*, New York: Harcourt, Brace and World, 1955. Packenham is very much indebted to Hartz.

28. Hunt, *Ideology and U.S. Foreign Policy*, p. 160.

29. Ali Mazrui, "Uncle Sam's Hearing Aid," in Ungar, *Estrangement*, pp. 179–192.

30. Frances FitzGerald argued this point in "The American Millennium," in Ungar, *Estrangement*, pp. 253–276.

31. Howard J. Wiarda, *Ethnocentrism in Foreign Policy*, Washington: American Enterprise Institute, 1985, p. 1.

32. Henry A. Kissinger, *The White House Years*, Boston: Little, Brown and Company, 1979, p. 130.

33. Philip L. Geyelin, "The Adams Doctrine and the Dream of Disengagement," in Ungar, *Estrangement*, p. 197.

34. Frances FitzGerald, "The American Millennium," in Ungar, *Estrangement*, p. 270.

35. Ibid., p. 271.

36. Initially the United States paid 38.89 percent of a budget of less than $20 million. As large as this percentage was, it was considerably smaller than the US assessment would have been had the principle of capacity to pay been strictly applied (49.89 percent).

37. Georges Langrod, *The International Civil Service*, Leyden, Holland: A. W. Sythoff, 1963, p. 176.

Chapter III

The Roots of Disenchantment

No state could realistically expect the United Nations always to reflect its views. Issues will be inscribed on the agenda that some states would prefer not to discuss or on which they would prefer not to take a position. Other issues to which some states attach a high priority will not be given the serious attention they believe those issues deserve. Some states will from time to time be discomforted by the tone of the debate, and they will, even in the best of circumstances, occasionally find themselves on the losing side of a vote. Some states will not always be satisfied with the way their assessed contributions to the organization are used. They may chafe under the frustrating requirements of multilateral diplomacy.

But if all states can expect to have bad moments at the United Nations, the United States might have been expected—and apparently did itself expect—to have fewer problems than most because of its great power and influence, the fact that the organization had been tailored in considerable measure to US expectations, and the luxury, denied to many lesser powers, of being able to achieve many of its objectives unilaterally without the need to mobilize support in the UN. Unfortunately, but not unpredictably, the United States has not, however, had fewer problems with the United Nations than most other states. It is difficult, of course, to gauge comparative discontent. Many states have had good and sufficient reason to view the UN as an inhospitable place: the Soviet Union when isolated in the early years, China as a result of its long ostracism, several European countries during the years when they were the target of the UN majority's unrelenting assault on colonialism, large numbers of Third World states for what they have regarded as the UN's inadequate response to their development problems, and Israel and South Africa for their treatment as pariah states.

Our purpose is not to determine which states have fared least well at the United Nations, but to explore the frustrations of the United States, which have arguably had more of an impact on the evolution of the UN than those of any other state and which have seemed so disproportionate to the reality of US power and influence in the world, which the UN has not in any way significantly diminished. At the root of US disenchantment with the UN have been US expectations, outlined in the previous chapter, which would appear to have almost certainly been excessive in view of the nature of the United Nations and of the changing systemic conditions in which the UN has had to function.

The United Nations possesses a number of fundamental characteristics that, by themselves, did not make the frustration of the United States with the global organization inevitable; however, they did—or at least some of them did—make it likely. Similarly, the international system in the decades after World War II evolved in ways that did not guarantee US antagonism toward the UN. They did, however, make it more probable. It was the intersection of these basic characteristics of the UN and the emergent and persistent features of the postwar international system that frustrated US expectations for the United Nations. Had the UN been so constructed as to render it largely immune to systemic developments that the United States opposed or, better yet from the US perspective, to enable it to channel those developments in directions compatible with US purposes, US-UN relations would have been far more amicable. Conversely, had systemic developments been more benign (from the US perspective), it would have mattered less to the United States how the UN was structured and what procedures were employed there.

But systemic developments were not, from the US point of view, always benign, and the United Nations possessed a number of characteristics that did not, as the United States had hoped, facilitate the realization of US objectives. Instead, they all too often seemed to amplify those disconcerting trends within the United Nations system. In retrospect, all of this was probably inevitable. But it may be useful to examine briefly both the major systemic developments of the postwar era and those fundamental characteristics of the UN that reflected, nurtured, and sometimes distorted them, producing along the way increasing US frustration and, ultimately, something very close to US abandonment of the belief that the United Nations had any meaningful role to play in the conduct of US foreign policy.

Fundamental Characteristics of the United Nations

The United Nations possesses—and has possessed since its founding—five characteristics of overriding importance: universality of membership, egalitarianism/majoritarianism, limited authority, great power responsibility and privilege, and a broad mandate. Some of these have contributed significantly to the defeat of US expectations for the UN, but even those that appear best suited to the protection of US interests and values have often in practice been at best a mixed blessing for US foreign policy.

Universality of Membership

In the standard typology for classifying international organizations, two dimensions are employed: manifest purposes of the organization (specific or general) and membership (limited or universal).[1] Limited membership organizations are typically regional in scope (e.g., the Organization of American States), or they may have relatively few members because only a relatively few states are engaged in the activity that led to the creation of the organization (e.g., the International Whaling Commission). The UN was never intended to be a limited membership organization in either of these two senses, and it was therefore always prospectively universal. Article 4 of the Charter does, however, stipulate two conditions that might have limited membership had they been interpreted differently. One is that a state seeking membership be peace-loving, the other that it be able and willing to carry out the obligations contained in the Charter.

The rationale for inclusion of the qualifying phrase "peace-loving states" was the exclusion of the defeated Axis states (as well as Spain), itself an important exception to the concept of universality. If one considers the many instances since the founding of the United Nations in which states have resorted to war to settle disputes or achieve national objectives, it becomes clear that a more literal reading of the "peace-loving" condition might have been used to further limit UN membership. Needless to say, such a reading of Article 4 was never seriously contemplated, although the Soviet Union and the United States did engage in what has been termed "competitive exclusion" of each other's candidates for membership in the early 1950s on not dissimilar grounds.[2]

The notion that states should be willing and able to fulfill Charter obligations could have been used to screen out applicants with tiny land areas, minuscule populations, and, the usual corollary of those conditions, minimal financial resources—the so-called microstates. The option of qualified or associate membership was in fact considered at the UN, but in view of the large number of fairly small states among the original members and the potency of the "sovereign equality of states" argument, not to mention the political calculus, size never became an impediment to universality.

The result is the one with which we are all familiar, a UN that counts among its members virtually every state in the world, a rich (or, depending on one's point of view, a rancid) stew of entities as diverse as Sweden and Iraq, the Seychelles and China.

Egalitarianism/Majoritarianism

Not only has any entity meeting the minimum legal standards of state sovereignty been eligible for UN membership; in addition, according to Article 18 (1), each member state, regardless of size or other attributes of power, casts one vote in the General Assembly. The corollary of egalitarianism, also enshrined in the Charter in Article 18 (2 and 3), is majoritarianism, that is, decisions may be arrived at by voting, in which process the vote of the smallest state counts for as much as the vote of the largest and the majority carries the day. These provisions of the Charter created a situation, often commented on by the UN's critics, in which issues can be decided by large and even overwhelming majorities consisting primarily of relatively small states. There were, of course, alternatives to one-state, one-vote, as the decisionmaking rules of the International Monetary Fund and World Bank, or, for that matter, the UN Security Council, demonstrate. But the drafters of the UN Charter, committed to the principle of sovereign equality of states and mindful of the fact that the UN's authority was to be limited in any event, took as their model the voting arrangements in parliamentary democracies. As Inis Claude once observed, this is an analogy of dubious merit. International majorities, he wrote, are likely to be "undemocratic in the sense that they do not represent a majority of the world's population, unrealistic in the sense that they do not reflect the greater portion of the world's real power, morally unimpressive in the sense that they cannot be identified as expressions of the dominant will of a genuine community."[3] Whether one agrees with Claude's conclusion that for all these reasons majority decisions in an egalitarian UN are both ineffectual and dangerous, it is clear that these attributes of the Charter have constituted both an invitation to the proliferation of sovereign states and a means whereby the rapidly growing multitude of sovereign states could control the UN agenda, challenge established norms, and seek to enlarge the Charter's limited grant of authority.

It should also be noted that UN egalitarianism has also meant that each member state, once again regardless of size or other attributes of power, is eligible to occupy a seat on the UN's limited membership organs, including, most significantly, the Security Council. The point is illustrated by the composition of the Council that adopted the several resolutions condemning Iraq's invasion and annexation of Kuwait and authorizing sanctions and "all necessary means" to secure Iraq's unconditional withdrawal.[4] The ten nonpermanent members of the Council participating in those decisions included Yemen, Malaysia, Cuba, Colombia, Ethiopia, Zaire, Côte d'Ivoire, Romania, Finland, and Canada. This roster provides persuasive evidence of the durability of the egalitarian principle.

Limited Authority

Both universality and egalitarianism plus majoritarianism were supported by the United States, but it is not difficult to see how they could have become problems for the hegemonic power. The UN's limited authority is a somewhat different matter. It is a characteristic of the United Nations that supports Lawrence Finkelstein's dictum regarding the unit veto—that states may not be bound by UN majorities without their consent—and therefore it is consistent with one of the US assumptions regarding a desirable (and an acceptable) UN. In fact, had the Charter granted the organs of the United Nations, and especially the General Assembly, substantially greater authority, the United States almost certainly would have insisted on some form of weighted voting. As Stephen Zamora has summarized the correlation between these two organizational features: "where states are most likely to surrender some autonomy to the international organization, one finds the highest incidence of voting safeguards to protect their interests."[5] In the main, Charter language makes clear that its organs have recommendatory power only. There are, however, important exceptions. There is, of course, the case of the Security Council, especially under Chapter 7 of the Charter. Here the United States enjoys the protection of the veto. But the General Assembly, in which the United States has a vote equal to that of Cuba (or Grenada or Guinea-Bissau), may under the Charter establish new institutions (Articles 22 and 68), approve the budget and apportion expenses (Article 17), and establish regulations according to which staff will be appointed (Article 101). These are not inconsiderable grants of authority.

But even if we set these exceptions aside, the limited authority of the United Nations has not been an unmixed blessing for the United States. It has meant not only that the United States could more easily not do what it did not want to do; it has also meant that the United States has often been unable to do what it has wanted to do, or, in order to achieve its objectives, has had to support expansive interpretations of the Charter with which it has later been uncomfortable.[6]

Great Power Responsibility and Privilege

The characteristic of the Charter regarding the privileged status of great powers has its expression in the permanent seats and veto rights on the Security Council for the so-called "Big Five." Thus in the area of what was to be the UN's primary function, the maintenance of peace and security, the second and third of the organization's fundamental attributes—egalitarianism and limited authority—are significantly qualified. In the Security

Council some states are unquestionably more equal than others, and when they are in agreement the Council may indeed authoritatively allocate values. The cases of Iraq and Somalia are only the most recent and in some ways the most dramatic demonstrations of this proposition.

The privileged position of the great powers (or at least those who were accorded that status in 1945) reflects the view that decisive action to deal with threats to the peace, breaches of the peace, and acts of aggression should not be undertaken unless those powers are prepared to support it. As Claude has observed, the founding fathers' "acceptance of the veto was a testament to their awareness that the great powers would not consent, on paper and still less in fact, to put their power resources at the disposal of a sheer majority for the implementation of decisions with which they might not be in accord."[7] The United States, no less than the Soviet Union, subscribed to this position. It wanted the United Nations to possess teeth in this, its most important area of responsibility, but it was not prepared to abdicate US national control over the most important of all sovereign prerogatives, the decision to keep peace or make war.

The price the United States paid for its privileged position—and ultimately paid willingly after some haggling over the question of whether a permanent member of the Council had to abstain from voting in disputes to which it was a party—was that other "powers" would be similarly able to block UN action in crisis situations. Thus a Charter provision that was quite consistent with US preferences often proved in practice to be a barrier to the realization of US purposes, especially in the hands of the Soviet Union.

The Broad Mandate

As noted above, the common typology for classifying international organizations breaks them down as to their manifest purposes. Do they have limited purposes or are they general purpose institutions? The United Nations, alone among the universal intergovernmental organizations, falls into the latter category, a point that is made abundantly clear in Article 1 and then amplified in the balance of the Charter. To be sure, the maintenance of peace and security was the UN's principal raison d'être. But unlike the other agencies in the UN system, the United Nations makes no pretense of functional specificity. The Charter was (and is) an all-purpose hunting license, and authorizes the UN to become deeply involved in issues far removed from traditional notions of peace and security and in ways much less identified with the maintenance of the status quo, which was such an important consideration for the United States.

The breadth of the UN mandate, like the other fundamental characteristics of the organization, was not only acceptable to the United States but actively supported by it. But the United States expected that the UN's responsibilities in areas other than peace and security (especially in the fields of economic and social cooperation) would be "ancillary and instrumental within the framework of the Charter,"[8] neither as important as the peace and security function nor a challenge to the primary role of more specialized agencies within the UN system. Yet the United States accepted classification of the Economic and Social Council (ECOSOC) as a principal organ of the UN, did not insist upon a guarantee of a seat for itself on that Council, endorsed one-state/one-vote and majority rule for the organs that would deal with economic and social issues (ECOSOC and the General Assembly), and countenanced "an open-ended authorization for the UN to create new institutions, hold conferences, draft conventions, and otherwise modify the institutional landscape for multilateral cooperation in the economic and social field."[9] It is small wonder that this last of the five fundamental characteristics of the United Nations, the broad mandate, would be a source of much frustration to the United States over the years.

Systemic Developments Affecting the United Nations

Systemic changes that took place over the years following the founding of the United Nations were inevitably reflected there. Indeed, the very nature of the UN—and especially its universality, its egalitarian/majoritarian decision rules, and its broad mandate—virtually guaranteed that these changes would be dramatized in UN chambers. Although the roster of systemic developments of consequence is, of course, much larger, four—the Cold War, the North-South conflict, the technology revolution, and the fact that the state is increasingly under siege—merit special attention.

The Cold War

The developments of the postwar period that most significantly affected the United Nations, and hence the US view of the UN, were, to use the conventional shorthand, the East-West and North-South conflicts. Both were challenges to the dominant position in the international system of the states of the North Atlantic community, the United States foremost among them, and each in its own way transformed the United Nations. Neither challenge was entirely new, but both gathered momentum during the decades following the defeat of the Axis powers and the creation of the United Nations.

The East-West conflict, or the Cold War, came with the collapse of the always strained and tenuous wartime cooperation among the allies and the emergence of a determined bid by the Soviet Union to achieve, if not dominion, as the Soviets may have hoped and the United States may have feared, at least parity. The challenge from Moscow was the first demonstration of a fact that later came to seem obvious but was initially difficult for the United States to acknowledge: That its great preponderance of power and claim to uncontested hegemony was the product of the special circumstances obtaining at the end of the war—a historical aberration, not the norm.

For more than forty years, the struggle between the two superpowers and between the coalitions they built and armed in this era of bipolarity was the single most important feature of the international system. It constituted the principal threat to world peace; it fostered an arms race, the prospectively devastating consequences of which are beyond imagining; it inflamed local conflicts in areas far removed from the vital interests of the United States and the Soviet Union. And it permeated the United Nations, turning the new institution with responsibility for maintaining the peace into an often virulent if verbal battleground.

The United Nations was not, of course, the most important place, much less the only place, where the Soviet challenge to the United States was played out. But it was impossible to keep the Cold War out of the UN, and the superpowers, rather than trying to insulate the global forum from the struggle in which they were engaged, turned the UN into a major arena for that struggle. The United States sought to enlist the United Nations against the challenge from the Communist bloc; the Soviet Union fought back, employing every available Charter weapon. The two powers both courted and threatened the so-called nonaligned states, turning one issue after another into a referendum on the Cold War. The roll call of UN crises resulting from the Cold War conflict is familiar to all students of this troubled era: The stalemate over the admission of new members, the bitter end of the stewardship first of Trygve Lie and then of Dag Hammarskjöld as Secretary-General, the response to the war in Korea and later to the breakdown of government authority in the Congo, the Article 19 crisis of the 1960s. These are only a few of the entries on a long list, which continued to grow almost until the eve of Iraq's invasion of Kuwait, overshadowing much of what the UN did or tried to do and contributing to the disillusionment of the United States with the United Nations.

The North-South Conflict

This second axis of global contention—the North-South conflict—came into sharp focus somewhat later than the struggle between East and West, and never constituted as much of a threat to world peace. But over time it actually displaced the East-West conflict as the principal focus of the

UN's agenda, generating angry debate, dramatic and controversial proposals, many new institutions, and accelerated budget growth. In fact, it is no exaggeration to say that this conflict between the established, industrialized, market economy states and the less-developed states of the so-called Third World would have been considerably more muted had the latter group of states not had the United Nations as a venue for expressing their grievances and promoting various changes in the international order that had been put in place after World War II.

The North-South conflict antedated the founding of the United Nations, but it was the inability of the colonial powers, weakened by the war, to retain their overseas possessions that propelled it into prominence as a global meta-issue. Once having obtained their independence, the many new states that emerged during the 1950s, 1960s, and 1970s discovered that true independence was a chimera, and they turned with increasing frustration and anger against the North (or more precisely the West) for redress of their growing list of grievances.

These states joined the UN, transforming it both quantitatively and qualitatively, and availed themselves of its egalitarian and majoritarian decision rules to press their case. And whereas the North-South conflict is normally associated with the economic development issue, the South was (and is) also interested in a number of other emotional and volatile issues that bring it into conflict with the North, including the fate of Palestinians and black South Africans, neocolonialism and cultural imperialism. These issues came to be linked repeatedly in rhetoric and resolution. The South seemed increasingly to take the view that the old order itself—the global order that the United States had done so much to establish—constituted "a threat to peace and security because it perpetuates hegemony and dependence, justifies intervention, sanctions racism, frustrates development, and fosters the conditions that breed disorder and violence."[10]

The United States was the principal target of this challenge, just as it was in the Cold War confrontation. The United States was, after all, the state that best symbolized the established order and, more than any other, seemed to thwart the aspirations of the South. It could, if it would, make the concessions necessary to usher in a new order. The United Nations not only amplified this challenge by providing a highly visible platform and a venue for concerted action among the tactically like-minded, it also conferred a kind of legitimacy upon the claims of the aspirant states. They had, after all, taken their case to a US-sanctioned forum, availed themselves of Charter procedures that the United States had sponsored or endorsed, developed a broad agenda reflecting what were indisputably most of the great issues of the day, and built impressive winning coalitions in support of their positions on those issues.

The Technology Revolution

A case can be made that contemporary history began with the second industrial revolution, which took place in the latter part of the nineteenth century. Geoffrey Barraclough made precisely that case when he argued that "the primary differentiating factor, marking off the new age from the old, was the impact of scientific and technological advance on society, both national and international."[11] It was Barraclough's thesis that the second industrial revolution—the scientific revolution—was "far quicker in its impact, far more prodigious in its results, far more revolutionary in its effects on people's lives and outlook"[12] than the first and more celebrated industrial revolution. This revolution ushered in the familiar twentieth-century age of steel and electricity, of oil and chemicals, of bacteriology and refrigeration.

Barraclough's slim but provocative little volume was published in the early 1960s, less than two decades after World War II came to a dramatic conclusion following the explosion of the atomic bombs over Hiroshima and Nagasaki. And already it has been overtaken by events; we are in the middle of another revolution of far-reaching implications, a revolution that many have characterized as postindustrial. This revolution has been driven by an explosion in scientific knowledge and technological innovation in the fields of information processing, telecommunications, and molecular and cellular biology. Its salient features include microchips and semiconductors, fiber optics, biosynthetics and artificial intelligence—a whole host of developments that have been transforming international relations in almost every sphere.[13]

This revolution in science and technology dramatically sped up the processes by which the world was shrinking. As Dennis Pirages observed, "nations once buffered from each other by oceans, mountains, and other natural obstacles are becoming part of an integrated 'global village' created by instantaneous communication, nearly immediate transportation, and integrated global markets."[14] Although these changes have undeniably brought with them many benefits, they have not been an unmixed blessing. This revolution has made even so-called conventional weapons more complex, more accurate, and more deadly, turning the international arms bazaar into a particularly chilling demonstration of interdependence. It has made state boundaries increasingly porous, placed the environment at risk in ways previously unimagined, and otherwise brought into focus a set of interrelated problems that have collectively been termed the "global problematique."[15]

Although this revolution has not convulsed the United Nations in the way that the Cold War and the North-South confrontation have, it has been an important contextual factor, exacerbating old problems and generating new ones. It made the Cold War more dangerous, widened the gap between developed and developing states, and raised difficult and divisive questions about the continuing validity of the industrial paradigm. All of these developments have been very much on display at the UN.

The State Under Siege

The great paradox of the late twentieth century is that at a time when there exists an unprecedentedly large number of sovereign states, the sovereign state is facing unprecedentedly serious challenges. It was fashionable a few years ago, with the rise to prominence of the transnational corporation, to speak of "sovereignty at bay" and to speculate about the coming end of the Westphalian system. But even though it is certainly too soon to write the obituary of the sovereign state, it is true that the state—and not only the small, weak state—is experiencing increasing difficulty maintaining and exercising the authority that has been the hallmark of sovereignty. The sovereign state is everywhere penetrated—by satellite surveillance, electronic banking, transboundary pollution, waves of refugees and peoples fleeing economic hardship, terrorists and drug traffickers, increasingly assertive and successful transnational corporations, and weapons delivery systems that easily span great distances. The list of agents that are no respecters of boundaries is growing and seems destined to continue to grow, in spite of the best efforts of governments to protect their states from these externally generated military, economic, political, and cultural shocks.

This assault on the integrity of the sovereign state came at a time when many newly independent states were demonstrably artificial, their boundaries a legacy of colonial rivalries embracing disparate peoples who felt no sense of common nationhood. The result in many places was struggle to create viable nation-states at the very time when the rationale of the Westphalian system was increasingly coming into question.

The survival of the nation-state was not, of course, ever an agenda item at the United Nations, where states for the most part were busy insisting on their sovereign prerogatives. But the problem of the not-quite-sovereign state was a factor in many UN debates on many UN agenda items, and the forces that were challenging state sovereignty gained increasing prominence on that agenda over the course of the UN's history. Moreover, the Charter's most explicit acknowledgment of the fact of sovereignty, Article 2 (7), came under attack even from states that would countenance no abridgement of their own sovereignty. This occurred in at least two categories of cases. One involved members' frustration with pariah states such as South Africa, which led them to make exceptions to the fundamental principle of Article 2 (7).[16] Another consisted of efforts by the Third World majority to use General Assembly resolutions to compel Western states to transfer resources. This attempt to create more authoritative international regimes included, paradoxically, measures that would insulate developing countries against interference by economically more powerful states, thereby strengthening the sovereign authority of the weak while limiting or conditioning that of the strong.[17]

It is probably human rights issues that constitute the area in which systemic trends have fostered the greatest challenge at the United Nations to the concept of state sovereignty. The UN has moved gradually "from promotion to protection—that is, from negotiating norms to supervising their implementation."[18] Initially this took the form of strong condemnation of the practices of certain politically vulnerable states, such as South Africa, Israel, and Chile, but more recently the rather considerable UN machinery in the human rights field has been used on a much broader front, and clearly reflects a growing if still cautiously exercised willingness to challenge traditional notions of state sovereignty.[19] The most recent evidence of this erosion of the protective shield of state sovereignty can be found in UN-sanctioned interventions in Iraq in the aftermath of Operation Desert Storm and in Somalia.

Impact on US Expectations

As suggested above, these several systemic trends or developments have interacted with the distinctive characteristics of the United Nations to produce UN practices and patterns that have, on balance, frustrated the United States and caused it to look much less favorably on the global organization than it did in the beginning. It will be useful to return to the set of assumptions and expectations the United States brought to its assessment of the United Nations, and to examine the ways in which they were affected over the years by systemic developments and the manner in which those trends were handled by the UN.

Hegemony

Robert Gilpin has argued that two of the principal components of governance in the international system are the distribution of power and the hierarchy of prestige.[20] When the United Nations was launched, the United States was indisputably the preeminent power with respect both to economic and military capabilities. Moreover, its power was ostensibly reinforced by its prestige, that is, by the credibility of that power and the resulting willingness of lesser states to identify their values and their interests with those of the United States. Its demonstrated willingness to supply public goods in the form of security and economic well-being would further have enhanced its prestige. The United States was, in effect, the hegemonic power in the emergent postwar international order.

But US hegemony proved to be ephemeral. It also proved to be largely irrelevant where the UN was concerned. The Marshall Plan, widely regarded as one of the most dramatic demonstrations of hegemonic power (and the willingness to spend prodigious amounts to realize the hegemon's goals), was negotiated and implemented without any reference to the UN. Even in the UN's early years, when the United States had not yet been significantly challenged militarily by the Soviet Union or economically by Japan or Western Europe, and when it typically commanded a huge majority in the UN's General Assembly, US power proved to be less fungible in the United Nations than it did when employed elsewhere, free of the UN's constraints. Gilpin suggested that "lesser states in an international system follow the leadership of more powerful states, in part because they accept the legitimacy and utility of the existing order."[21] But US prestige was not sufficiently compelling to overcome reservations among many UN members regarding the legitimacy and the utility of the US-supported world order.

The United States could hardly be said to have played Gulliver to the rest of the world's Lilliputians at the UN, but it discovered early on that, however dominant the US position in world affairs, it would not always be easy to mobilize the United Nations in the pursuit of US goals. The rapid deterioration of East-West relations into a bitter Cold War and the chaos and disorder that accompanied the breakup of the colonial empires quickly demonstrated that UN structures and processes would not always be responsive to US leadership. Early successes, such as the withdrawal of the Soviet Union from Iran's Azerbaijan region and the creation of the United Nations Truce Supervisory Organization (UNTSO) to preserve the armistice in the first Arab-Israeli war, provided initial grounds for optimism. But as Thomas Franck argued, "while during its inceptive years the UN may occasionally have succeeded in applying its principles and procedures, the successes tended to be serendipitous, the failures fundamental."[22]

The limits of hegemonic power—both within the UN and beyond its walls—were dramatically demonstrated by the Soviet-backed coup in Czechoslovakia in 1948, only three years after the San Francisco Conference. Although there would be more victories for the United States at the United Nations in the years ahead, they would be fewer than US interests demanded, they would be progressively harder to achieve, and they would often be the result of fortuitous circumstances unlikely to recur. The classic case of such fortuitous circumstances was, of course, the absence of the Soviet Union from the Security Council when North Korea invaded South Korea on June 25, 1950, enabling a US-sponsored resolution invoking collective security under Chapter 7 of the Charter to be adopted by a vote of 9 to 0 with one abstention.[23]

The United States did bear disproportionate costs at the United Nations in the early years, as befits a hegemon, although such costs were obviously inconsequential when compared with those incurred in reviving the world economy. But the returns on even that modest investment looked less and less impressive as challenges from the Communist bloc and the Third World were mounted, the former employing the Soviet veto in the Security Council and the latter taking advantage of the egalitarian/majoritarian decision rules in the General Assembly either to block US initiatives or to adopt resolutions opposed by the United States. Disillusionment set in early and, as Franck contended, "the United States began to abandon its commitment to the system some years before we ceased to control it."[24]

Hegemonic stability theorists typically stress what they refer to as the hegemon's dilemma—that the hegemon's efforts to sustain the system (and the costs incurred in doing so) lead inevitably to its own decline. US hegemony, never as strong or convincing as talk of a Pax Americana would have it and always a misnomer where the UN was concerned, did atrophy over time as the United States became overextended and other power centers emerged. The UN itself had nothing to do with this relative decline in US power, but in spite of its reputation as a mirror that distorts the realities of the international system, the UN fairly accurately reflected this decline and US frustrations resulting from it.

Congruence

All states would like the United Nations to support programs, endorse resolutions, and achieve results that are responsive to their own needs and reflect their own interests and values. All states, in other words, want a UN that is congruent with their needs, interests and values, and quite obviously that is an impossibility. US expectations in this regard appeared to have a stronger foundation than those of most other states, but those expectations were not always realized, and the situation only worsened over time. US power did not produce the desired deference.

As noted in Chapter II of the Charter, congruence implies two things: that the United Nations would reflect the preferences of the United States and that it would not affect US power. Given the protections afforded by its veto in the Security Council and the absence of centralized decision authority in the General Assembly, the United States had little or no cause to worry about the second of the two conditions for congruence. It would be difficult to make a case that the UN diminished US power, although it has quite obviously demonstrated on occasion the limitations of that power.

But the UN has certainly not always reflected US preferences, and until relatively recently it seemed to reflect those preferences less and less on more and more issues. In that sense, the US expectation regarding congruence was not realized. The United States was—and is—always able to block Security Council action that is contrary to its interests and to opt out of compliance with what are essentially hortatory General Assembly resolutions. But it was not able to prevent the UN's majority from adopting resolution after resolution that were anathema to Washington—resolutions condemning Israel and supporting the Palestine Liberation Organization, calling for strong measures to force South Africa's hand on the issue of apartheid, ascribing blame for the failure of development and laying out an agenda for a new international economic order, and so on in a lengthy list, which makes the unmistakable point that the UN had from the US perspective become incongruent.

Even the dramatic instances of congruence proved to be transitory. The Security Council supported the United States in the Korean War, and when the Soviet Union resumed its seat there, the General Assembly endorsed the US-sponsored Uniting for Peace resolution, thereby circumventing the Soviet veto by shifting responsibility for managing collective security to the plenary body.[25] But many members quickly began to have second thoughts about the wisdom of having the UN take sides in the most dangerous of Cold War conflicts, and the US-led Korean exercise turned out to be a one-of-a-kind use of UN authority. The UN response to the Suez crisis of 1956 was also congruent with US preferences, thanks in good measure to the convergence of US and Soviet interests, and as a result the United Nations embarked on its precedent-setting experiment with peacekeeping forces. But congruence between US interests and UN positions in international crises became increasingly rare in succeeding decades, and replicating the success of the United Nations Emergency Force (UNEF) model in subsequent crises proved increasingly difficult to do.[26]

The source of the US problem was not, of course, the United Nations. US preferences on important issues were simply not those of a great many other states. But the United Nations, by its very nature, made it easy for those states to demonstrate their disagreement with the United States and to leave a record of that disagreement. The US government inevitably had to deal with the reality of incongruence—with the Communist bloc, with Marxist regimes in the Third World, with some of its trading partners, even with its allies. It came to resent the need also to deal with what it perceived as the inflation of that incongruence at the UN, where many states, encouraged by the protection of numbers, seemed emboldened to challenge the United States more forcefully than they could through bilateral channels. At the nadir of US-UN relations, the United States often found itself in near complete isolation in a body of more than 150 members.[27] Expectations regarding a congruent UN had clearly been misplaced.

The Status Quo

The erosion of US dominance and the increasing incongruence between US preferences and UN positions translated into a challenge—or rather a series of challenges—to the postwar status quo. While many of the differences between the United States and the UN majority posed no threat to the international order that the United States had done so much to establish, some did.

The conflict between the United States and the Soviet Union, initially the UN's most significant division, concerned fundamental principles and norms, but Moscow was rarely in a position to play more than a negative, obstructionist role at the UN except when it aligned itself with the large and growing bloc of developing or Third World states. This group of states was both opposed to many of the basic features of the status quo *and* capable of enlisting the UN in efforts to bring about significant change. Of the fifty-one original members of the United Nations, thirty-one were developing countries. But twenty of the thirty-one were old, well-established Latin American states, not then regarded as hostile to the status quo. Asia and Africa were poorly represented at the United Nations. By the end of the 16th General Assembly session in 1960, the UN's membership had grown to an even hundred, of which sixty-six or almost two-thirds were developing countries. More significantly, forty-six of the sixty-six were Asian or African, the overwhelming majority of them former colonies of European states, now newly independent.

The ascendancy at the UN of recently independent Third World states continued until by 1980 more than half of the total membership had not even existed as sovereign states at the time of the San Francisco conference in 1945. They had not been present at the creation of the United Nations; the status quo was not one they had had any part either in designing or endorsing when the postwar order was being established. Dissatisfied with their lot within that order, they mounted challenges to some of its most basic features.

The most sweeping of these challenges was contained in the 1974 Charter of Economic Rights and Duties of States,[28] which asserted new rights (for developing countries that had not participated in the creation of the liberal order) and new duties (for developed countries which had created the liberal order with their own interests and needs in mind). The New International Economic Order (NIEO) was the plan for putting those rights and duties into practice.[29]

These were not the only attacks on the status quo, although they were the most sweeping in scope. Such attacks did not alter the real world status quo, although they may have dented it in places. But they did, in US eyes at least, have the effect of creating a presumption that the status quo was not legitimate—a presumption the United States would not concede. And they certainly altered the status quo at the United Nations, where such bodies as the United Nations Conference on Trade and Development (UNCTAD) and the Committee of 24,[30] created at the urging of large

Third World majorities, shouldered aside older and more conservative UN bodies, developed relatively coherent ideological arguments in support of their revisionist demands, and put the United States and other defenders of the status quo on the defensive.

The regimes that the United States played such a large role in establishing after the war have, of course, undergone dramatic changes, but for the most part those changes are not attributable to the United Nations. The United States itself has been an important change agent: President Nixon's action in suspending the convertibility of dollars into gold in 1971 dealt a far greater blow to the status quo than the Group of 77's call for an NIEO, for example. Yet the UN's persistent and often strident rejection of important elements of the US-supported status quo has been a major factor contributing to US disenchantment with the global organization.

The Unit Veto

In his assessment of the politics of value allocation in the United Nations, Lawrence Finkelstein spoke of an "intermediate zone of struggle" between decisions that depend for their authority on the consent of member states and decisions that do not.[31] Both Finkelstein's argument and the reality of UN politics tell us that the boundaries are not determinate. But this is precisely the problem from the US point of view. The United States assumed that it would not be bound by the overwhelming majority of UN decisions unless it chose to accept those decisions as binding. It was a strict constructionist where the Charter was concerned, and Charter language seemed quite unambiguous: The General Assembly was authorized to "discuss," "consider," and "recommend." The United States was free to opt out of compliance with decisions by the UN majority at will.

There were, to be sure, exceptions, but they, too, were well defined. The Assembly could create subsidiary bodies, approve the budget, apportion expenses, establish regulations for appointment of staff, and, of course, set the agenda and adopt its own rules of procedure. In these specific instances, centralized decisions by majorities (or qualified majorities) were provided for by the Charter. But the United States initially appeared to view decisions in these categories as housekeeping decisions and no threat to its interests. It certainly did not believe that the list of centralized decisions could grow at the expense of the much larger list in which the unit veto was available.

However, those states that were dissatisfied with the status quo—and they turned out to be a rather substantial majority of the members—sought to use the UN as a vehicle for change because its egalitarian/majoritarian decision rules gave them leverage, first to set the agenda for change and then to register overwhelming support for specific changes. But, not surprisingly, the UN majority was not satisfied with only moral victories. It wanted the overwhelming votes for change to be treated as authoritative. As a former Algerian Ambassador to the United Nations argued, the Third World possessed a "right to the creation of law thanks to the strength of its numbers."[32] According to this line of reasoning, UN resolutions calling for changes in the status quo are more than mere recommendations; they should be binding if adopted by compelling majorities.

Third World diplomats and their governments did not really believe that the United States and other members in the minority on such issues would meekly comply, although they frequently argued, to the obvious annoyance of Washington, that all that was lacking was political will. But the majority nonetheless pursued what Stephen Krasner has termed a metapower strategy,[33] that is, seeking to change the rules governing international transactions by employing what in the game of basketball might be termed a full-court press. This consisted of dressing up its demands in language that sounds authoritative, such as the *Charter* of Economic Rights and Duties of States; reiterating those demands in resolution after resolution, each of which is crafted in such a way as to create a presumption that the UN had already decided those matters; cross-referencing demands in other forums; and using such authority as the majority does possess—to set the agenda, adopt the budget, establish supportive committees, instruct the secretariat, and convene ad hoc conferences—to ratchet up the pressure on the custodians of the old order.

The result has not been the demise of the unit veto, but constant struggle over the location of the boundary between decisions subject to the unit veto and decisions whose authority derives from majority votes—a struggle that has taken its toll on US patience. Moreover, even where the majority cannot compel dissenting states to act in particular ways, it can chip away at the legitimacy of their positions or, conversely, build up a presumption of legitimacy for the majority's positions. That the United States understands this is illustrated by the tenacity with which it regularly challenged such things as the "Zionism is racism" resolutions;[34] the repeated references to the New International Economic Order, always in caps as if the content of such an order had already been decided; and the efforts of the Committee of 24 to treat the status of Puerto Rico as an egregious example of colonialism.[35]

Functional Specificity

The division of labor among UN system agencies was never watertight. The United Nations was always a multipurpose organization, and the mandate of the UN Educational, Scientific, and Cultural Organization (UNESCO), although narrower than that of the UN, has always been relatively broad and by its nature easily stretched. As independent states with very low per capita income, negligible industrial capabilities, and dependence on unstable earnings from such commodities as copper, tin, coffee, cocoa, sugar, rubber, and jute became more numerous, pressure mounted across the spectrum of UN-system agencies to make economic development a high priority. The result was the overlapping and interlocking of agendas, as well as increasing competition in the field from UN agencies, each anxious to assume the role of favored provider of technical assistance in developing countries. By the time the campaign for an NIEO was launched, it would not be an exaggeration to say that most UN system agencies were in important respects development agencies. Their membership (clientele) made it inevitable.

In those cases in which international organizations were disinclined to regard themselves as development agencies, efforts were made to convert them to that cause. The International Monetary Fund (IMF) is a conspicuous case in point. Whereas the World Bank had fairly easily made the transition from a bank for reconstruction to a bank for development (although with doctrine and conditions that have sometimes frustrated developing countries), the IMF has always insisted that it is not in the business of lending for development. But developing countries have tried to push and prod the IMF in that direction, often availing themselves of the favorable political climate and decision rules of the UN General Assembly and UNCTAD for the purpose and using those forums to pronounce upon matters traditionally within the purview of the IMF. During the years when the NIEO was an active issue, for example, the UN majority argued that the IMF should create a so-called SDR-aid link, that is, use special drawing rights (SDR) for development assistance as well as for coping with balance-of-payments problems. Not surprisingly, this did not sit well with the United States, which not only strongly disapproved of the idea but also resented the intrusion into the IMF's domain by an organization whose personnel, both delegates and staff, were seen as generalists, lacking the specialized expertise and outlook of their counterparts at the IMF.

Functional specificity among UN agencies broke down along two fault lines. On the one hand, as illustrated by the UN's forays into the IMF's jurisdiction, the general purpose organization challenged the regimes established at the end of World War II by taking exception to the institutional custodians of those regimes. On the other hand, the revisionist majority, intent on giving its message the widest possible hearing, either dismissed the view that the specialized agencies should consider matters falling only within their areas of specialization or rationalized that the issues they raised were of transcendent importance and were therefore germane in any forum.

Thus the issue of the Palestinians was not confined to the UN, where the United States found it difficult enough to deal with, but was broached in virtually all UN system agencies. The United States called this politicization, by which it meant that the agencies were straying from their assigned functional niches and dabbling in matters that should be addressed, if at all, in other, more appropriate forums. A major reason given for US disillusionment with UNESCO, for example, was the allegation that it was poaching upon the turf of other organizations, for example, the UN itself in the matter of arms control and disarmament (although the record will show that the United States was not enthusiastic about much of what the UN itself said and tried to do in this field).

Among the factors undermining the US preference for functionally specific institutions were also the ongoing revolution in science and technology and an awareness of the increasing vulnerability of the sovereign state on a shrinking planet. The former repeatedly demonstrated the interconnectedness among problems, making it increasingly apparent that they could not be effectively addressed in isolation from each other. The latter produced a healthy respect for the phenomenon of negative side effects and a growing sense, at least in some quarters, that the industrial paradigm just might no longer serve the human interest in a world of finite resources and environmental fragility. The reports of the Club of Rome and other organizations with a holistic vision that began surfacing in the 1970s were not addressed to the agenda of any one institution; they directed attention instead to the need for a broader perspective, one that inevitably made the sectoral boundaries within the UN system seem more artificial.

But whether the erosion of boundaries among UN agencies was the product of political calculation by frustrated majorities of member states or inexorable long-term trends in the global problematique, the United States was frequently discomforted by the process. It felt the need to mount damage-control efforts on more issues in more places than it had expected to when the UN system was being created. As with other attempts to change the status quo, this development produced more rhetorical heat than tangible results, but the United States felt compelled to offer resistance out of a concern that silence would be construed as acquiescence in unwanted regime change.

The Market

The recent collapse of any pretense that Communism is a viable economic alternative to capitalism, much less the wave of the future, has apparently made the issue surrounding this particular US assumption moot, at least for the time being. But for a good portion of the UN's existence, the conflict between US insistence on primacy of the market and vigorous challenges to that view by a great many UN members produced one of the principal causes of US disaffection with the global organization. Deeply rooted suspicion of capitalism at the United Nations for much of its history can be attributed to (1) the reaction of the many newly independent members against colonial exploitation; (2) the appeal of the Soviet model, with its promise of more rapid economic progress and more equitable distribution of its benefits than capitalism could provide; and (3) the widespread concern among Third World leaders that a market economy would mean rival centers of power and influence, which might threaten the regime during the difficult period of postindependence nation-building.

As a result, the UN became not only a place where states with a strong commitment to a market economy were outnumbered, but a place where the alleged defects and evils of capitalism were regularly denounced and the virtues of socialism in its various forms (e.g., African socialism) were regularly proclaimed. This was not a situation designed to make the UN popular with the US government at any time, and even less so during the years when its principal rival was a militantly communist state aggressively proclaiming the superiority of its system.

But the more important problem from the US point of view was not the nature of the domestic economy of UN members, but the plans the UN majority had for restructuring the international economy. UNCTAD was created to generate and legitimate different "knowledge" regarding trade and development issues than that emanating from the General Agreement on Tariffs and Trade (GATT) and the IMF (both dominated by Western market-economy states), the Organization for Economic Cooperation and Development (OECD, an exclusively Western club), and even ECOSOC (which had been a disappointment to the growing majority of Third World states at the UN). That different knowledge was ultimately codified in the Charter of Economic Rights and Duties of States and the Declaration and Program of Action for Creation of a New International Economic Order, and it was conspicuously favorable to authoritative as opposed to market allocation of economic goods and services.

This particular manifestation of the assault on the status quo can be seen in such proposals as the Lima Declaration of 1972, with its stipulation that the developing countries' share of the world's manufacturing output be increased to 25 percent by the year 2000,[36] a target that could not possibly be met without massive government intervention in the working of the free market. Even more threatening were provisions of the Law of the Sea Treaty, negotiated under the auspices of the United Nations, which obligates private corporations to make seabed mining technology available to an international enterprise (and to groups of developing countries) and provides for limits on the production of seabed nodules so that earnings of land-based producers will not be adversely affected.[37] Whereas yet another of the "new order" proposals, the Common Fund for Commodities, posed no real challenge to the market in its final form, the original version, vigorously promoted by the UNCTAD Secretariat and the Group of 77, would have authorized a new international institution to intervene in the market to support prices of a number of commodities of special importance to developing countries.[38]

Such measures were designed to overcome the political and economic weaknesses of developing countries—weaknesses, they argued, that made it virtually impossible for them to compete effectively in a market-oriented system. But although government intervention in the marketplace is far from unknown in the United States, the US government was unprepared to scrap the principle of market allocation in such precedent-setting ways. It was convinced that these prescriptions for speeding the process of Third World development would not produce the desired results, that they would damage the interests of the United States and US-based corporations, and that any exceptions to market principles should be ad hoc and situationally specific and not take the form of sweeping regime changes, codified in treaties and broadly applicable to all states regardless of the nature of their particular economic situations.

This issue, perhaps more than any other, demonstrated to the United States the problematic nature of a Charter that allows majorities to define priorities, create new organs to pursue those priorities, and allocate budget resources to promote them. UNCTAD has been a prime example of the problem, in Washington's view. The United States was not enthusiastic about its creation in the first place, but came more and more to resent UNCTAD's role as a think tank for developing countries and a principal incubator of proposals that championed authoritative over market allocation. Whereas, other Western states were variously willing to make concessions to the Group of 77 in UNCTAD and the General Assembly, the United States rarely deigned to treat Third World demands (or the UN's contribution to the formulation of those demands) seriously. Its hostility to the UN over this issue owed less to a concern that the liberal economic order was actually threatened than it did to contempt for the ideas launched and embraced there, as well as resentment that it had to take time to refute those ideas and see its budget assessments channeled into such an endeavor.

Pluralism

The challenge to capitalism was, of course, a challenge to the kind of pluralistic society the United States fervently espoused. But from the US point of view the problem was not only that the UN majority was not sufficiently supportive of the free market. Throughout much of the UN's history the majority of its members were not democracies as the US understands the term, and this undemocratic majority grew appreciably with the influx of new postcolonial states. The result of this trend was a UN, many of whose members had little tolerance for private enterprise, free trade unions, elections based on competition among several political parties, media independent of government control, and other features of a pluralistic society.

There have always been a fair number of traditional dictatorships among the UN member states, whose leaders were more interested in self-aggrandizement than the welfare of their societies. No one has ever confused such states with Western-style democracies, but there has typically been at least a modicum of pluralism in nonpolitical spheres in such states, as long as no challenge was mounted to the dictator. The United States has typically tolerated such regimes, which have not been in the vanguard of those advocating dramatic changes in the international status quo and which have often been US clients.

Much less acceptable to the United States have been the modern dictatorships, mobilization regimes that are typically committed to the radical transformation of their countries, which have at their disposal modern methods of communication and control, and which have often displayed a virulent strain of anti-Americanism.[39] Such states have typically been more vigorous in their challenge to US interests and values, and they have not troubled to disguise their contempt for pluralism. Moreover, they have frequently assumed leadership roles at the UN, their status enhanced by credentials earned in the struggle for independence and the forcefulness of their challenge to an international order that they had no part in creating. Cuba, and to a lesser extent Algeria, have been cases in point, aggressive leaders of the Non-Aligned Movement during the height of the assault on US values at the UN during the 1970s.

One manifestation of the statist mentality the United States has found so troubling has been the UN majority's approach to the human rights issue. The Charter, in Articles 55 and 56, seeks to promote human rights, and the United States has had no problem with that objective, provided that a UN-based regime did not subject US practices to international scrutiny; indeed, it played an important role in the drafting of the Universal Declaration of Human Rights, adopted in 1948.[40] Human rights in many different categories have since been codified in UN-approved treaties.[41] But the UN's record in monitoring compliance with these many rights has been at best highly uneven.

Some part of that record may be understandable, given the tenacity with which sovereign states resist interference in what they regard as their domestic affairs, but the United States has been deeply disappointed with the UN's performance. Part of the problem, as perceived in the United States, is that, regardless of rhetorical support for such political rights as freedom of speech, assembly, and religion, the presumption of innocence, a fair trial, and self-government through free elections, a majority of UN members have not really accepted such limitations upon the authority of the government. For such states, government is the source of rights, not the agent whose potential for misrule and abuse is the justification for individual rights. The UN's mandate in the human rights field has not, therefore, been the vehicle for achieving pluralism that the United States might have hoped it would be.

The rights that over the years have really aroused the emotions of the UN's majority have more often than not been group rights—such as the right of self-determination (at least for people living under colonial rule) and the right not to be subjected to a regime of apartheid—and economic and social rights—such as the right to work, the right to an adequate standard of living, and the right to the highest attainable standard of physical and mental health. The UN's promotion of group rights, which in Washington's view are not controversial per se, has often been resented because it has in effect been a demand that the Western powers take actions the United States regards as imprudent or counterproductive.

Economic and social rights, on the other hand, are treated by the United States more as goals than as rights. The UN majority has often taken the position that the great majority of states cannot now meet those goals because they labor under the crippling disadvantages imposed by the liberal international economic order. The proposed solution has been the acceptance by the West of the Charter of Economic Rights and Duties of States, a solution the United States has never accepted.

In the area of greatest concern to the United States, civil and political rights, UN performance has improved substantially in recent years. But for much of the UN's history, the various UN bodies involved in the field were highly selective in investigating and censuring human rights violations. The issue that rankled the United States more than any other was the repeated condemnation of Israel, the Middle East's only pluralistic democratic country. Israel's policies, especially in the occupied territories, certainly merited attention on occasion, but what angered the United States was the double standard whereby other more egregious offenders were not similarly criticized. For the United States, this combination of statism and hypocrisy contributed significantly to its disenchantment with the United Nations.

Reform, Not Revolution

The US aversion to violent revolution and radicalism, shaped by the lessons learned from its own historical experience and hardened by the Soviet challenge, was tested frequently throughout the years at the United Nations. Although the United States desired the end of colonial empires, it was uncomfortable with the violent process by which some colonies achieved their independence and with the radical rhetoric that accompanied that violence. Too often, from the US perspective, liberation movements were run by self-proclaimed communists or were supplied with arms and other forms of assistance by the Soviet bloc. The alarm felt by the United States was not due just to the violence, but to the credentials and the postindependence goals of the insurgents as well. A case in point was Namibia. The United States supported its independence from South Africa, but serious reservations about the South West African People's Organization (SWAPO) conditioned that support and for years put the United States at odds with the UN's majority on tactics.

The same was true in other struggles where colonialism per se was not the issue, such as those involving the quest for a Palestinian state and the end of apartheid in South Africa. These two cases have been among the most durable, frustrating, and impervious to solution of any on the UN's agenda. In both, the United States has wanted to pursue solutions via diplomacy and negotiation, whereas the great majority of UN members have been willing (some, Washington believed, even eager) to press the issue through all available means. The tactics of both the Palestine Liberation Organization (PLO) and the African National Congress (ANC) have been (and in the case of the PLO still are) anathema to the United States, but have been embraced by the UN in numerous resolutions, almost always over strenuous US objections. Indeed, the UN has granted observer status to these two movements, declared its solidarity with them, created special bodies to help them in their respective struggles, and endorsed armed struggle for the realization of their goals.

From the US perspective, what the United Nations has done, under relentless pressure from a Third World majority hostile to both Israel and South Africa, has been to legitimize radical approaches to difficult, complex problems and, in the process, cause serious harm to the very principles on which the UN is based. The treatment of Israel, perhaps more than any other single factor, has long alienated the United States and convinced it that the majority is all too willing to substitute radical rhetoric for rational debate. Nor does the US government believe that such rhetoric, while offensive, is essentially harmless; as Thomas Franck argued, there has been a sustained attempt "to liquidate the symbols by which the world acknowledges (Israel's) statehood."[42] As recently as 1983, Israel was charged with genocide in the General Assembly and an unsuccessful motion to reject its credentials obtained a total of forty-three votes, which with twenty-nine abstentions meant that nearly 50 percent of those states voting were willing to countenance Israel's exclusion from the UN.[43]

Confronted with radical rhetoric, advocating radical means to achieve radical ends, the United States was rapidly losing patience with the United Nations even before the Reagan-Kirkpatrick "revolution" of the 1980s.

Preemptive Imperialism

The long twilight zone between peace and war, which we know as the Cold War, was not a foregone conclusion when the United Nations was created, but it was a distinct possibility and it quickly became a reality. Chapter 7 of the Charter was clearly an insufficient barrier against unambiguous Soviet aggression, a fact that was established beyond doubt in 1956 when the UN stood helplessly by while Soviet tanks rolled across Hungary. The United States was no more eager than any other state to march into war with the Soviet Union under the UN flag, and has been willing to settle for what Alan James called "creed protection"[44]—UN resolutions that condemn those actions that violate Charter norms, especially when stronger measures are neither possible nor prudent.

Unfortunately, the US view of the UN's proper role often encountered two problems. The first is that the UN majority was not always sufficiently vigorous and explicit in denouncing behavior of the Soviet Union and its clients, which the United States regarded as a violation of Charter norms (as well as a threat to US interests and values). The second is that that same majority was not always willing to endorse unilateral action by the United States aimed at arresting or reversing such behavior, but instead frequently criticized US action on the ground that *it* violated Charter norms.

What the United States wanted from the United Nations was the international community's support for its resistance to the spread of international communism, which it regarded as by far the most serious threat to the status quo throughout the Cold War years. In effect, it wanted the UN to accept its view that the Soviet Union was an imperialist state, committed to an adventurous foreign policy that fished in the troubled waters so common in many parts of the Third World, promoted Marxism-Leninism, stirred up anti-US sentiment, and created client states, dependent on and supportive of the Soviet Union, wherever it could. Washington took the view that the UN should be prepared to oppose Soviet imperialism and support US policies with that objective.

The UN did, to be sure, censure Soviet aggression in a number of instances, from Hungary in 1956 to Afghanistan in 1979, and thereafter.[45] Creed protection in the latter case was most welcome from the US perspective, because it had become convinced that the UN majority had settled into a double standard in this area much as it had in the area of human rights, treating the Soviet Union with kid gloves while showing little or no compunction about criticizing the United States. But in order to obtain broad backing for General Assembly resolutions critical of the Soviet Union (the veto effectively blocked Security Council action), the United States typically had to settle for language that was less sharp and less direct than it would have liked. Thus the resolutions dealing with the presence of

Soviet forces in Afghanistan never mentioned the Soviet Union by name, calling instead for the withdrawal of foreign forces.

But even more important to the United States was the issue of support for its own unilateral efforts to check the spread of communist (read Soviet) influence. Such support was forthcoming in the early case of the North Korean invasion of South Korea, when the Security Council and later the General Assembly adopted resolutions that purported to invoke the Charter's collective security measures, but can more accurately be described as protective cover for US intervention in support of South Korea. In later years, US intervention to arrest what it perceived as the spread of Soviet/communist influence failed to receive the blessing of the United Nations. Although it was the dogged resistance of what US President Lyndon Johnson called that "raggedy-ass little fourth-rate country" and the rising tide of domestic opposition that doomed US intervention in Vietnam, the UN in the person of Secretary-General U Thant angered Washington with his outspoken advocacy of a political rather than a military solution in the Vietnam War.[46]

Whereas the conflict with Thant marked a low point in US government relations with the office of the UN Secretary-General, the hostility of large majorities in the UN's intergovernmental organs to US anticommunist interventions in the Third World, and especially in the Western Hemisphere, was even more frustrating. Grenada and Nicaragua are cases in point. In both instances, the Reagan administration took the position that it was acting to check the spread of Soviet (and Cuban) influence; in both instances, the UN majority rejected that rationale for intervention, contending that the US action constituted a violation of international law and the norms of the Charter. The General Assembly did not name the United States, but otherwise minced no words in affirming "the sovereign and inalienable right of Grenada freely to determine its own political, economic and social system, and to develop its international relations without outside intervention, interference, subversion, coercion or threat in any form whatsoever."[47] The resolution calling for the immediate withdrawal of foreign troops was adopted by the overwhelming margin of 108 in favor, 9 against, and 27 abstentions.

The US invasion of Grenada came to a quick and successful conclusion and was enormously popular in the United States, circumstances that made the General Assembly's criticism doubly irritating. Nicaragua was a different story, the president's policy having encountered strong opposition in the Congress and a decidedly mixed reaction from the public.[48] But here, too, the UN was unsympathetic. The United States was compelled to use its veto to block Security Council decisions calling for a halt to military attacks on Nicaragua and for compliance with the World Court ruling that supported Nicaragua's charges against the United States.[49]

The record is clear that the United Nations has been relatively even-handed in its criticism of Soviet and US violations of Article 2(4) of the Charter. But US administrations have typically rejected what amounted to a doctrine of moral equivalence. They believed that Soviet intentions were malevolent, their own benign. The very stability of the international system was threatened by international Communism, directed and/or nurtured by Moscow, and the international community ought to recognize that fact and support US efforts to combat the spreading cancer. Soviet imperialism was bad, US preemptive imperialism a necessary antidote. The failure of the UN to acknowledge the merits of this thesis and to act on it was an important factor in the souring of US-UN relations.

Efficiency, Frugality

Considering the broad scope of its mandate, the seriousness of many of the issues before it, and the near universal membership it must try to serve, the UN's budget has never been all that large. In 1992, the regular budget (the portion for which members are assessed) totaled approximately $1.1 billion, a seemingly impressive figure that shrinks dramatically in significance when compared with the cost of such things as a B-1 bomber or a Trident submarine.

The US assessment has always been by far the largest of that for any state, reflecting the fact that the United States has the greatest capacity to pay (the principal criterion employed by the organization in determining the scale of assessments). Originally close to 40 percent of the regular budget, the US assessment has been scaled down in steps to its present level of 25 percent. It should be noted that this percentage is actually *less* than would be the case if the principle of capacity to pay had been rigorously applied, the United States having managed to negotiate a lower assessment for itself. It is also worth noting that the UN regular budget constitutes only about .00005 percent of the US gross national product, with each US citizen paying a mere $0.88 as his or her share of the US assessment.[50]

But these figures notwithstanding, the United States has long been dissatisfied with the level of the UN budget. Although the United States did not withhold a percentage of its assessment until the 1970s and did not resort to truly substantial withholding until the 1980s, the US government had been complaining about waste, inefficiency, and mismanagement at the UN for many years before that. These charges mirrored growing dissatisfaction with UN programs, and hence with the agenda of a majority increasingly at odds with the United States over UN purposes and priorities. But while the US critique of UN management was in considerable measure a critique of UN politics and policies, the United States was genuinely convinced that the global organization was badly run.

In this US view, programmatic decisions were increasingly made by the political organs without reference to feasibility or cost. The responsibility for carrying out those decisions was entrusted to a secretariat that was becoming, in US eyes, less professionally and administratively sound as a result of the requirements of geographic distribution and short-term contracts, not to mention poor management practices. The Secretary-General and his principal subordinates were too often seen as captives of a political process they could not control and irresponsible governments to which they could not say no. In effect, the United States was disappointed in the realities of international administration. In addition to the inherent difficulty of integrating the functioning of personnel from many different cultures and administrative systems, there were a host of other problems the United States found frustrating. Among them were a bloated and top-heavy secretariat; secretariat members who were little more than agents of their home countries or whose appointments were clearly based on considerations other than merit; the absence of a clear, coherent relationship between program planning and budget; the proliferation of committees, commissions, and other bodies of marginal utility, often with overlapping and even redundant responsibilities; and excessive meetings and documentation.

The United States pursued its criticism of what it regarded as waste and inefficiency in the General Assembly's Fifth Committee, the Advisory Committee on Administrative and Budgetary Questions (ACABQ), and the Committee on Program and Coordination (CPC), as well as through consultations with other major contributors to the UN's budget. But it regularly encountered resistance from a UN majority that suspected the US concern with waste and inefficiency was simply rationalization and that the real US objective was to subvert the will of the majority. Each of the UN's several restructuring efforts underscored this conflict, the Third World majority wanting to use restructuring to speed the process of development, the United States viewing it as an occasion for administrative reform. Not surprisingly, there has been little restructuring of the United Nations in spite of numerous reports and debates on the subject.[51]

Elements of the National Character

Those elements of national character alluded to in Chapter II—optimism, naiveté, impatience, and a tendency to premillennialism—have all come into play as the United States has struggled with its disappointment with the UN's performance.

US optimism—the belief that progress is easy and that all good things go together—has been severely tested by events since World War II. Because those events have frequently been dramatized, and on occasion exaggerated, on the UN stage, the UN has acquired a negative image—things that should be relatively simple are unnecessarily complicated. That progress toward the solution of global problems is *not* easy is certainly understood by most US leaders, but that does not mean that they or the US public must like it. And the UN's reputation has been tarnished by the fact that it has been a constant reminder that some problems are indeed intractable. The UN's agenda has been clogged with issues that go back many years and produce predictable—and for the United States boring—debate year after year; there is no sunset law at the United Nations.

In a world as complex as the one in which we live, there are bound to be failures of understanding between states with different histories, cultures, economic conditions, political systems, rivalries, values, interests, and problems. In effect, all states are probably more ethnocentric and less well-informed than is desirable for optimally clearheaded and productive diplomacy. This is inevitably a recipe for frustration and occasionally for surprise, and the United States is not immune. In fact, as suggested in Chapter II, the United States may labor under a special handicap as a result of its own relatively insular history and, until recently, limited interaction with many non-Western peoples.

As with US optimism, the problem of a certain naiveté about the world is not, of course, confined to the United Nations, but has affected US policy in a variety of bilateral contexts as well. But the UN tends to magnify the problem. The UN is not a cozy club of the like-minded or the similarly situated. It has, for example, a very large population of states that are predominantly Muslim; the United States has only recently begun to understand these states, and then only imperfectly. African states constitute nearly one-third of the UN's membership, and unlike the British and French, the United States has little familiarity with the African continent and its diversity, which is arguably even greater than that of the world of Islam. Yet these two large and overlapping groups of states have been at the center of most of the UN's most emotional and contentious debates—those concerned with the volatile Middle East, Africa's troubled southern quadrant, economic development, self-determination, and terrorism. The United States has, of course, taken positions on this broad and contentious agenda—positions very often at odds with those preferred by the UN's majority—but it has had a much harder time understanding the forces that shape that agenda.

Ali Mazrui argued that this "lack of understanding is one part of the US insensibility to outsiders, part of the phenomenon of its deaf ear."[52] Mazrui, among others, has charged that US foreign policy is characterized by racism and intolerance of cultural pluralism, a more serious charge than naiveté and one with which many in the Third World would agree. Among the most commonly cited illustrations of that thesis has been nearly reflexive US support for Israel, a Western outpost in a region of darker-skinned peoples whose faith is Islam, a predominantly Afro-Asian religion, and whose culture is strange to virtually the entire US public. The conviction that this pro-Israel, anti-Arab policy is often contrary to real US interests has only helped to make Mazrui's point for Third World critics. And the resulting dialogue of the deaf has only served to further alienate the United States from the United Nations.

It has been argued that impatience is another aspect of the US national character. "The difficult we do immediately, the impossible takes a little longer"—the World War II motto of the Seabees—captures the traditional can-do attitude the United States has typically brought to the conference table. Unfortunately, the United Nations rarely does anything immediately, and some things do not get done at all. This is not, of course, solely or even primarily the fault of the UN per se, although its structures and processes and institutionalized work habits have all contributed to the problem. But the UN, perhaps inevitably, came to symbolize the more complex reality of 150-odd states[53] with very different interests struggling to find common ground and an agreed strategy for reaching it, and on occasion even seeking to dramatize differences rather than compromising them. Not surprisingly, the United States frequently preferred to pursue its policy objectives in settings where it did not have to mobilize support from among so many states of such diverse persuasions.

US impatience has also been on display, of course, when the United States is on the defensive, trying to prevent the adoption of resolutions it opposes, or, at a minimum, to maintain a losing coalition of respectable size and composition. This was the more common experience over the years, and the United States became increasingly impatient with the effort required, especially in view of the marginal results. The impatience was the greater when the effort had to be expended in rebutting "lies." Daniel Patrick Moynihan, in perhaps his most eloquent moment as US ambassador to the UN, expressed it best in his 1975 speech after the adoption of the "Zionism is racism" resolution: "The terrible lie that has been told here today will have terrible consequences. Not only will people begin to say, indeed they have already begun to say, that the United Nations is a place where lies are told. . . ."[54]

Moynihan had, of course, argued that the United States should neither acquiesce in such distortion of language nor abandon the field, but instead stay and fight (or go into opposition, as he urged in the essay that earned him his post as ambassador). And the United States did stay and fight. But its impatience with what was happening there—with respect to language and many other things, some of them quite tangible—would lead eventually to the crisis of the 1980s.

And then there is the matter of that hint of premillennialism in the US approach to world affairs. As we have noted, the United States wanted the

United Nations to join with it in supporting the status quo, and particularly in containing the Soviet Union and rejecting radical solutions to the numerous crises besetting states in the Third World. When the UN instead gave support to the idea of moral equivalence when it was not actually endorsing Soviet-supported causes and clients, the United States tended to react as if the global body were legitimizing evil rather than simply reflecting the interests of its members. US President Dwight Eisenhower's secretary of state, John Foster Dulles, argued precisely this point in attacking nonalignment, a movement that began outside of the UN but soon found in the UN the most effective platform for presenting its case and demonstrating broad support for its positions on the crucial issues of the day. After all, if US causes were good and those of the communist powers were evil, neutrality was not a morally acceptable position.

This attitude also intensified US impatience with UN tolerance of certain Soviet practices. It was no secret that the Soviet Union made no distinction between those of its citizens working in its mission to the UN and those serving in the UN Secretariat, requiring the latter to live in the Soviet compound along with the former and otherwise making a mockery of the concept of an international civil service. The Soviet Union refused to let its nationals accept permanent contracts in the Secretariat, and insisted on what amounted to a claim in perpetuity to certain Secretariat posts. As far as Washington was concerned, Soviets serving in the UN Secretariat were in effect Soviet spies. The fact that US hands were not entirely clean where the concept of an international civil service is concerned, or that other countries have also manipulated the service for their own advantage, is beside the point. It was Soviet behavior and UN acquiescence in it that particularly rankled the United States, and the explanation lies in that premillenniarian perspective which distinguishes evil intent from garden-variety abuses of the system. The latter may be offensive (when others do it), but the former is intolerable.

* * *

In all of these many ways, the United Nations was for many years a chronic source of frustration to the United States. Were we to graph that frustration over time, we would find peaks and valleys—periods of time when US-UN relations were reasonably amicable, or at least less strained, alternating with periods when the global organization and its most important member were on a collision course. But the trend line was largely negative. US expectations for the United Nations had been repeatedly, if not invariably, disappointed, and although the need to stay and defend vital interests always outweighed the urge to walk away from what seemed increasingly to be a failed organization, the United States grew steadily more impatient with the UN and the UN became less and less important in US foreign policy calculations. Finally, in the 1980s, US impatience reached a breaking point.

Notes

1. Harold K. Jacobson, *Networks of Interdependence,* 2nd ed., New York: Alfred A. Knopf, 1984, pp. 11–13.

2. For a discussion of the membership stalemate, see Inis L. Claude, Jr., *Swords into Plowshares,* 3rd ed., New York: Random House, 1964, pp. 83–86.

3. Ibid., p. 119.

4. See Chapter V in this book for a discussion of these resolutions.

5. Stephen Zamora, "Voting in International Economic Organizations," *American Journal of International Law* 74 (1980), p. 608.

6. See, for example, the so-called Uniting for Peace Resolution, GA Res. 377 (V), November 3, 1950.

7. Claude, *Swords into Plowshares,* p. 139.

8. Robert W. Gregg, "The Politics of International Economic Cooperation and Development," in Lawrence S. Finkelstein, ed., *Politics in the United Nations System,* Durham, N.C.: Duke University Press, 1988, p. 116.

9. Ibid.

10. Ibid., p. 115.

11. Geoffrey Barraclough, *An Introduction to Contemporary History,* New York: Penguin Books, 1964, p. 45.

12. Ibid., p. 44.

13. For a recent survey of scientific and technological trends that are transforming international relations, see Kenneth Keller, "Science and Technology," *Foreign Affairs* 69, 4 (Fall 1990).

14. Dennis Pirages, *Global Technopolitics,* Pacific Grove, Calif.: Brooks/Cole Publishing Co., 1989, p. 2.

15. The term is John Gerard Ruggie's. See "On the Problem of the 'Global Problematique': What Role for International Organizations?" *Alternatives* 5 (May 1980), pp. 517–550.

16. In addition to adopting a long series of resolutions condemning South Africa for the practice of apartheid, the General Assembly began in 1974 to refuse to accept the credentials of delegates from the Pretoria government.

17. This theme is explored in Stephen D. Krasner, *Structural Conflict,* Berkeley: University of California Press, 1985.

18. David P. Forsythe, "The Politics of Efficacy," in Finkelstein, *Politics in the United Nations System,* p. 247.

19. See the running account of the expansion of UN efforts in the human rights field in the annual publication of the United Nations Association of the United States entitled *Issues Before the (46th) General Assembly of the United Nations,* now published by the University Press of America, Lanham, Md.

20. Robert Gilpin, *War and Change in World Politics,* Cambridge: Cambridge University Press, 1981.

21. Ibid., p. 30.

22. Thomas M. Franck, *Nation Against Nation,* New York: Oxford University Press, 1985, p. 45.

23. SC Res. 1501, June 25, 1950.

24. Franck, *Nation Against Nation,* p. 59.

25. GA Res. 377 (V), November 3, 1950.

26. The difficulties in replicating the success of UNEF I were quickly apparent in the Congo crisis, when the United Nations once again placed a peacekeeping force in the field with results that came close to destroying the global organization.

27. See Miguel Marin-Bosch, "How Nations Vote in the General Assembly of the United Nations," *International Organization* 41, 4 (Autumn 1987). Marin-Bosch's analysis of General Assembly voting behavior showed that in the 1980s (prior to his essay) the United States cast the lone negative vote 98 times, or twice as many times as all other UN members combined.

28. GA Res. 3281 (XXIX), December 6, 1974.

29. GA Res. 3201 and 3202 (S-VI), May 1, 1974.

30. See GA Res. 1654 (XVI), November 27, 1961. This Committee (originally of 17) was to assume responsibility for realizing the goals of the Declaration on the Granting of Independence to Colonial Countries and Peoples, GA Res. 1514 (XV), December 14, 1960.

31. Lawrence S. Finkelstein, "The Politics of Value Allocation in the UN System," in Finkelstein, *Politics in the United Nations System,* pp. 1–40.

32. Mohammed Bedjaoui, *Towards a New International Economic Order,* New York: Holmes and Meier, 1979, p. 142.

33. Krasner, *Structural Conflict,* pp. 13–18.

34. GA Res. 3379 (XXX), November 10, 1975.

35. Franck recounted this struggle in *Nation Against Nation,* pp. 195–199.

36. The Lima Declaration and Plan of Action on Industrial Development and Cooperation was endorsed at the Second General Conference of the United Nations Industrial Development Organization (UNIDO) in 1975 and quickly became an integral part of the NIEO agenda.

37. See United Nations Convention on the Law of the Sea, Part XI, especially Section 3 and Annex III.

38. For analysis of the Common Fund negotiations, see Robert L. Rothstein, *Global Bargaining,* Princeton, N.J.: Princeton University Press, 1979, as well as his subsequent articles, "Regime Creation by a Coalition of the Weak," *International Studies Quarterly* 28 (Autumn 1984), and "Consensual Knowledge and International Collaboration: Some Lessons from the Commodity Negotiations," *International Organization* 38, 4 (Autumn 1984).

39. See Barry Rubin, *Modern Dictators,* New York: McGraw-Hill, 1987.

40. GA Res. 217A (III), December 10, 1948.

41. See especially the International Covenant on Economic, Social and Cultural Rights and the International Covenant on Civil and Political Rights, both adopted in GA Res. 2200A (XXI), December 16, 1966. Other human rights treaties have been adopted in the fields of torture, racial discrimination, and gender discrimination, as well as on the subject of apartheid.

42. Franck, *Nation Against Nation,* p. 216.

43. Ibid., p. 217.

44. Alan M. James, "Unit Veto Dominance in United Nations Peace-Keeping," in Finkelstein, *Politics in the United Nations System,* pp. 82–83.

45. On Hungary, see GA Res. 1004 (ES-11), November 4, 1956. On Afghanistan, the Assembly first addressed the issue in GA Res. (ES-VI), January 4, 1980.

46. This episode in US-UN relations is well described by Franck, *Nation Against Nation,* pp. 153–158, and by Max Harrelson, *Fires All Around the Horizon,* New York: Praeger, 1989, pp. 157–166.

47. GA Res. 38/7, November 2, 1983.

48. A good account of this story is to be found in Cynthia J. Arnson, *Cross-Roads,* New York: Pantheon Books, 1989.

49. The General Assembly did adopt a resolution demanding compliance with the ICJ ruling. See GA Res. 41/31, June 27, 1986.

50. David P. Forsythe, *The Politics of International Law,* Boulder, Colo.: Lynne Rienner, 1990, p. 118.

51. Restructuring did not become a serious issue at the UN until the mid-1970s, in the context of debate about a New International Economic Order. The most ambitious reforms did not occur, however, until the financial crisis of the 1980s and early 1990s, and these were largely limited to the secretariat rather than to the multiplicity of intergovernmental bodies that have grown up within the UN system and the UN itself over the years.

52. Ali Mazrui, "Uncle Sam's Hearing Aid," in Sanford J. Ungar, ed., *Estrangement: America and the World,* New York: Oxford University Press, 1985, p. 188.

53. UN membership stood for some time at 159; the breakup of the Soviet Union and Yugoslavia, together with the end of the Cold War, has in the 1990s pushed that number above 180.

54. Daniel Patrick Moynihan, *A Dangerous Place,* Boston: Little, Brown and Company, 1978, p. 198.

Chapter IV

The Financial Crisis:
The United States Versus
the United Nations

The landslide victory scored by Ronald Reagan over Jimmy Carter in the 1980 presidential election was, in important respects, a watershed event for the United States. The emphasis on supply-side economics, government deregulation, dramatically increased defense spending, and the Armageddon-like struggle with the "evil empire" of the Soviet Union has been much commented on by both supporters and critics of the Reagan revolution. The rapidly escalating budget deficit that resulted from these policies has generated an enormous amount of publicity, if very little in the way of effective corrective measures. And taxes, always unpopular but the acknowledged means of paying for civilized society, had acquired such a bad odor as a result of Reagan-era rhetoric that few politicians in the land any longer have had the political courage to speak of raising them to address either the deficit or society's needs.[1]

These landmark changes in US political and economic life so dominated public discourse in the 1980s that relatively little attention was paid to another important shift in US policy. It was at this time that the United States turned up the heat, as it were, on the United Nations, resorting to tactics far stronger than rhetorical condemnation. The United States, in effect, undertook to bend UN practice to US political will by playing the most potent card in the US hand—the leverage resulting from the fact that the United States pays 25 percent of the UN's regular budget.

A case can be made, of course, that the change in US policy toward the UN during the Reagan administration was more one of degree than one of kind. After all, neither the failures of the United Nations to measure up to US expectations nor expressions of US disenchantment with the global body were new. The change in policy may have seemed more dramatic because the Carter administration had consciously sought to send a signal that the UN would have a more prominent place in the conduct of US foreign policy. Tensions in US-UN relations had been eased by the appointment of Andrew Young as the US ambassador to the United Nations. Young had "talked of redeeming the United States at the UN and the UN in the United States, of putting the United States on 'the right side of the moral issues of the world.'"[2] During his stewardship there, he made it clear that the United States wanted to make greater use of the UN, and he adopted a diplomatic style that underscored that intent.

But the Carter-Young interlude should not be construed as a major turning point in US-UN relations; rather, it should be seen as an attempt, against the grain, to redirect US foreign policy and to use the UN as one vehicle for doing so. How ephemeral that attempt was became apparent shortly after the election of 1980. Having said that, however, it remains true that what happened to the US approach to the United Nations during the Reagan administration did constitute a rather significant departure from earlier practice. The United States had long resisted majority-sponsored resolutions, endorsing ideas and calling for actions it found unacceptable, and had found itself on the losing end of the vote count on such resolutions with increasing frequency. It had long complained about a variety of UN practices and argued for reforms, only to discover that what it regarded as meaningful reform was almost impossible to achieve in the prevailing political climate at the UN. The US response in the past had been to take a principled stand, seeking to persuade and, failing that, registering its objections, the meanwhile distancing itself from the organization and discounting its importance in the conduct of US foreign policy.

The United States might have been expected to do something very much like this during the Reagan era. But it did something else as well. It undertook to compel the UN to change its ways by withholding a sizable portion of its sizable financial assessment. This was not the first time that the United States had resorted to this tactic, but it was the first time that it had done so on a scale that made clear that it was not only registering its displeasure but also trying to force the UN to perform as the United States wanted it to perform. The United States decided to play hardball.

The story of US policy toward the United Nations during the Reagan years is, of course, more complicated than is suggested by the use of the familiar sports metaphor. It is a story that encompasses the sometimes strained relationship between the executive and legislative branches of the US government, as well as the complexities of the legislative process, especially where budget issues are concerned. And it is a story that necessarily focuses on the interplay between the representative subsystem in Washington and the participant subsystem in New York.[3] In other words, the conflict between the United States and the United Nations during the 1980s can be viewed as an action-reaction process or feedback loop. Decisions reached at the UN stimulated factions within the US government to greater (and more negative) activity, resulting eventually in rejection of the obligation to pay the full US assessment. This policy, in turn, stimulated reaction at the United Nations, leading to a qualified adjustment of the rules governing the process of UN budget making. And those changes in New York in their turn led to a new round of debate within the US representative subsystem and a further modification of the US position. This action-reaction process was on display throughout much of the Reagan presidency; its results are still with us, and they both support cautious optimism regarding the future of US-UN relations and present problems for the UN as it tries to assume a more positive role in the post–Cold War era.

Financial Obligations Under the UN Charter

Decisions of the United Nations fall into two categories: Those of external application and those of internal application. Decisions in the former, with rare exceptions, do not bind member states without their consent.[4] They are symbolic in character, mere tests of international opinion. There are, of course, those who will argue that such decisions, especially when reiterated many times by overwhelming majorities or by consensus, should enjoy the status of international law.[5] But the language and the logic of the Charter argue otherwise, and states can and do ignore such decisions, not only with impunity but with ample legal justification.

Decisions of internal application are another matter. Most such decisions are either specifically authorized by the Charter, in which case they enjoy the legal standing of the Charter itself, an international treaty, or they are logically inferred from specific Charter provisions. These decisions have standing in international law that decisions of external application do not. The most conspicuous example of decisions of internal application are General Assembly resolutions that adopt the organization's budget and set members' assessments.

Article 17 of the UN Charter is explicit about this. It stipulates that "the General Assembly shall consider and approve the budget of the Organization" and that "the expenses of the Organization shall be borne by the Members as apportioned by the General Assembly." One does not need to read between the lines or argue in this case that a general grant of authority, to be effective, requires a specific (and possibly controversial) interpretation. Nor is this a case in which the Charter appears to send a mixed message, as it does, for example, in Article 2 (4) with its requirement that "all members shall refrain in their international relations from the threat or use of force" and in Article 51 with its provision that "nothing in the present Charter shall impair the inherent right of individual or collective self-defense."

The intent of Article 17 is clear. The fact that Article 18 (2) classifies budgetary questions as important ones, to be made by a two-thirds majority of the members present and voting, tends to reinforce the view that the drafters of the Charter understood full well what they were doing in Article 17. And if there were any doubt, it would seem to be dispelled by Article 19, with its provision that states falling two years in arrears in the payment of their financial contributions shall lose their vote in the General Assembly. Only in Articles 5 and 6 is so explicit and severe a penalty specified for failure to comply with one of the provisions of this treaty.[6] States that ratified the Charter and became members of the United Nations undertook to be bound by its provisions, including Article 17.

This is the situation in law. In practice, as we know, things have been quite different. Over the years, many states have paid less than their full assessment as approved by the General Assembly under Article 17. Their reasons for doing so have varied, but in the main have been the result either of an alleged inability to pay or of a demonstrated unwillingness to pay, based on strong disagreement with the purposes for which the money was to be spent or the processes by which those expenditures were approved. The former explanation for nonpayment may be acceptable under the Charter; the latter is not.

But the fact that majority decisions are authoritative on matters pertaining to the budget has not meant that some states have not exercised a unit veto. There have been two major assaults on the General Assembly's authority in this area, one occurring principally in the 1960s and the other—the focus of this case study—in the 1980s. They make the point, and make it convincingly, that the struggle over the capacity of the UN General Assembly authoritatively to allocate values is a two-way street. The majoritarian camp may have been tenacious in its demands for more centralization of authority, but defenders of the unit veto have not only resisted those demands but have actually challenged the authority of the majority in the area where it would appear to be strongest under the Charter—control over the budget.

In the 1960s and again in the 1980s, the General Assembly majority's control over the UN budget was challenged, in the first instance by the Soviet Union and other Communist bloc states and by France, and in the second by the United States. In both cases, actions in violation of obligations incurred by becoming members of the United Nations proved to be powerful means of coercing changes in the rules governing budget making. In the ongoing struggle over capacity of the United Nations authoritatively to allocate values, those who wished to reduce that authority were in a stronger position than those who wished to expand it. Capabilities are decidedly asymmetrical at the United Nations.

The first of the UN's two major financial crises, the one which rocked the organization in the 1960s, was the result of the refusal of several states, the Soviet Union and France foremost among them, to pay assessments for one or more peacekeeping forces.[7] This case is distinguishable from the crisis of the 1980s in that nonpayment was justified in part on the ground that the peacekeeping operations were themselves illegal. The Soviet Union and France took the position that under the Charter only the Security Council could authorize peacekeeping forces, whereas it was the General Assembly, acting under the Uniting for Peace resolution, that had done so in the Suez and Congo crises. The United States made no such claim of illegality when it withheld portions of its assessments in the 1980s. Moreover, the costs of both the United Nations Emergency Force and the United Nations Operation in the Congo (ONUC) were financed out of separate accounts, thereby differentiating them from the regular budget. However, these costs were treated as UN expenditures within the scope and intent of Article 17 of the Charter, both by the Secretary-General and the General Assembly; an advisory opinion of the World Court declared them to be legally binding[8] and an overwhelming majority of the membership supported a resolution accepting the Court's opinion[9]—all of which suggests that those who refused to pay were in effect acting to reduce the scope of centralized authority and setting a precedent of sorts for US withholding in the 1980s.

The penalty prescribed in Article 19 was never invoked against the Soviet Union, even though its refusal to pay assessments for the peacekeeping forces placed it more than two years in arrears. The UN went to great lengths to avoid a showdown over this important constitutional issue, transacting business during the 1964 General Assembly session by substituting "laboriously negotiated consensus" for voting.[10] Whereas the United States had initially been adamant about the importance of upholding the Charter, in the end it concluded that the costs of forcing an issue that it could not be sure of winning in any event were simply too high.

One factor in the US abandonment of its support for the letter of the Charter and for the International Court of Justice advisory opinion was almost certainly a growing awareness that an authoritative General Assembly might not always be in the best interests of the United States. Ambassador Arthur Goldberg made a point of noting the precedential quality of the Assembly's failure to apply the Article 19 penalty to the defaulters in 1964, declaring that "if any member can insist on making an exception to the principle of collective financial responsibility with respect to certain activities of the Organization, the United States reserves the same option to make exceptions if, in our view, strong and compelling reasons exist for doing so."[11] In 1964, the US position was not that Articles 17 and 19 had been "repealed" or that the General Assembly's authority had been trimmed in this critical area. But a shadow of doubt had been cast on the obligation to pay assessments voted by the requisite majority of the General Assembly. Whether the Charter had been amended de facto remained a debatable question well into the 1980s, and indeed is still an open question.

What is clear is that the United States did not invoke the Goldberg doctrine for many years, even when it found itself in disagreement with the UN majority on budget issues, which was often. Instead, the government typically made its case in the Fifth Committee of the General Assembly (and in other subsidiary committees with responsibility for aspects of the budget process) and then abstained and grumbled about the result. The presumption that there was a legal obligation to pay was a strong one, and no direct challenge was mounted against centralized authority on budget matters for a considerable period of time after the Article 19 crisis.

As we shall see, even in the 1980s, when the United States became much more aggressively confrontational with respect to the United Nations, the president (or at least the executive branch) took pains to stress that the United States had a legal obligation to pay assessments voted by the General Assembly. It never argued that the obligation to pay had become a casualty of custom, that because states had not been penalized for failure to meet their financial obligations, Article 17 no longer meant quite what it said and states are no longer required under the Charter to pay what the General Assembly assesses them to finance the budget it has approved. Indeed, it would have been difficult to make an empirical case for such an argument, given the fact that UN members that were more than two years in arrears had in fact been deprived of their votes in the General Assembly by the simple expedient of turning off the electronic voting mechanism at their seats.

But the obligation to pay, while never denied by the US government, was eroded by two developments in the 1980s: One was the evolution of the practice of selective withholding by the administration and the other was the introduction of the practice of dramatic, across-the-board withholding as a result of action by the Congress. These are closely related phenomena that at one and the same time tell us much about the conflict between the executive and legislative branches of the US government in the conduct of US foreign policy and just as much or more about the symbiotic relationship between the two branches at a time when US-UN relations had reached their nadir.

The Reagan Administration and the United Nations

As we have noted, US-UN relations had been deteriorating over the years, and in spite of efforts by Carter administration people, notably Ambassadors Andrew Young and Donald McHenry and Assistant Secretary of State for International Organization Affairs C. William Maynes, the United States entered the 1990s with a substantial catalogue of grievances against the United Nations. The UN's agenda had come more and more to reflect the preoccupations of the Third World majority, and both the ends and the means advocated by that majority, aided and abetted by the Soviet Union, were difficult for US policymakers to accept. The UN budget inevitably reflected these developments; the rate of growth of the budget, spurred by the ever-growing Third World constituency, was perceived in Washington as out of control. Many of the purposes for which US assessments were being spent severely strained the tolerance of key figures in both branches of the government. Nor was the problem limited to the United Nations itself. Disenchantment with other agencies within the UN system was also on the rise, especially for the Congress. Testimony to this mood may be found in such documents as the so-called Ribicoff Report of 1977,[12] which catalogued a whole series of grievances against the way the system was working.

Events of the 1970s foreshadowed the abandonment by the United States in the 1980s of a willingness to accept responsibility for its financial obligations. It was during that decade that the Congress, in its handling of appropriations for both the International Labour Organisation (ILO) and UNESCO, established a precedent for its attack on the UN assessment. In 1970, seven years before the United States withdrew from the ILO, the Congress reduced by half the president's request for funds for that organization. In 1971 it appropriated no funds whatsoever. In 1974, ten years before pulling out of UNESCO, the Congress stipulated that no funds were to be obligated or spent to support that organization until the president certified that it had ceased certain anti-Israel actions.[13] In both cases, funds were released well before the United States fell two years behind in its payments, suggesting that both branches of the government were mindful of the country's legal obligation. But the United States had taken the first steps down the slippery slope. Moreover, the Congress in 1972 had adopted legislation stipulating that the US contribution to the UN budget, then set at 31.52 percent of the whole, be reduced to 25 percent by the end of 1973.[14] The House of Representatives had earlier in that same year approved a bill that would have achieved the same result immediately, placing the United States in violation of the Charter, and there is strong likelihood that the US would have unilaterally reduced its assessment the following year had not the 27th General Assembly voted to bow to US pressure and accept the 25 percent ceiling.[15] Thus there was no violation of the Charter and no formal refusal to accept a decision of the General Assembly regarding the budget as binding. But it was a close call. Already in 1972, as John Stoessinger has observed, "a large number of American legislators had come to perceive the United Nations as, at least, a wasteful and inefficient body and, at worst, an organization that in the wake of the American defeat over the Chinese representation issue, had become inimical to the national interest."[16]

And this was before the "Zionism is a form of racism" resolution. It was before the campaign for a New International Economic Order and before the resolution on a Charter of Economic Rights and Duties of States was adopted, blaming the Western market economy states for failure of Third World development, demanding sweeping changes in the structure of the world economy, and insisting on the equivalent of an affirmative action program for developing countries. It was before US labor's dissatisfaction with the policies of the ILO led to the temporary withdrawal from that agency, and before charges of politicization and frustration over a New World Information Order undermined support for UNESCO and helped create the climate of negative opinion that in the 1980s supported the decision to withdraw from that organization as well.[17] It was before US Ambassador Daniel Patrick Moynihan, calling the UN a dangerous place, urged the United States to go into opposition at the UN.[18]

In effect, the years immediately prior to the advent of the Reagan era were a period of growing disillusionment the UN system, a disillusionment the Carter administration was unable to dispel and to which it may even have inadvertently contributed.[19] It was a disillusionment tinged with anger—anger at perceived politicization; at double standards; at programs that seemed to violate the principle that the activities of these organizations would be beneficial to all members; at an increasing emphasis on statism; at secretariats that were regarded as biased, incompetent, and disloyal to the ethic of a truly international civil service; at mismanagement or worse by executive heads; and at persistent and seemingly perverse hostility to US views and values. When the United States acted in the 1980s to withhold monies from the UN, it acted in the context of years of cumulative disappointments and frustrations with the global organization.

In retrospect, one of the most important previews of the events of the 1980s was provided by the contretemps over the so-called Helms amendment in 1978. This congressional assault on the principle that full payment of assessments is a legal obligation took the form of efforts to cut appropriations by an amount equivalent to the portion of UN agency budgets devoted to technical assistance. The argument in this case was that technical assistance should be funded through voluntary contributions to programs such as the United Nations Development Program. In that way the United States could control the level of its commitment and frustrate Third World efforts to achieve automaticity of resource transfers through the regular budgets of the UN and the specialized agencies. This issue, which threatened to become a hardy perennial, came to a head in 1978 with the adoption of an amendment by Senator Jesse Helms (R-N.C.) to the FY 1979 appropriations bill for the Departments of Commerce, Justice, and State, which deleted nearly $28 million and added a proviso that the US contribution to the regular budget could not be used for technical assistance purposes.[20] The "treaty obligation" argument initially prevailed in the House, but ultimately, during consideration of the conference report, the House voted to accept the Senate (i.e., the Helms) version. President Carter opposed this action, both on the ground that it was illegal and because he, like all presidents, disliked micromanagement of foreign policy by the Congress. But he signed the appropriations bill nonetheless, indicating that he would ask the 96th Congress to repeal the restriction.

UN officials indicated that they could not accept earmarked funds, and the president was unable to certify that none of the US contribution would be used for technical assistance programs; as a result, the law had the effect of freezing the entire US contribution to the affected agencies. The funds were eventually restored, but it was a closely contested struggle between those who argued that the United States had an obligation to pay its assessment and increasingly assertive conservatives who denied any such obligation and were openly seeking more control over UN system expenditures by the United States (and by the Congress).

The tenor of the arguments being advanced by the UN's congressional critics was reflected in the charge of Congressman John Rousselot (R-Calif.) that assessments amount to mandatory taxes collected by the UN tax man and in Senator Helms's assertion that these assessments are an international tax that US taxpayers do not owe.[21] This line of argument would be heard again in the 1980s when US hostility to both the United Nations and taxes generally peaked during the Reagan presidency. Although the Congress did subsequently modify its position on this issue and never formally sought to make the case that the UN had exceeded its authority, it had effectively implemented the Goldberg doctrine and set the stage for a more serious challenge to the United Nations, which was to come during the Reagan presidency.

Responsibility for the stepped-up assault on the United Nations in the 1980s has been the subject of considerable debate. In the final analysis, however, the executive and legislative branches of the government must share responsibility. The massive US withholding of funds from the United Nations is typically attributed to the Kassebaum amendment, so-called because the sponsor of the measure that most dramatically restricted the US contribution was Senator Nancy Kassebaum (R-Kan.).[22] This would seem to suggest that it was the Congress, not the White House, that was primarily responsible for the confrontation that brought the UN to the edge of bankruptcy. But although it is true that anti-UN sentiment ran high on Capitol Hill and that for a time Congress took the initiative away from the administration on the matter of the US assessment, as it had in the 1970s, President Reagan and his appointees were key players in that confrontation. They set the tone for US-UN relations in the 1980s; Congress was quick to pick up the cue.

By 1980 the national mood had changed, and the president himself personified and reflected that new mood. Whatever the words used to describe that mood and the president's articulation of it—assertive, tough, a nation once again standing tall—they suggest a declining tolerance for business as usual at the UN, where the United States seemed to have taken up residence as a permanent, defensive, and often lonely minority. An administration that was "the most unilateralist, nationalistic, and ideological of any presidential team since at least 1945"[23] had little need for such an organization. The Heritage Foundation, once an organization on the outer fringe of respectability, gained credibility and influence as a think tank that had the ear of the new administration; its United Nations Studies project, with its barrage of anti-UN monographs and backgrounders, captured the growing resentment with the global organization and channeled it into policy recommendations.[24]

The much heightened hostility to the UN had its personification in the appointment of Professor Jeane Kirkpatrick as the US ambassador there. Kirkpatrick, who shared much of the Heritage Foundation's dissatisfaction with the UN, was an ideal spokesperson for the administration she served. Both the message she carried to the UN and the style in which she delivered it were well attuned to the new national mood.[25] She made full use of her post to castigate the UN for what she saw as the defects of both its processes and its policies, and because she was perceived to be close to the president her indictment carried much weight.

Moreover, Ambassador Kirkpatrick brought into the government, both at the mission in New York and in the Bureau of International Organization Affairs in the Department of State, a group of like-minded people, some of them from the Heritage Foundation, who collectively produced a decidedly anti-UN tilt within the government. These were the people who were called upon to craft US policy toward the United Nations and to testify on Capitol Hill on UN-related matters, budget included, and inevitably their negative message had an impact. Whereas other members of her team, including a string of hard-liners who served as assistant secretaries of state, had more to do with shaping that message in Washington, it was her colleague, Ambassador Charles Lichenstein, Kirkpatrick's alter ego at the Security Council, who made the biggest headline. In remarks later characterized as "off the cuff" and not approved by the White House, he had this to say:

> If in the judicious determination of the members of the UN, they feel they are not welcome and they are not being treated with the hostly consideration that is their due, then the US strongly encourages such member states seriously to consider removing themselves and their organization from the United States. We will put no impediment in your way, and we will be at dockside bidding you a fond farewell as you set off into the sunset.[26]

Unfortunately, but not surprisingly, President Reagan chose to dignify this irresponsible speech just two days later, saying that Lichenstein "had the hearty approval of most people in America in his suggestion that we weren't asking anyone to leave, but if they chose to leave, goodbye."[27]

Nor was administration hostility reserved for the United Nations alone. International organizations generally came in for rough treatment from an administration that was even more sensitive than its predecessors had been to a perceived lack of respect for US interests and values. It was during the Reagan era that the United States reversed policy at the UN Law of the Sea Conference, abandoning support for a treaty that previous US administrations had played such an important role in drafting; withdrew from UNESCO just as that UN system agency was beginning to make significant progress in addressing US complaints; cast the only vote against a World Health Organization resolution that sought to restrict the marketing of infant formula in developing countries; and even turned sour on the World Bank and the IMF for lending and regulatory practices that were deemed insufficiently supportive of free market principles. It was not a propitious time for US relations either with the UN or with the UN system.

The fact that the representative subsystem for US participation in the UN was so much more openly hostile to the UN during the Reagan presidency created a situation in which it became increasingly difficult for the view to prevail that the United States had a treaty obligation to pay its assessed share of the UN budget. Initially, withholding was selective, as it had been in the case of the Helms amendment when Carter was in the White House. An early and enduring example of such selective withholding has been the refusal to pay that portion of the US assessment that would have been used to finance programs beneficial to the PLO (e.g., the Division on Palestinian Rights in the UN Secretariat and the General Assembly Committee on the Exercise of the Inalienable Rights of the Palestinian People). Another example has been the withholding of funds equal to the US share of the annual cost of the Preparatory Committee responsible for drafting rules for implementation of the Law of the Sea Treaty. These instances of withholding have different origins. The first is attributable to a congressional initiative, the second to a decision taken in the executive branch. But the result is the same: nonpayment of a small but symbolically important part of the US assessment.

At least these instances of withholding are consistent with the norm developed in the financial crisis of the 1960s and enunciated in the Goldberg doctrine. They constitute refusal to pay for specific activities that the United States opposes (or believes to be in violation of the Charter). Ambassador Kirkpatrick argued the legitimacy of such withholdings in testimony before the Congress:

> I think that it is appropriate for us to withhold contributions from the
> United Nations when the purposes for which they are being spent are not
> consistent with the goals of the Charter. Those assessed funds are, after all,
> assessed in relationship to some specific goals, and those goals are stated in
> the Charter, and if programs are proposed that are themselves inconsistent
> with the Charter and American values, I think it is appropriate for the
> United States under those circumstances to withhold.[28]

Whether such withholding constitutes a responsible exercise of US power
is, of course, another matter. But refusal to pay for programs that support
the PLO or the Law of the Sea Preparatory Committee is a far cry from
blanket withholding. This was yet to come, and it was not long in coming.

The attack on the UN budget, as opposed to specific line items in that
budget, escalated rapidly in the 1980s. Near the end of President Reagan's
first year in office, the United States, for the first time in the UN's history,
cast a vote against the UN budget in its entirety.[29] That this was a perfectly
legal exercise of US power, an attempt to influence the UN majority and
the Secretary-General to rein in budget growth, is not in dispute. Moreover, the United States had the support of other major contributors in opposing the UN budget. But it is clear that US patience was fast approaching a breaking point. Given the prevailing attitude within the government
and the Congress, together with the steady erosion of traditional restraints,
it seemed probable that the United States would soon refuse to comply
with budget decisions of the UN majority unless significant and timely
concessions were made in New York.

Another straw in the wind was the Reagan administration's decision to
begin delaying the date of payment of its annual contribution to the UN.
Reagan had come into office committed to cutting government expenditures, and although the UN was not a special target (the assessment was
too small to make much of a dent in the US budget), steps taken to reduce
federal spending and induce restraint at the UN did contribute to an undermining of respect and support for US treaty obligations. Under UN
rules, payment of the annual assessment in full is due within thirty days
of receiving the Secretary-General's letter requesting it. That letter is typically sent in January. Under the change instituted by the Reagan administration, the United States now defers payment until the fourth quarter of
the calendar year. Even though this shift had only a bookkeeping rationale
in Washington, it had the effect of creating cash flow problems at the UN.

In the early 1980s, Congress also signalled a readiness to expand the
scope of the Goldberg doctrine and begin generalized withholding. It
passed a law that stipulated the United States should cease participation
in and withhold financial support from the UN or any UN-system agency
that denies participation to Israel.[30] The Department of State quickly fell
into line with this congressional mandate and invoked the policy in the
case of the International Atomic Energy Agency in 1982.[31]

This action by Congress reflected a growing unwillingness to be bound by decisions of the UN majority and contributed to a sense that the United Nations and the United States were on a collision course. It also indicated that the Congress was quite prepared to confront the UN on its own, independently of the position of the executive branch. And although the executive branch inevitably had problems with congressional assertions of independence, its own rhetoric and actions had more than a little to do with the performance by the Congress. After all, Reagan was the first president to withhold UN assessments without congressional mandate.

The Kassebaum Amendment

All of this skirmishing came to a head in 1985 in the form of an amendment to the Foreign Relations Authorization bill, introduced by the junior senator from Kansas, Nancy Kassebaum.[32] It is ironic that this most serious of US challenges to its obligations under the UN Charter should be associated with Senator Kassebaum. She is not, and was not at the time, a member of the reflexively anti-UN camp in the Congress. Most Hill watchers claim that her initiative, successful in considerable measure because of the respect accorded her as a nonideological pragmatist, owed much to the diligent and persuasive work of a much more ideological member of her staff. In any event, it was her amendment that came to be identified with the nadir in US-UN relations.

Senator Kassebaum's amendment was not aimed at any one instance of UN malfeasance or any one UN position that the US found objectionable. It was concerned instead with an overall pattern of excess and waste, and with the fact that the United States, in spite of its role as the largest contributor by far to the UN budget, was unable to exercise proportionate influence over the global organization's spending priorities and practices. What she sought was reform in the process by which the United Nations approved its budget. The means she proposed for achieving the goal of UN reform involved an across-the-board reduction in the US contribution. The earmarked withholdings, which until then had been the vehicle for expression of US dissatisfaction, could and presumably would continue, but they clearly did not constitute sufficient leverage for genuine reform. The Kassebaum amendment provided that leverage. It called for a 20 percent reduction in the US contribution (from 25 percent to 20 percent of the UN's budget) and it stipulated that the reduction should remain in effect until the UN (and its specialized agencies) introduced weighted voting on budgetary matters. In other words, the United States would have the equivalent of 25 percent of the votes when decisions regarding the budget were being made. If it did not, it would unilaterally reduce its assessment to 20 percent of the UN budget.

The demand that weighted voting replace one-state/one-vote in decisionmaking regarding the budget was tantamount to an insistence on a change in the regime for financing the UN system. In fact, regime theorists would argue that the United States was insisting on a change *of* the regime itself, because it would override one of the fundamental principles on which the regime was based, the principle of equality of states. Weighted voting may, of course, coexist with a requirement that decisions be reached by a majority (simple or extraordinary) of votes cast. That is the situation in the IMF and the World Bank. But those majorities would be very different from those that have heretofore approved UN budgets. As a practical matter, weighted voting would give a de facto veto to the principal donor states if their votes were weighted more or less proportionately to the size of their contribution to the budget.[33] A quick glance at the list of states voting against the United Nations budgets in the years preceding the adoption of the Kassebaum amendment makes it quite clear that those budgets would have been rejected (or tailored to satisfy the objections of the major donors) under a system of weighted voting.[34] So the US action was nothing less than a direct challenge to one of the UN's basic premises and a bold attempt to shrink substantially the scope of such centralized authority as the UN possesses under the Charter.

There was, of course, no prospect whatsoever that weighted voting could be adopted by the United Nations, given the conditions for amending the Charter.[35] Elliott Richardson, chairman of the United Nations Association of the United States, said as much when he observed that demanding what is unachievable only complicates the task of improving UN performance.[36] And inasmuch as Senator Kassebaum and a majority of the members of the Congress were more interested in reforming the UN than killing it, there was a willingness to reconsider the Kassebaum language when the UN General Assembly responded to US pressure by agreeing to reforms in the UN's budget process.

The UN Response to US Pressure

The Kassebaum amendment, coming as it did on the heels of a growing list of US withholdings for specific purposes, focused the attention of the UN membership as few other developments in recent UN history had. By the time the Kassebaum amendment took effect, the UN already faced a deficit and cash flow problem as a result of various other withholdings and unpaid assessments by a number of countries in respect to both the regular budget and peacekeeping forces.[37] The Secretary-General had been reporting annually to the General Assembly on the organization's deteriorating financial situation, and he had taken steps to reduce spending, including a freeze on hiring, wage increases, and promotions, and the imposition of new limits on travel, paperwork, overtime, and consultants.[38] By fall 1986, a serious question had arisen as to whether the United Nations would be able to pay its bills and meet its payroll.

During its 41st Session, the General Assembly received the report of the eighteen-member Group of High-Level Intergovernmental Experts, which it had established during the 40th Session in fall 1985 to identify measures for improving the efficiency of the UN's administrative and financial functioning.[39] The posture adopted by the United States had imparted a special sense of urgency to this task, and the Group of 18 responded with a number of significant recommendations concerning the size of the UN Secretariat and the desirable mix of permanent and fixed-term positions in the Secretariat. However, the Group of 18 was unable to reach agreement on the most important matter of immediate concern: The rules governing decisionmaking regarding the budget.

In light of the not-so-subtle threat contained in the Kassebaum amendment, the General Assembly had to come to closure on this issue. It did so late in its 41st Session in Resolution 41/213.[40] This resolution is arguably one of the most important adopted by the General Assembly in many years. Although it does not address all of the concerns expressed by US critics, it does attempt to rationalize the UN budget process. While not recommending the adoption of weighted voting on budget decisions, as required by the Kassebaum amendment, it called for the institutionalization of consensus at an important stage of that process. The UN had long been poorly organized to integrate programmatic and budgetary decisions; by strengthening the Committee on Program and Coordination and giving it the responsibility for making recommendations to the Fifth Committee of the General Assembly regarding the budget ceiling and budget priorities, Resolution 41/213 represented an important step toward making the UN budget a serious policy tool, independently of whether it would satisfy the US Congress.[41] But by calling for the adoption of these critical budget decisions by consensus, Resolution 41/213 did give the United States something very much like a de facto veto over the UN budget and hence appeared to achieve the avowed objective of the Kassebaum amendment by means other than weighted voting.

Armed with the leverage of withholding, the United States had tried to use the bargaining process in the Group of 18 and in the General Assembly to gain a considerably greater measure of control over the UN budget and thus over the UN itself. As one US official put it quite candidly to the author, the United States wanted to build a machine it could drive. Stated quite simply, the United States wanted to put an end to budget making by UN majorities. It was not clear, however, whether a consensus requirement would provide the United States with a sufficiently powerful device for blocking budgets and hence programmatic activities it deemed unacceptable. Resolution 41/213 had introduced consensus only in the CPC, not in the Fifth Committee or the General Assembly meeting in plenary. Some skeptics argued at the time that nothing much had changed, inasmuch as the CPC had customarily reached decisions by consensus anyway, even before the adoption of Resolution 41/213.

This argument was disingenuous in 1986, and subsequent experience has done nothing to lend it more credence. Consensus, previously an informal understanding, was codified by Resolution 41/213. Moreover, the procedure now obtains in a form demonstrably more powerful than it was before. But those who harbored doubts about the efficacy of consensus thought they had some reason to be worried. Pressures to enlarge the CPC developed immediately, and the 42nd General Assembly acted, over US opposition, to achieve that objective, voting to increase the CPC's membership from twenty-one to thirty-four.[42] To UN critics in Washington, this development, hard on the heels of the adoption of reform legislation, looked suspiciously like an attempt to subvert that reform by packing the CPC with members who would insist on ambitious and controversial programs that the United States and other major contributors would then be expected to fund.

Even prior to the adoption of Resolution 41/213 there had been some modest erosion of majoritarian control over an area of decisionmaking that had traditionally been an exception to the prevailing unit veto system. The Group of 18, which played such an important role in setting the agenda for the debate in the General Assembly on budget reform, was itself not the kind of body to which the UN majority likes to entrust such important matters, given its small size and a composition that favored relatively large and "important" states.[43] And the CPC, with its limited membership and proportionately greater voice for states with large assessments, is a standing challenge to the majoritarian ethos. The decision to enlarge the CPC was unquestionably an expression of concern about the erosion of the majority's authority, but it did not mean that the majority would not take reform seriously. The majority in the General Assembly retained the capacity to reject CPC recommendations and adopt a budget unacceptable to the United States and/or other major contributors, but the result of such a move would almost certainly have been continued or renewed withholding and a worsening of the budget crisis. US leverage remained intact, with the UN's commitment to consensus the best deterrent, if not a certain guarantee, against a further tightening of the budgetary screws in Washington.

The US Response to UN Reform

It was a widely held view at the United Nations that the General Assembly had gone a long way to meet US conditions, in spite of strong resentment of US tactics and against deeply ingrained reluctance on the part of the majority to yield its numerical advantage. Having done so, the members expected the United States to reciprocate—to keep its part of the bargain and pay its assessments.

The US response to the adoption and implementation of Resolution 41/213 is instructive in that it demonstrated several things: (1) that budget reform would not satisfy many of those whose objections to the United Nations are political in nature; (2) that divisions within the government, within the Congress, and between the two branches over US participation in the UN are deep-seated and hard to overcome; (3) that skepticism regarding the UN's commitment to reform would not be easily exorcised; (4) that policies, once set in motion, acquire a life of their own, making them hard to reverse even when the conditions that produced those policies no longer exist; and (5) that new or newly potent independent variables (in this case the US budget deficit and the strictures of the Gramm-Rudman-Hollings Budget Deficit Reduction Act) intrude and affect US reaction to UN reform.

Eventually the United States announced that not only would it resume full payment of its assessment, but it would pay the arrearages that had accumulated while the Kassebaum amendment was in effect (not, however, those resulting from withholdings for specific purposes such as the Law of the Sea Preparatory Committee and assistance to the PLO). But the road to that announcement was a rocky one, which warrants comment inasmuch as it tells us much about the US-UN relationship and the complex process by which the United States arrives at its UN policy or policies.

The Kassebaum amendment had stipulated that the United States would withhold 20 percent of its assessment until the UN adopted weighted voting. Not only had the UN not adopted weighted voting, it had approved a reform measure that did not absolutely guarantee the result the Congress so obviously had in mind. Inevitably, there were many on Capitol Hill who remained unconvinced that reform was more than cosmetic, and who were therefore prepared to believe that the UN could be expected to continue to do business as usual, in ways quite unsatisfactory to the United States.

In the end, after a protracted debate on the adequacy of Resolution 41/213, which exposed the diverse motives of the supporters of the original Kassebaum amendment, the Congress adopted the position that the reform process at the UN merited recognition, but that it also required continued congressional oversight. The administration, which had initially been critical of the action of the Congress, took the initiative in seeking modification of the Kassebaum amendment. The Congress, responding in part to the urging of Senator Kassebaum herself and in spite of mixed signals from the administration, ultimately rewrote the authorizing legislation.

Consensus, assuming that the CPC continued to employ it and that the General Assembly honored CPC recommendations, was to be treated as an acceptable substitute for weighted voting. But the Congress was not prepared to trust either the UN's or the administration's interpretation of the adequacy of reform. It rejected an administration recommendation that would merely have required presidential certification for restoration of the US assessed contribution at a level above 20 percent, and substituted in the end a proposal by Senator Kassebaum that called for a three-stage payment of the US assessment. This formula stipulated that the president could release 40 percent of the appropriated funds on October 1, the beginning of the US fiscal year, but that an additional 40 percent could not be released to the UN until the president had certified that the UN was making progress in realizing reform goals (late in December, after General Assembly action on the UN budget). The release of the final 20 percent could not occur until the Congress had had 30 days in which to express its independent judgment as to the adequacy of the reforms.[44]

The 40-40-20 formula was acknowledged to be a device for retaining congressional leverage. By itself, however, it was not enough for many members, especially those who saw the issue as much more than the reform of the UN budget process. As a result, modification of the Kassebaum amendment quickly became an exercise in laying out even more detailed conditions; it attracted amendments that were to make the Foreign Relations Authorization Act for Fiscal Years 1988 and 1989 as much of a straitjacket for the administration as the original Kassebaum amendment had been. The thrust of several of these amendments is contained in the law, which made release of US assessments conditional upon presidential certification that three things had taken place. The president had to determine—and so report to the Congress—that:

- The consensus based decision-making procedure established by General Assembly Resolution 41/213 is being implemented and its results respected by the General Assembly.
- Progress is being made toward the 50 percent limitation on seconded employees of the Secretariat as called for by the Group of High Level Intergovernmental Experts to Review the Efficiency of the Administrative and Financial Functioning of the United Nations (Group of 18).
- The 15 percent reduction in the staff of the Secretariat (recommendations 56 and 57 of the Group of 18) is being implemented and that such a reduction is being equitably applied among the nationals on such staff.[45]

The first of these conditions is essentially the revised version of the original Kassebaum amendment. The other two reflect perennial concerns of several members who had repeatedly sought to use the leverage of withholding to change UN personnel policies, especially those that were deemed favorable to the Soviet Union. It was clear that the congressional concern for UN reform would not be easily satisfied by a UN decision to employ consensus in budget making in a body called the Committee on Program and Coordination.

Confusion Compounded

At the time of the adoption of the first version of the Kassebaum amendment in 1985, the United States had developed a modest arrearage in its UN assessment, the result of congressionally mandated withholdings for UN programs beneficial to the PLO and SWAPO, an administration withholding for the Preparatory Commission on the Law of the Sea Treaty, and a sum that reflected administration disagreement with the UN over the relatively arcane matter of tax equalization. The Kassebaum language stipulated that withholding was to commence at the beginning of FY 1987, October 1, 1986, at which time the United States would normally be paying its UN assessment for the calendar year 1986. So the effect of the Kassebaum amendment was not felt until late in 1986, by which time the General Assembly was struggling to agree on a formula for reform that would both satisfy the United States and preserve the prerogatives of the UN majority—the formula contained in Resolution 41/213. Unfortunately for the UN, Kassebaum-mandated withholdings took effect in the same year that US budget deficit reduction efforts first produced further reductions in the appropriation, with the result that the United States was able to contribute only $100 million of an assessment in excess of $200 million.

This drastic shortfall in itself was problem enough for the UN; but it also meant that the base against which subsequent authorization requests and appropriations would be made was so low that, barring herculean efforts by the administration and extraordinary restraint by the Congress, the problem would only become worse. And it did become worse before it became better.

The adoption of reform Resolution 41/213 by the General Assembly came on December 19, 1986, too late to be factored into the Department of State's request for funds for UN calendar year 1987. Rather than request full funding, which could subsequently have been withheld had reform not materialized, the administration reduced the request by the amount specified by Kassebaum. It was not until July of 1987 that a supplemental request went forward to Capitol Hill, and at no time did the administration request funds to meet the shortfall for calendar year 1986. Inevitably, this led to confusion and disorder in congressional efforts to adopt authorizing legislation.[46]

As noted above, agreement was finally reached at the end of 1987 on revision of the strictures of the Kassebaum amendment. This meant that funds excluded in the FY 1987 appropriation could be added for FY 1988, but it also meant that they could not be released to the UN until the new conditions had been met. Although $144 million was eventually appropriated, neither an authorization nor an appropriation bill had been passed by the beginning of FY 1988. The United States was able to squeeze out a $10 million payment to the UN in November from funds made available under a continuing resolution; in December an additional $90 million was contributed, although the payment required special approval by the Office of Management and Budget and elicited a chorus of disapproval from UN critics on Capitol Hill.[47] Thus by the end of UN calendar year 1987 the United States had accumulated arrearages in its UN assessment of $253 million, more than $200 million of those arrearages in the two years since the adoption of the Kassebaum amendment.[48]

Although the FY 1988/1989 authorization act, when finally adopted, provided for close to full funding for the UN, thereby permitting the administration to seek additional appropriations, the US budget summit in late 1987 produced an agreement that limited increases for Function 150, which includes the UN assessment, to 2 percent. This agreement, reached in the wake of the stock market crash of that fall, meant that there would be an FY 1989 appropriation for the UN assessment of $144 million, the exact figure appropriated for FY 1988 and a far cry from full funding. While the administration defended its request for $144 million, $70 million short of the assessment for calendar year 1988, it argued that it was merely honoring the budget summit agreement, not indicating lack of support for the United Nations.

Just as 1987 had been taken up with achieving agreement on language modifying the Kassebaum amendment, so was 1988 occupied with waiting for and trying to influence the president's determination regarding UN reform. In July, a sense of the Congress resolution was adopted calling upon the United States to pay its full UN assessment for calendar year 1988,[49] yet in August the Senate Appropriations Committee voted to refuse to waive presidential certification in order to permit the immediate release of $44 million already appropriated to meet calendar year 1987 obligations.[50] Congressional critics of the pace and adequacy of UN reform were numerous and vocal, in spite of the call for full funding.

Finally, on September 13, 1988, President Reagan issued the long-awaited certification, which had the effect of releasing the previously appropriated $44 million.[51] He also indicated that he was requesting full funding for FY 1990 and that he was going to create an independent study group to seek ways to pay accumulated US arrearages. This was good news for the UN, both because it brought an immediate infusion of dollars and because it seemed to augur well for the future after two years of budget brinkmanship. A second presidential certification, still necessary for payment of the balance due for calendar year 1988, was made in late December after the General Assembly, for the first time since 1946, approved a budget resolution by consensus.[52]

This brief account of the tortured struggle over UN financing makes clear that what had begun as a strategy for compelling the United Nations to pay more attention to US interests soon degenerated into a parody of responsible decisionmaking. Nor did the trouble end with presidential certification that revised congressional conditions had been met. US arrearages continued to mount even as the Congress lost interest in the confrontation with the UN; at the very time when President Bush was assiduously seeking UN support for measures that would remove Saddam Hussein's armies from Kuwait, those arrearages had climbed to more than $450 million.

The Tenacity of Anti-UN Sentiment

How is one to account for this disorderly process—a process devoid of leadership, a process that repeatedly sent mixed messages and too few dollars to the United Nations? One explanation is that it is extremely difficult, at least in the short run, to reverse a tide of negative criticism. The UN was not exactly a popular institution in the United States when the Reagan administration took office. But Ambassador Kirkpatrick and her protégés in the government did much to further diminish the reputation of the global organization. One example among many of the influence of her stewardship is the annual Report to Congress on the Voting Practices in the United Nations, prepared by the Department of State pursuant to legislation Kirkpatrick had promoted.[53] This document was not intended to be a useful reference for US diplomats engaged in coalition-building at the UN. They would be presumed to be thoroughly familiar with the voting practices of UN members. It was, rather, a yardstick with which to measure support for US positions on critical issues and a club with which to punish those states deemed insufficiently supportive, presumably through reductions in foreign aid. There is little evidence that the results have been an important, much less a decisive, factor in determining the recipients of US foreign assistance; but the report helped to make the point that the United Nations was a place where a great many states regularly have an opportunity to demonstrate their lack of respect for US interests and values.

This annual report was far from being the most important legacy of the Kirkpatrick tenure, but it symbolizes the mood of the time. The barrage of negative speeches and testimony by the ambassador and her colleagues sent a message that had resonance among members of a Congress already less than enamored with the United Nations. It was a message the administration found it hard to countermand when it decided that it wanted full funding and a better relationship with the global body.

Both the president and the secretary of state expressed their strong support for the reforms adopted at the United Nations, and Vernon Walters, who succeeded Kirkpatrick, worked indefatigably to persuade the Congress to respond positively to those reforms. In the end, Walters's efforts began to pay dividends, but it was not easy to convince the Congress, especially in light of the fact that several members of the Kirkpatrick team remained on board after her departure, their conversion to support for full funding of the UN not entirely convincing. The best evidence that this conversion had been largely cosmetic was provided by Alan Keyes, who as assistant secretary of state for international organization affairs had dutifully carried the administration's message to Capitol Hill. After resigning from the government in fall 1987, Keyes wrote a bitter op ed piece in the *Washington Post*, which in effect charged the government with abandoning its opposition to UN abuses and anti-US bias, thereby sending "a clear signal to the officials and delegates in New York: they can safely continue with business as usual." And, he added, "they will."[54]

Keyes's statement, together with several of Kirkpatrick's syndicated columns and a denunciation of the UN by Charles Krauthammer in a widely discussed essay in *The New Republic*,[55] illustrate one of the lessons from the battle over the US assessment: the administrative and budgetary reforms in New York, even if they were to prove substantial and enduring, would not satisfy many of the UN's critics, including a sizable number on Capitol Hill. For such people, issues related to the budget, including waste, inefficiency, inflated salary scales, and the overall size of the UN budget, were not the real cause of discontent. Their grievances seemed sure to survive long after the specific concerns of the senator from Kansas were met. This point was made by Krauthammer when he argued:

> the UN problem is not an accounting problem, although it is an American propensity to see life's failures that way. . . . The issue is not improving UN efficiency. Do we really want an organization more efficient in undermining Western values, devaluing the language of Western liberalism, attacking Western allies, condemning Western economic and social practices, and exacerbating the few conflicts to which it does turn its attention?[56]

Krauthammer had much more to say, and his is an indictment with which many agreed, although few expressed it in such caustic and colorful language—the UN "as a playpen created by the adult powers for the children"; a forum providing "therapeutic recreation for the have-not countries"; a place whose language of discourse "is the twisted Orwellian dialect of UNese"; an institution, in brief, where the US presence "lends the outrages [of the UN majority] a legitimacy and credibility they would otherwise lack."[57]

This is the United Nations that its detractors were convinced would not be reformed by Resolution 41/213. One high-ranking UN official said as much to the author when he argued that because nearly 80 percent of the UN's budget is used to pay salaries, the result of reform would be only to trim the UN Secretariat, not modify the behavior of the members. Indeed, this official claimed that the reason the Third World majority eventually went along with Resolution 41/213 was that they realized that its impact would be on the bureaucracy, not on the ability of the majority to invoke world opinion and set the agenda.

It is widely accepted among people who deal with UN affairs in Washington that knowledge of the UN among members of the Congress is very limited, with superficial generalizations substituting for thoughtful analysis in a great many cases. Although this is hardly surprising, and is almost certainly true with respect to many a complex issue on the congressional agenda, it has had a bearing on the way in which the Congress deals with UN financing. The benefits of US participation in the United Nations are frequently hard to measure; defenders of the organization often find that their arguments, which stress intangibles and collective goods, do not impress members who are looking for something much more concrete to justify the annual outlay of hundreds of millions of dollars (the budget for the UN system as a whole is, of course, substantially larger than that for the UN itself, and the differences among the UN-system agencies are not always well understood by many members). There is no substantial pro-UN constituency, so that attacking the UN or trimming its assessment is largely cost-free in a political sense. Indeed, some members have found the opposite to be true—that there is political mileage in being a UN opponent *and* saving money in the process.

Against this background, a decision such as the one the United Nations took to build a new conference center for its Economic Commission for Africa in Addis Ababa, Ethiopia, assumed the proportions of a last straw. Not in itself a significant issue—and a relatively inexpensive one at $73.5 million—the center symbolized much that the Congress believed was wrong with the UN: It appeared to be a misplaced priority, especially at a time when the UN was under pressure to rein in budget growth; it was more evidence that the UN catered uncritically to Third World interests; and it was to be built in a country that at the time was an unpopular Soviet client and had been manipulating famine for political ends. Senator Kassebaum made use of the Ethiopian conference center to galvanize support for congressional action to achieve reform of the UN budget process, but her initiative and the alacrity with which the Congress responded must be viewed in the context of cumulative frustration with the UN *and* the nature of the Congress and the condition of relations between that body and the executive branch where money matters are concerned.

Congress Versus the Executive Branch

The participation of the Congress in the process of approving the US contributions to the United Nations is, of course, constitutionally mandated. The Congress must appropriate the money with which the United States pays its assessment. If the Congress viewed payment of the assessment as a legal obligation—that is, as an uncontrollable such as payment of interest on the national debt or certain entitlements—there would be no issue. But the Congress as a whole has not seen it that way. Even so, it has not followed automatically that the Congress should see its role in the budget process as a license to challenge either the assessment or the administration's request for funding. The fact that it has come to do so is related in part to the adversarial relationship between the legislative and executive branches and to the great importance the Congress as a body attaches to the power of the purse. The Congress, like the president, is acutely aware that the budget is a most powerful policy tool and that programs are no stronger than the money available to finance them. Given its disenchantment with the United Nations and the absence of leadership with either the institutional tools or the will to insist that the assessment shall be paid in full, it is not surprising that it should try to use the power of the purse as leverage to effect changes at the United Nations and, if necessary, to force the administration's hand on the issue.

The challenge to the president, or at least to the executive branch, is part of a much discussed pattern, latent in a system that divides power and invites competition, but very much in evidence since the Vietnam War. Popular as Ronald Reagan was, we were all witness to the fact that the Congress repeatedly denied the president funds he wanted in order to support the Contras in Nicaragua. And while the issue was much less visible and the stakes were perceived to be smaller, UN financing also produced a congressional challenge to presidential prerogative. No longer willing to defer quietly to the executive branch on foreign policy issues and very much concerned to maintain its own oversight of activities of which it was skeptical, the Congress found the authorization-appropriation process a convenient vehicle for managing US-UN relations. That the administration had itself engaged in UN-bashing and sent mixed signals to Capitol Hill only served to make it easier for the Congress to do what many of its members were inclined to do in any event.

The tension between executive and legislative branches over UN funding cannot be explained by reference to the fact that a Republican sat in the White House whereas Democrats controlled the Congress. It was congressional Republicans who took the lead in stipulating the conditions that had to be met before full funding would be restored; the Democrats, if anything, might have been expected to stake out a position more supportive of the UN than the one adopted by Reagan's team. Nor were executive-legislative tensions simply one more example of Vietnam-conditioned reflexes. The State Department, which has the task of defending the administration's requests for UN assessments before relevant congressional committees, has frequently had a problem on Capitol Hill that transcends party lines. In part, this is simply a matter of roles and styles. Edward Derwinski, a former congressman who later served in the State Department, said it succinctly:

> Congressmen tend to approach issues that fall into black and white categories. The approach of the State Department is to look at all sides, study all options, try for compromise. Well, when you're in the political world, you approach things in a more precise and hard-nosed fashion. You either come down for or against aid to Turkey or Greece, for or against a base agreement with the Philippines.[58]

Derwinski might as well have been talking about the United Nations, about which many in the Congress believe the State Department (and its Bureau of International Organization Affairs) is equivocal, too ready to understand and explain the organization rather than move decisively to change it, and insufficiently diligent in pursuing matters of concern to Capitol Hill. Two of the UN's severest critics in the Congress, Senator Robert Kasten (R-Wisc.) and Representative Donald Sundquist (R-Tenn.), illustrated this last point in the 1980s with their scathing criticism of the State Department for its failure to take steps expeditiously to deal with the problem of alleged kickbacks to their governments by communist bloc nationals working for the UN Secretariat.[59]

The congressional problem with the State Department did not disappear with the arrival on the scene of Ambassador Kirkpatrick's people. The department's reputation was too well established for that to happen, and it had the difficult task of simultaneously denouncing the United Nations, insisting that the administration should and could manage the troubled relationship with the global organization, and interpreting the progress of reform there. Congressman Dan Mica (D-Fla.) reflected congressional frustration when, defending the Congress against a *New York Times* charge that it was responsible for inadequate UN funding, he blamed inadequate requests and mixed signals from the administration.[60]

The institutional problem has been exacerbated on occasion by personality conflicts. One of these broke out during the period in question between the chairman of the House Foreign Affairs Subcommittee (Congressman

Mica) and the assistant secretary of state for international organization affairs (Alan Keyes). Persons who were involved in the authorization process at the time claim that the conflict between the two men was so acute that it made cooperation in that process, and hence between the two branches of government, exceedingly difficult (one participant described it as "virtually impossible").

Throughout this period of intense US confrontation with the United Nations, relatively few in the Congress were willing to rise to the defense of the proposition that the United States had a treaty obligation to pay its full assessment. There were, to be sure, some members who, although not unmindful of the UN's flaws, remained strongly committed to the organization and to the Charter requirement that dues be paid as assessed. But they were outnumbered by their colleagues in three other discernible categories: Those who shared the Krauthammer view and were convinced that "reform" would only be cosmetic; those who advocated "tough love" and believed that the United States had to do something to shake up the UN, but who, having done so, were willing to give reform a chance; and those, predominantly Democrats, who were internationalists and supporters of the UN but who saw no need to take the lead in a fight for full funding when the president's own party was disinclined to do so. This last group might be called the "tar baby" school for its aversion to becoming too closely identified with an issue with such limited appeal, especially in a time of budget stringency.

The Congress may have been divided in its assessment of the value of the United Nations to the United States and how to strengthen the global organization, but the record is clear that it was committed to micromanagement in this area of foreign policy, as in other fields. All of the statutory restrictions mandated by the Congress are a form of micromanagement. The Congress came to see itself as the pivotal player in the campaign for UN reform. The president and the Department of State might have wanted reform, but they were not going to make it happen; the Congress would. Senator Kassebaum made the point in proposing her amendment, arguing that "the history of the UN has shown conclusively that it requires Congress rather than executive branch action to bring the UN and its agencies under control."[61] And Congressman Mica, while serving with the US delegation to the 40th General Assembly, left no doubt as to the primacy of the Congress in the process. "We in Congress," he announced, "have every intention of reducing our financial contribution to this body unless genuine budgetary reforms are instituted."[62]

Even in the process of abandoning the Kassebaum amendment, the Congress was not prepared to turn the business of judging the adequacy of reform completely over to the executive branch. Kassebaum's about-face, Walters's intensive lobbying, Keyes's departure, and a combination of movements toward reform in New York and a residual sense of obligation in Washington produced in the end a partial restoration of funding for the United Nations. But it was a restoration on the installment plan. Advocates of tough love and those who wanted to avoid the tar-baby effect were willing to put US-UN relations back on track. But the tensions inherent in executive-legislative relations, the complexities of the budget process, and the constraints imposed by the Balanced Budget and Emergency Deficit Reduction Act, commonly referred to as Gramm-Rudman-Hollings, conspired to prevent the US government from moving quickly to restore full funding.

The Congressional Budget Gauntlet

When Congressman Mica spoke of "we in Congress" being determined to achieve UN budgetary reform, or Senator Kassebaum referred to the role of the Congress in bringing the UN under control, the implication seemed to be that the Congress is a monolith, speaking with one voice. This is, of course, patently untrue, as critics of the Congress's role in foreign policy are fond of telling us with their references to 535 secretaries of state. While the situation is considerably less chaotic than that number would suggest, the participation of the Congress in foreign policymaking is highly fragmented, and that has been an important factor in the handling of the UN assessment, as it has been in almost every other policy area. Walter Oleszek described the situation:

> This congressional decision-making process is constantly evolving, but it has certain enduring features that affect consideration of all legislation. The first is the decentralized power structure of Congress, characterized by numerous specialized committees and a central party leadership that struggles to promote party and policy coherence. A second feature is the existence of multiple decision points for every piece of legislation.[63]

As Oleszek reminds us, decentralization means that policymaking is subject to various disintegrative processes. In the case of the UN assessment, its fate is determined by six committees—two authorizing committees (the House Foreign Affairs Committee and the Senate Foreign Relations Committee), two appropriations committees (one in each house), and two budget committees (one in each house), together with their specialized subcommittees. Although these committees each have their own roles to perform in the legislative process, all of them are involved in making spending decisions and they are in point of fact rivals in that process. The authorizing committees are the substantive legislative panels; appropriations committees are not supposed to make policy. But in practice they often do make policy, and in recent years, under conditions of fiscal austerity, the authorizing committees have lost influence to their appropriating counterparts.

In the conventional wisdom, the Foreign Affairs Committee and the Foreign Relations Committee would be program advocates, their members typically more liberal and internationalist in outlook than the membership of the two houses as a whole. The appropriations committees would be advocates of spending restraint, setting up a struggle between the two sets of committees. However, conditions of fiscal austerity have modified the role of the authorizing committees, making them more negative, conditioning them to accept reduced levels of resources for programs within their jurisdictions. Congressional disenchantment with the United Nations has made the task easier, especially among their Republican members.

Moreover, the budget committees have contributed to the erosion of the role of the authorizing committees, especially in the context of large budget deficits and the strictures of Gramm-Rudman-Hollings. The congressional budget resolution, which is the product of the budget committees' efforts, creates a framework within which other committees must work. Cuts must be made, whether by negotiated agreement or sequestration. Under the deficit neutrality of Gramm-Rudman-Hollings, if more is to be spent on one program, less must be spent on another, a situation not designed to benefit departments and functions without strong constituencies.

The problem has been compounded by the fact that appropriations for the Department of State, including international organizations and conferences, are part of an appropriations bill, one of thirteen, which embraces the Departments of Commerce and Justice and the federal judiciary, as well as the Department of State. In this company, the Department of State (including the UN) is vulnerable. During the hectic struggle to produce legislation for FY 1988, described above, the competition for appropriations between foreign relations and domestic programs came to the surface when the President threatened to veto the House-passed measure because it made drastic cuts in the Department of State appropriations (21 percent less than the administration had requested, which translated into a cut of $88 million in the assessed contributions for intergovernmental organizations).[64] Defending this action, the floor manager of the measure, Representative Neal Smith (D-Ia.), noted that the administration had omitted from his request a number of programs that were important to members of the Congress, including the Economic Development Administration, the Legal Services Corporation, and the Juvenile Justice Program. These, he explained, had to be funded, and given the budget realities, that could not be accomplished unless some other programs were trimmed. Assessments for international organizations, which lacked popularity and constituency support, were among the obvious candidates.[65] This episode not only illustrates the perennial conflict between the two branches, it also underscores the fact that the budget process is a gauntlet, containing numerous points at which the UN assessment can be manhandled. Moreover, the process is one that the several committees, whose efforts are already poorly coordinated, do not wholly control. Fragmentation of congressional attention to an issue such as the UN assessment is further exacerbated by the declining deference members pay to committee decisions. Rank-and-file members have increasingly resorted to legislating by amendment from the floor. Many of the amendments that have been aimed at US participation in the UN have come from the floor, especially at the appropriations stage, as members who do not serve on the key panels and do not claim any special expertise in the matter take advantage of the openness of the process to leave their imprint on fiscal policy or score points against the unpopular UN or both.

Some of these amendments are representative of an ongoing but unsuccessful attempt to find a formula more favorable to the United States than capacity to pay, and most would produce results considerably more inimical to US interests than the situation they would change. Some proposals seem to have been aimed at nothing less than emasculation of the UN. Although many of these obviously "hostile" amendments have been rejected, others have been adopted, often by voice vote, without serious effort by the leadership to block their passage. Frequently such amendments are dropped in conference, but some have become law and even those that have not seem to have had a distorting impact on congressional consideration of US financial obligations.

Many of the hostile amendments, such as Sundquist's on kickbacks or Helms's on technical assistance or Kasten's on secondment, are attributable in considerable part to another congressional development, the dramatic increase in staff. The catalyst for member activism is typically a zealous staff assistant who latches onto a particular issue, as was the case with Senator Kassebaum's initiative on reform of the UN budget-making process. A case can be made that the decline in deference to committees and leadership is inversely proportional to the growth in size (and hence in knowledge and expertise) of staff, although the causes of fragmentation in the congressional decision process are obviously more complex.

This fragmented budget process also has had as a result the phenomenon of missed deadlines. The Congress finds it extremely difficult to meet its own schedule, which calls for a budget resolution, then authorization, and finally appropriation. The result is that government must often be funded by continuing resolution, which adds yet one more obstacle to prompt and full payment of the UN assessment. The deficit and Gramm-Rudman-Hollings have the effect of making an already complex process even more difficult.

The challenge to the United Nations mounted by the United States in the 1980s was both a continuation, albeit in heightened form, of an old, familiar quarrel with the global organization and a manifestation of a more ideological style in US politics and of frustrations resulting from constraints imposed by a mounting budget deficit. It was a challenge in which both the White House and the Congress conspired. The form the challenge took—across-the-board withholding of a substantial portion of the US assessment—was the doing of the Congress, and demonstrated the extent to which US relations with the UN are hostage to the phenomena of divided government, the weakened state of congressional leadership, and a complex and disorderly budget process. But even though the administration would presumably not have resorted to the tactic of withholding à la Kassebaum, and it certainly resented congressional micromanagement of the issue, it did set the tone for the confrontation with the United Nations. Moreover, the Reagan administration bears much of the responsibility for the dramatic increase in the US budget deficit, a development that made it easier to justify cuts in programs with limited constituency support.

When George Bush assumed office, the government had already announced its intention to resume full funding and to pay the arrearages that had accumulated during the 1980s. The congressional frenzy over the United Nations had also abated, in part because reforms had been instituted in New York, but also because changes in government personnel had a calming effect and UN bashing seemed to have yielded up about as much political mileage as most members of the Congress could expect to gain from it. But the problems that had plagued the US relationship with the United Nations for so many years had not disappeared overnight. The legacy of disappointed expectations remained, now compounded by a new legacy: A large bill due the United Nations, a bill that would not be paid quickly and could be expected to cloud US-UN relations well into the 1990s.

Some of the factors that had generated and sustained US disillusionment with the UN in the first four decades of that organization's existence began to undergo change at the very time that the United States chose to adopt a more confrontational stance. Those changes were not due solely or even primarily to US policy. But they did open up possibilities for a rapprochement between the United Nations and its most important member state—possibilities that were prominently on display during the Gulf crisis of 1990–1991.

Notes

1. President Bill Clinton did propose substantial tax increases in his initial State of the Economy address to the Congress, and then faced the difficult task of building support for this aspect of his deficit reduction plan among citizens conditioned by years of antitax rhetoric. President Bush paid heavily in political capital for his abandonment of a "no taxes" pledge; it may have been a decisive factor in

his loss of the presidency in 1992. Walter Mondale's 1984 promise to raise taxes almost certainly doomed whatever remote chance he might have had of upsetting Ronald Reagan.

2. Seymour Maxwell Finger, *Your Man at the U.N.*, New York: New York University Press, 1980, p. 261.

3. This distinction is discussed in Harold K. Jacobson, *Networks of Interdependence*, 2nd ed., New York: Alfred A. Knopf, 1984, pp. 110–114.

4. Enforcement measures under Chapter 7 constitute the most conspicuous exception.

5. See, for example, Mohammed Bedjaoui, *Towards a New International Economic Order*, New York: Holmes and Meier, 1979.

6. Article 5 countenances suspension of the rights and privileges of membership of states against which enforcement action has been taken, and Article 6 speaks of expulsion of a state that has persistently violated Charter principles.

7. The story of the UN's first financial crisis has been told in many places. A good succinct summary is provided in John G. Stoessinger, *The United Nations and the Superpowers*, 4th ed., New York: Random House, 1977, pp. 121–145.

8. *Certain Expenses of the United Nations*, Advisory Opinion of July 20, 1962, I. C. J. Reports, 1962.

9. GA Res. 1854 (XVII), December 19, 1962.

10. See Stoessinger, *The United Nations and the Superpowers*, pp. 121–145, and Thomas M. Franck, *Nation Against Nation*, New York: Oxford University Press, 1985, pp. 82–87.

11. *New York Times*, August 17, 1965, A6.

12. *U. S. Participation in International Organizations*, United States Senate, Committee on Government Operations, 95th Congress, 1st Session, 1977.

13. The action with respect to the ILO is contained in PL 91-472, and in the case of UNESCO in PL 93-559.

14. PL 92-554, October 25, 1972.

15. See Stoessinger, *The United Nations and the Superpowers*, pp. 142–144.

16. Ibid., p. 143.

17. The fullest account of US withdrawal from the ILO is to be found in Walter Galenson, *The International Labor Organization*, Madison: University of Wisconsin Press, 1981. US-UNESCO relations have been dissected by many; see, for example, Roger Coate, *Unilateralism, Ideology, and United States Foreign Policy: The U. S. In and Out of UNESCO*, Boulder, Colo.: Lynne Rienner, 1988.

18. Daniel Patrick Moynihan, *A Dangerous Place*, Boston: Little, Brown and Company, 1978.

19. Although Ambassador Andrew Young earned respect at the UN, especially among African and other Third World delegates, his penchant for what Seymour Maxwell Finger has called "open mouth diplomacy" not only hurt Carter but created problems for the public perception of the UN (for example, his comment that Cubans were a stabilizing factor in Angola and, most damaging, his remark to a reporter that "there are hundreds, perhaps thousands of political prisoners in the United States"). See Finger, *Your Man at the U.N.*, pp. 267, 283–286.

20. This episode and the implications for US-UN relations are the subject of a brief case study in Charles W. Whalen, Jr., *The House and Foreign Policy: The Irony of Congressional Reform*, Chapel Hill: University of North Carolina Press, 1982, pp. 92–95.

21. *Congressional Quarterly Almanac*, 96th Congress, 1st Session, 1979, pp. 134, 136.

22. To be precise, the measure should be called the Kassebaum-Solomon Amendment, inasmuch as Congressman Gerald Solomon (R-N.Y.), was the author of the original House version. That version was dropped in conference, so that it was essentially the language proposed by the Senator from Kansas that became law.

23. David P. Forsythe, *The Politics of International Law,* Boulder, Colo.: Lynne Rienner, 1990, p. 122.

24. The Heritage Foundation's studies of the UN (and UN-system agencies) included such monographs as Arieh Eilan, *The General Assembly: Can It Be Salvaged?* and Burton Yale Pines, ed., *The U. S. and the U.N.: A Balance Sheet;* such backgrounders as Juliana Pilon, *Moscow's UN Outpost,* and Roger Brooks, *The U.N. Department of Public Information;* and such executive memoranda as Juliana Pilon, *Breaking the Law: The State Department Helps the PLO,* and Thomas Dewey, *The U.N. Makes a Deal with the Soviets.*

25. See Seymour Maxwell Finger, "The Reagan-Kirkpatrick Policies and the United Nations," *Foreign Affairs* 62, 3 (Winter 1983/1984), pp. 436–457.

26. These remarks are reprinted in "The U. S. Role in the United Nations," *Hearings,* House Subcommittee on Human Rights and International Organizations, 98th Congress, 1st Session, Washington: GPO, 1984, Appendix 2.

27. Ibid., Appendix 4.

28. "U. S. Financial and Political Involvement in the United Nations," *Hearings,* Senate Committee on Government Affairs, 99th Congress, 1st Session, Washington: GPO, 1985, p. 25.

29. See *Issues Before the 37th General Assembly of the United Nations,* UNA-USA, 1982, p. 145.

30. H. Cong. Res. 322, S. Cong. Res. 68, 97th Cong., 2nd Session: *Congressional Record* (House), 128: H1943, May 10, 1982.

31. See speech by Gregory Newell, Assistant Secretary of State for International Organization Affairs, US Department of State, at the 24th Annual Conference of the International Studies Association, April 8, 1983.

32. This amendment would ultimately become Section 143 of the Foreign Relations Authorization Act, Fiscal Years 1986 and 1987 (PL 99-93), August 16, 1986.

33. At the time the Kassebaum amendment was adopted, the United States and the Soviet Union could together cast more than a blocking one-third of the votes if votes were the equivalent of assessments. The same would have been true of the United States and Japan, or the United States and the Federal Republic of Germany, or any of a number of combinations of Western countries.

34. A good illustration is GA Res. 41/211, by which the General Assembly adopted a revised budget for the 1986–87 biennium entailing an increase of more than $48 million over the originally approved budget. This practice of adding to the UN's budget has been a particular concern of the US government, and it treated this vote as one of the ten key votes in the 41st General Assembly. The resolution was adopted by a vote of 122 to 13, with 10 abstentions. The combined assessment of the 13 states opposing the resolution was 47.16 percent of the total, and the combined assessment of the 10 states abstaining was 35.09 percent. The 122 states that supported this resolution had a combined assessment totaling only 17.18 percent of the whole.

35. According to Article 108, a two-thirds vote of the General Assembly is required for adoption, followed by ratification by two-thirds of the UN's membership, including all permanent members of the Security Council.

36. Quoted in the *Washington Weekly Report,* UNA-USA, XI-37, November 1, 1985.

37. As of December 31, 1986, the UN's short-term deficit was estimated at $392.8 million, including both the regular budget and the budget for peacekeeping operations. See *Report of the Secretary-General on the Financial Emergency,* UN Doc. A/C. 5/41/24, October 27, 1986.

38. For a brief summary of measures taken by the Secretary-General to stave off bankruptcy in the mid-1980s, see *Financing the United Nations,* a UNA-USA Fact Sheet, n.d.

39. The Group of 18 was established by GA Res. 40/237, December 18, 1985. The Report of the Group of 18 is to be found in GAOR (XLI), Supplement No. 49 (A/41/49), August 15, 1986.

40. GA Res. 41/213, December 19, 1986.

41. There was widespread agreement among officials interviewed by the author, both in the UN Secretariat and in the US government, that the revised mandate of the CPC and the attendant changes in the structure of the Secretariat could contribute significantly to making the UN budget process more rational. The Secretary-General created, within the Department of Administration and Management, an Office for Programme Planning, Budgeting, Monitoring, and Evaluation, which consolidated planning/coordination and budgeting functions previously handled in different units of the Secretariat. See UN Doc. A/42/234, April 23, 1987.

42. GA Res. 42/450, December 17, 1987. The United States cast the only vote in opposition. From this time forward, geographical distribution in the CPC was to be fixed as follows: nine seats for African states, seven for Asian, seven for Latin American and Caribbean, seven for Western European and other, four for Eastern European.

43. The Group of 18, with less than 12 percent of the UN's membership, represented 62.68 percent of the assessment for the regular budget; five of the top six states in the scale of assessment were represented and with few exceptions the representatives from the various regions were the states with the largest assessments, such as Argentina, Brazil, Mexico, India, and Nigeria. Similarly, even the enlarged CPC is not a microcosm of the General Assembly, but a body that gives more weight to states with relatively large assessments. At the time of the enlargement of the CPC, its thirty-four members constituted approximately 22 percent of the UN's total membership, but had a combined assessment of almost 77 percent of the total.

44. See Section 602 of PL 100-204, December 14, 1987.

45. Ibid.

46. This struggle is well captured in successive issues of the *Washington Weekly Report* of the UNA-USA.

47. Critics included, significantly, Senator Robert Dole (R-Kan.), not normally among those in the vanguard of the attack on administration policy in this area.

48. This is the UN's figure. The United States regularly places its obligations at a slightly lower level. The distinction is made each year in the annual report by the Department of State entitled *United States Contributions to International Organizations.* For example, in the Report to the Congress for the Fiscal Year 1987, the administration identified the net requirement at a 25 percent assessment rate, then subtracted administrative and statutory withholdings and arrived at what it called "the total U. S. estimated requirement." Where the contribution is less because of a shortfall in appropriated funds, as there was for that year, the shortfall

is acknowledged. It would seem that, at a minimum, the administration regards its own obligation as assessment less its own withholdings.

49. See *Washington Weekly Report,* UNA-USA, XIV-26, July 29, 1987.

50. The vote, during markup of the FY 1988 supplemental appropriation on a request from the Senate Foreign Relations Committee, was eight to seven.

51. The formal determination bears the number 88-23, and is reported in the *Washington Weekly Report,* UNA-USA, XIV-28, August 12, 1988. It calls attention to UN successes in the peacekeeping field as well as in the areas mandated in Section 702 of PL 100-204.

52. See Press Release from the UN Information Center, "UN General Assembly Adopts Key Budget Decisions by Consensus," January 3, 1989.

53. PL 98-164, Section 117, November 22, 1983. For commentary on the utility of this report, see Thomas M. Franck, *Nation Against Nation,* New York, Oxford University Press, 1985, pp. 267–269.

54. *Washington Post,* January 21, 1988, p. A23.

55. Charles Krauthammer, "Let It Sink," *The New Republic,* August 24, 1987, pp. 18–23.

56. Ibid., pp. 19, 22.

57. Ibid., pp. 20–21.

58. Quoted in I. M. Destler, Leslie H. Gelb, and Anthony Lake, *Our Own Worst Enemy,* New York: Simon and Schuster, 1984, p. 282.

59. The kickback issue is addressed in Section 151 of PL 99-93, the Foreign Relations Authorization Act of FY 1986–1987. It resurfaced in Section 703 of PL 100-204, the Foreign Relations Authorization Act for FY 1988/1989, seeking in the latter case a "rental reduction" from the pay of any international civil servant who receives a housing allowance from any member state.

60. Reported in *Washington Weekly Report,* UNA-USA, XIV-7, February 26, 1988.

61. See *Congressional Record,* June 7, 1985, S 7793. Jeane Kirkpatrick, shortly after leaving her UN post, reinforced this view in testimony before the Senate Foreign Relations Committee (April 19, 1986), arguing that it is appropriate for the legislative branch to withhold contributions to UN budgets.

62. These comments were made before the Fifth Committee of the General Assembly on October 18, 1985. Quoted in *Washington Weekly Report,* UNA-USA, XI-37, November 1, 1985.

63. Walter J. Oleszek, *Congressional Procedures, and the Policy Process,* 3rd ed., Washington: CQ Press, 1989, p. 15.

64. See *Washington Weekly Report,* UNA-USA, XIII-24, July 10, 1987.

65. Ibid.

Chapter V

The Gulf Crisis:
The United States Leads
the United Nations

Most analysts of the events that followed Iraq's miscalculated invasion and annexation of Kuwait have concluded that it was the United States that called the tune. In this view, the role of the United Nations was secondary; the United States, in a masterful demonstration of diplomatic skill, secured UN legitimation for US objectives and for the means by which those objectives were achieved. In other words, the United States wanted—some would say needed—UN support and, playing the Security Council like a violin, obtained that support in a series of resolutions that were both forceful in their treatment of Iraq and permissive in the latitude they gave to US policymakers.

An alternative view gives more credit to the United Nations. It sees the Gulf crisis as the UN's finest hour in a long time, and the near unanimity of the Security Council in defending Charter principles and authorizing enforcement action as evidence that the global body is alive and well and ready to assume the role mapped out it by its framers nearly half a century ago. In this view, the United States was in the end an agent of the United Nations; its military might and leadership of the coalition provided the means whereby the will of the international community was carried out. Just as in the predominant view the United States needed the UN, so in this view did the UN need the United States.

Although the two perspectives differ, both underscore the importance of the US-UN relationship, and both acknowledge that in this very important test of that relationship the two worked well together. Because the Gulf crisis focused attention on the United Nations and US policy toward the UN as no other event had in many years, there is an understandable tendency to see it as a dramatic watershed, one of those events that wrenches the parties to a dispute out of old and unproductive patterns of mutual recrimination and confronts them with unanticipated opportunities for cooperation. Indeed, before Kuwait, this was a relationship in the doldrums, one that had actually been deteriorating; after Kuwait, a relationship of great promise, one that could be the cornerstone of a new world order.

Iraq's invasion of Kuwait and the efforts of the United States and the United Nations to force Iraq out of Kuwait were, in important respects, a turning point in the US-UN relationship. But it is necessary to note that the ground had been prepared for the cooperation between the United Nations and the United States to which we were all witness in the months during which the diplomatic screws were tightened and military force ultimately brought to bear against Iraq. Much of the US public may have been surprised to see the United Nations prominently, continually, and favorably in the news again after years of relative neglect; however, those who follow UN affairs more closely were aware that the global body was showing signs of life and that there was reason to believe that the United States might well find the UN a more congenial place to pursue its foreign policy objectives than it had in quite some time.

Transition at the United Nations

Several factors contributed to this transformation of the UN into a more congenial place for US interests and values. The most important by far, of course, was the winding down of the Cold War and its corollary, the Soviet Union's greater readiness to approach the United Nations as an arena of accommodation rather than confrontation. But the UN was already showing signs of movement in directions favored by the United States—or at least less unfavorable to the United States—even before it had become clear that the Soviet Union could no longer sustain the Cold War. The changes taking place at the United Nations—or in the ways that member states chose to use the United Nations—were typically tentative and incremental. Some were more atmospheric than tangible. And because they were modest and seemingly reversible, and because the United States had distanced itself from the UN except for the purposes of damage limitation, there was typically a lag between developments in New York and Geneva and an acknowledgment in Washington that the situation had indeed improved sufficiently to justify a rethinking of the US-UN relationship.

These changes at the UN, or in the political climate within which the UN functions, are several in number, although they tend to be interrelated. It may be useful to identify some of the factors that, with the outbreak of the Gulf crisis, helped to make the UN a more promising venue for the US-led effort to expel Saddam Hussein from Kuwait.

Mikhail Gorbachev's rise to power in the Soviet Union led quickly and dramatically to major changes in that country's domestic and foreign policies. Among the less heralded of these changes was a striking reversal of the Soviet approach to the United Nations. For much of the UN's history, as US policymakers were only too well aware, the Soviet Union had "viewed the world body as little more than a convenient platform from which to take rhetorical shots at American and Western policy, thereby forging a convenient solidarity with the Third World."[1] It had been a cynical performance, compounded by blatant disrespect for the concept of an international civil service, failure to pay assessments, and a lengthy litany of platitudinous proposals that Moscow never expected to be adopted and would have disavowed had they been adopted. Indeed, a major reason for the poor state of US-UN relations was Soviet behavior.

Gorbachev moved promptly to change all that. Even before politicians and pundits were declaring that the Cold War was over, the Soviet Union began to show a very different face at the United Nations. It abandoned the harsh rhetoric that had been a staple of its diplomatic style. It began to pay bills it had owed for years. It allowed nationals who worked for the UN Secretariat to seek living accommodations outside of the complex maintained for its UN mission. It announced that it would permit some of its nationals working for the Secretariat to accept long-term contracts. It introduced a number of concrete proposals designed to improve the functioning of the organization, especially in the area of peacekeeping, and those proposals were clearly meant to be taken seriously. It worked cooperatively with the other permanent members of the Security Council to launch five significant peacekeeping missions. In brief, the Soviet Union demonstrated by word and deed that it intended to give the United Nations a much more important place in its foreign policy and that it would approach the UN in a much more constructive and collegial spirit than it had in the past.[2]

This reversal was, if anything, even more startling than that of the United States, and although welcome, it was initially greeted with some skepticism in Washington. But it gradually became apparent that the Soviet Union did indeed wish to end the Cold War, and that a different posture at the United Nations would very probably serve its interests better than the costly and largely failed policies of adventurism and military assistance in the Third World. Not only did the Soviet Union give evidence of this policy change by withdrawing its troops from Afghanistan, it supported the creation of the United Nations Good Offices Mission for Afghanistan and Pakistan (UNGOMAP), a peacekeeping operation with the express purpose of monitoring that withdrawal.[3]

This flurry of Soviet initiatives, begun at the same time that the effects of the Kassebaum amendment were first being felt at the UN, facilitated a thaw in US-UN relations and helped set the stage for the cooperation between the superpowers, which was essential for the Security Council's response to Iraq's invasion of Kuwait. Although that cooperation made enforcement action against Saddam Hussein possible in 1990 and 1991, it had first borne fruit in 1988 and 1989 with the creation of several new peacekeeping missions, another of the important factors making the UN a more attractive place from the US point of view.

In 1988, UN peacekeepers were awarded the Nobel Peace Prize. Somewhat ironically, the prize anticipated rather than followed the most creative use of UN peacekeepers since the Suez crisis of 1956. But if some of the operations honored retrospectively by the prize had been at best qualified successes (ONUC, UNFICYP, and UNIFIL[4] come to mind), they may have "preserved through a dangerous generation of bipolarity the 1945 dream of the United Nations as the central arbiter of global security."[5] In any event, the award of the Nobel Peace Prize came at a time when the United Nations was not only about to embark upon an unprecedented number of peacekeeping missions, but at a time when the very concept of peacekeeping was undergoing a remarkable transformation.

Peacekeeping forces were still being used to separate opposing forces and observer missions were still being called upon to monitor cease-fires. But late in the 1980s the UN Security Council began to broaden the range of duties of observers and peacekeepers. They were charged with overseeing the withdrawal of Soviet troops from Afghanistan and Cuban troops from Angola,[6] with supervising free and fair elections and the transition to independence of Namibia,[7] with the demobilization of the Nicaraguan resistance forces in Honduras,[8] and with monitoring of the electoral process in both Nicaragua[9] and Haiti.[10] During this same period, plans for the United Nations to assume major new roles in long-running and seemingly intractable conflicts in Cambodia, the Western Sahara, and El Salvador were also gaining momentum.[11]

It would be a mistake, of course, to give the United Nations all of the credit for this welcome burst of creative activity in the area of its primary responsibility under the Charter. In some situations, the parties to the conflict had simply reached the point of exhaustion and, unable to achieve their goals, were ready to countenance a UN role. In virtually all situations, events within the Soviet Union, together with their overseas ramifications, served to defuse conflicts sufficiently to create room for a UN presence. Moreover, Soviet diplomacy was instrumental in persuading client states to participate in negotiations leading to the creation of UN missions.[12] But the important point is that the United Nations was once again a viable vehicle for conflict management in a number of the world's hot spots, and the government of the United States had reason to be pleased with that new reality.

This appeared to be the case even in Central America, where the United States had resisted UN encroachment for decades. With the Soviet

Union no longer willing, and perhaps no longer able, to support communist regimes in the Western Hemisphere and now playing a more benign role at the UN, the United States could more comfortably contemplate the presence of UN peacekeepers in its own backyard. In sum, the creation of these several new and varied peacekeeping ventures by a Security Council newly freed from the suspicions and paralysis of the Cold War made the switch in US policy from confrontation to courtship of the UN considerably easier than it otherwise would have been.

Some of the factors that facilitated resumption of a cooperative relationship had little to do with the shift in Soviet attitude toward the UN. Some, such as the muting of the North-South conflict, antedated the Gorbachev era. The Third World's litany of demands for redistribution of the world's wealth had by the 1980s become a chronic source of irritation for the United States, which rejected not only the substance of most of those demands but their underlying assumptions as well. But the campaign for a new international economic order had peaked in the 1970s and was already fast losing steam when Ronald Reagan was inaugurated for the first time in 1981. The last major push came at the 11th Special Session of the General Assembly in 1980, but the global negotiations which the UN majority hoped would follow never came about.

Although the problems that stimulated developing country claims against the Western world remained, and in many cases actually became worse, the futility of an aggressive assault on the liberal economic order was acknowledged and the dialogue became less heated and more desultory. The debt crisis, with its high stakes for developed and developing countries alike, preempted increasingly sterile debate about commodity price stabilization and technology transfer and other features of the NIEO, which looked very much like zero-sum proposals in Washington. Moreover, the debt crisis shifted attention away from UN forums and the Group of 77 to international financial institutions and bilateral negotiations with the large debtor countries such as Mexico and Brazil.

On the eve of the Gulf crisis, the United States was very much preoccupied with its own unprecedentedly large budget deficit and was less disposed than ever to treat the United Nations as a significant development forum. The fact that demands for resource transfers and a global affirmative action program were heard less frequently and less stridently at the UN helped to set the stage for improvement in the US-UN relationship.

Another factor making it somewhat easier for the United States to resume a cooperative relationship with the United Nations was the emergence at the UN of a somewhat more even-handed approach to the discussion of human rights violations as well as greater attention to the matter of enforcement. A pattern had been established throughout the years whereby egregious violators of rights the United States regarded as basic were effectively spared criticism for their behavior in UN forums, whereas a handful of unpopular regimes, several of which enjoyed US support, were regularly excoriated—the double standard to which the United States had so often and so strenuously objected. But in the 1980s some modest progress could be observed—progress that was insufficient to bridge the vast gulf between the US view of human rights and that of most UN members, but progress nonetheless. As David Forsythe has observed,

> the UN regime had shown increased balance compared with the 1960s and early 1970s. Independent rapporteurs and working groups were used to bypass the 'tyranny of the majority'; both Communist and Third World violations were addressed to at least some extent; and new norms and agencies were established, as on torture.[13]

In spite of this heightened concern for the development of enforcement procedures and a new willingness to make use of such rudimentary procedures in cases involving previously "immune" governments, the UN core regime on human rights remained weak and problematical. But with the amelioration of some of the worst features of the UN's performance in this field and a modest if still fragile and reversible trend toward more democratic governments in several regions of the world, the United States had reason to view the UN as a slightly less dangerous place, even before Saddam Hussein's aggression sent the Bush administration hastening off to New York in search of UN support.

The ending of the East-West conflict and the shifting of the North-South conflict to a back burner meant that debate at the United Nations was less shrill and in some instances more civil. One other factor contributing to a less heated dialogue was progress toward the dismantling of apartheid in South Africa. One of the most intransigent problems on the UN's agenda has long been Pretoria's apartheid regime. It has shared with Israel's occupation of the West Bank and Gaza and opposition to creation of a Palestinian state a place at the top of any list of the most emotional issues confronting and dividing the global organization. No progress was achieved on the latter problem during the 1980s, but the lifting of the ban on the African National Congress and the release from prison of ANC leader Nelson Mandela raised hopes for an early end of apartheid.

These developments did not satisfy the great majority of UN members, who have annually adopted resolutions condemning apartheid in language clearly reflecting their hostility to the South African government and their frustration over their inability to effect more dramatic change more quickly. But they did ease the pressure on the United States somewhat, partially defusing an issue that had frequently found US policies under attack from the UN's Third World majority, and never more so than during the Reagan administration's experiment with the policy of constructive engagement.

In this area as in others, it is of less note that problems were resolved than that the atmosphere in which debate took place became less acrimonious. Developments that took place outside of the United Nations and had relatively little to do with anything the UN itself had said or done provided grounds for cautious optimism and reduced incentives for recriminations. The United States, of course, believed that its approach had been vindicated. Whether that view is warranted or not, breathing space was created at the UN, to the benefit of the US-UN relationship.

The stewardship of Perez de Cuellar as Secretary-General also facilitated rapprochement between the United States and the United Nations. The Reagan era was also the era of most of Perez de Cuellar's tenure. Although the fifth Secretary-General, like all of his predecessors, had his share of critics, he was widely regarded as a dedicated international civil servant and very probably the most effective executive head the UN had had since Dag Hammarskjöld in the years before the Congo crisis. Perez de Cuellar was, of course, the beneficiary of the lessening of East-West and North-South tensions, but he also demonstrated considerable diplomatic skills in turning the thaw in the Cold War into opportunities for the UN. Not only was he a tireless and frequently effective diplomat, using his good offices and personal representatives to facilitate the movement of warring forces from stubborn intransigence to wary negotiation, he also handled the prickly relationship with the United States during the financial crisis with considerable poise and patience, defending the institution and at the same time taking steps to reduce the size of the Secretariat and otherwise addressing complaints regarding organizational bloat and inefficiency.

In many respects, Perez de Cuellar was the kind of Secretary-General with whom the United States could feel comfortable, and US criticisms of the UN were not directed at him, even if there were those who wished he would read the riot act to the Soviet Union and be a tougher manager of a multinational Secretariat with whose habits and culture many in Washington had little patience. Later, in the aftermath of Operation Desert Storm and amid talk of a new world order, the United States would indicate its preference for a younger and more vigorous Secretary-General. A senior US official, commenting on US disappointment in the election of Boutros-Ghali in 1991, provided a succinct and telling picture of Washington's view of the outgoing Secretary-General, noting that his successor "comes from the same generation of old-fashioned, traditionalist diplomacy that Perez de Cuellar exemplified. Our fear is that he will prove to be warmed-over Perez de Cuellar."[14] But that was 1991. At the turn of the decade, when the frenzy of UN bashing subsided at the US mission and in the Congress, the Secretary-General was ready to assist the transition to a more amicable relationship and the United States was prepared to support him.

Finally, there was the matter of budget reform. Although efficiency and money were not necessarily at the heart of the US quarrel with the

UN, as argued by Charles Krauthammer, the inability of the United States to control the size or shape of the UN budget had become the surrogate for a whole host of US complaints about the organization. Therefore, it was important at both ends of Pennsylvania Avenue that the leverage of the Kassebaum amendment work and that the United States gain effective control over UN spending.

By the end of the second Reagan term it was clear that the United Nations was committed to reform, and the president so certified. The consensus procedure in the Committee on Program and Coordination was holding, and the General Assembly had not tried to undo the CPC's work. In addition, US concerns regarding the UN's overall budget ceiling and cost add-ons after budget approval were being met, as was US insistence on something very close to zero growth in that budget. Similarly, on the personnel side, Secretariat posts were being trimmed. None of these elements of the reform package had progressed to a point where results could be considered conclusive. And there were plenty of critics who were ready to dismiss reform as woefully inadequate or superficial or even irrelevant; they would have preferred to keep pressure on the UN through continued withholding and were doubtlessly pleased that the United States was unable to pay arrearages quickly. But, on balance, the reforms begun as a result of US pressure—whether that pressure was illegal or not—also helped to create a situation in which the UN was once again a more attractive venue for US foreign policy.

Residual Problems for US-UN Relations

When Iraqi forces poured into Kuwait on August 2, 1990, the relationship between the United States and the United Nations could best be described as awkward. On the one hand it was not as strained as it had been throughout much of the previous decade, when in both word and deed the administration and the Congress had made it clear that the United States much preferred unilateral to multilateral diplomacy and was disinclined to make much use of the UN as a vehicle for such multilateral diplomacy as it did conduct unless the global body changed its ways. As a result of the end of the Cold War, several successes on the peacekeeping front, the easing of tensions over several hardy perennials on the UN agenda, and some modest reforms in budget and personnel practices, the UN became more acceptable to all but its severest critics in Washington. The United States had challenged the UN in about as dramatic a way as it could, short of withdrawing, and the UN had responded in ways that enhanced US leverage. The Soviet Union had embraced the UN and multilateralism, reversing four decades of policy and removing a principal source of US frustration.

And the election of George Bush, the only US president ever to have served as ambassador to the United Nations, seemed to augur well for a further strengthening of the US commitment to the UN.

But the relationship with the UN, no longer as cold as it had been in the middle 1980s, was nevertheless no more than lukewarm on the eve of the Gulf crisis. Some old problems, resistant to the winds of change blowing through UN chambers and corridors, continued to plague US-UN relations. And new problems continued to surface, providing ammunition for the UN's critics in the United States and reminding all parties that the path to normalization of US-UN relations would be uneven and occasionally rocky.

One of the more dramatic of these reminders that the United States and the UN majority still marched to different drummers was the flap in 1988 over Yasser Arafat's plans to address the 43rd General Assembly. The government of the United States decided not to grant Arafat a visa, a position the UN's legal counsel and the UN membership as a whole regarded as a violation of host country obligations under the Headquarters Agreement. The US position was straightforward and unequivocal:

> Having found that Mr. Arafat, as Chairman of the PLO, knows of, condones, and lends support to terrorism against Americans, the United States found that Mr. Arafat is an accessory to such terrorism and accordingly denied the visa. This is an action fully consistent with the Headquarters Agreement between the United States and the United Nations and this includes our right to protect our national security, established precedent thereunder, and the widely recognized, inherent right of any host State to protect its national security.[15]

The General Assembly vote on a resolution deploring the US action was just one more in a series that demonstrated how isolated the United States could be within the global body. Only Israel joined the United States in opposing the resolution (the United Kingdom abstained), and 151 states supported it.[16] The General Assembly then repaired to Geneva for three days of meetings so that Arafat could speak.

Progress toward US-UN rapprochement was also slowed by US actions in Central America and the response to those actions by the General Assembly. US policy in Nicaragua was a target of the UN majority right up until the time of the implementation of the Esquipulas II Agreement[17] and the announcement by the Nicaraguan government that it was calling general and free elections. Prior to that breakthrough in 1989 and the subsequent creation of ONUVEN and ONUCA, the United Nations was still roundly condemning the United States for its trade embargo and its support of paramilitary activities against Nicaragua, demanding that it comply with the World Court's ruling of June 27, 1986, and calling upon it to pay reparations to Nicaragua.[18]

If the success of the peace process in Nicaragua ultimately defused US-UN tensions on that front, the Bush administration's invasion of Panama in December 1989 served to rekindle tensions just over a month after the creation of ONUCA had seemed to usher in a new era of US-UN cooperation in the Western Hemisphere. Whatever the merits of the US case for its invasion of Panama,[19] the majority in the General Assembly saw it as a violation of the UN Charter and strongly deplored it by a vote of seventy-five to twenty, with forty abstentions.[20] In this instance, as in the mining of Nicaragua's harbors, the bombing of Libya, and other cases, the US conception of its rights and obligations regarding the use of force under international law clearly differed from that of the UN majority.

Indeed, the first post–Cold War session of the General Assembly produced a number of resolutions that highlighted the still large gap between some of the goals and tactics being promoted by the UN's majority and those the United States found acceptable.[21] These included resolutions calling for observance of international law and condemning the acquisition of territory by force.[22] US opposition to such resolutions, typically with very minimal support, could be explained by the fact that they were thinly disguised or even very explicit attacks on US and Israeli policies. As such, they were a reminder—if any were needed—that the Middle East remained a major stumbling block to the more rapid improvement of US-UN relations. One year later, Saddam Hussein would single-handedly change that, at least for the moment.

The other explanation for the tepid nature of the US-UN relationship on the eve of the Gulf crisis was that the United States, in spite of government promises to restore full funding and pay arrearages, had not yet made good on those promises. The administration had committed itself to repayment of the arrearages over a five-year period, so at the time Saddam Hussein invaded Kuwait, the United States still owed the United Nations. The excuse, of course, was that the US budget deficit made it impossible to retire the arrearage immediately. However, many at the UN (both in the Secretariat and in the diplomatic corps) were angry that the United States, having illegally withheld assessments and coerced the UN into unpopular changes in budget-making procedures, was now not fulfilling its part of the bargain and bringing the UN back from the brink of financial ruin. It was hard for many in the UN community to believe that the United States, with its great wealth and superpower status, could not find a way to meet its relatively modest financial obligations if it really wanted to.

Ambassador Vernon Walters addressed this problem with some plain talk when he appeared before the Subcommittees on Human Rights and International Organizations and on International Operations of the House Foreign Affairs Committee in February 1988. Speaking some months before President Reagan certified that the conditions of the Kassebaum amendment had been met, Walters initiated what would be an ongoing series of appeals to the Congress by the Reagan and Bush administrations for full funding of the UN. He stated that

> if the United States intends to use the United Nations as a serious arm of our foreign policy in Iran/Iraq, the Middle East, Afghanistan, and other areas, we must treat it as a serious institution. We cannot continue to neglect our financial commitments to the United Nations and then expect that our opinions, policies, and positions will carry their former weight in the world body. The United Nations is not a perfect organization, politically or administratively, from the U.S. perspective, nor will it ever be. After all, the world is hardly a perfect place, so the United Nations could hardly be otherwise. It is the organization of 159 independent countries who gather to discuss problems of common concern. We must work to improve the way it serves our needs, but with realistic expectations for the results that will be achieved.[23]

This appeal to the Congress, so different in tone from that of Walters's predecessor, Ambassador Kirkpatrick, reflected both the encouraging fact that reform efforts were under way at the UN and a pragmatic acknowledgment that the UN would be a congenial place for the pursuit of US interests only if the United States paid its dues. Walters's successors and others have been making this same point ever since, but appropriations have regularly fallen well short of obligations.[24]

By the time the Bush administration had settled in Washington, it was possible to make the following observations regarding US-UN relations:

- UN-bashing by the United States, at least in the often virulent form it had assumed in the mid-1980s, had ended.
- The Heritage Foundation crowd had departed and more pragmatic and diplomatic people had replaced them, both at the mission in New York and in the State Department.
- Budgetary reform had taken hold at the UN, and although the results were not entirely satisfactory to the United States, the new procedures seemed to be working satisfactorily.
- The Soviet Union, in both word and deed, had begun to take the United Nations seriously, signaling that it would no longer be a forum for waging cold war.
- Peacekeeping had earned a new lease on life, demonstrating not only that the UN was capable of making a contribution to stability in several of the world's hot spots, but that its capacity for task expansion was far from exhausted.
- The Third World's assault on the liberal economic order and on Western values generally had abated somewhat, a victim of its lack of success and declining cohesion within the ranks of the UN's majority.
- Deep divisions within the UN persisted nonetheless, some of them hardy perennials largely unaffected by the easing of Cold War

tensions and others reflecting the frustration of the majority with its inability to turn its votes into concrete results and of the minority with the hypervigilance required to defend its interests and values.

The balance sheet seemed to favor both improved US-UN relations and a more relevant and effective UN, although it also demonstrated that the United Nations was emerging from the doldrums of the previous decade in a financially weakened condition and with a great many latent problems that could easily reverse an otherwise positive trend. The frustration and anger that had characterized US policy toward the UN throughout much of the 1980s had largely dissipated by the beginning of the century's last decade. But frustration and anger had not yet been replaced by an eagerness to see the United Nations as a preferred venue for the conduct of US foreign policy. The government said the appropriate things, and anyone inferring US policy from speeches delivered before the assembled nations at the UN by President Bush might have believed that the United States had espoused multilateralism with great enthusiasm. His address before the General Assembly on October 1, 1990, although obviously influenced by the Security Council's response to Iraq's aggression, is a dramatic case in point. He began by stating that he had "never been prouder to have once served within your ranks and never been prouder that the United States is the host country for the United Nations."[25] And he concluded with these words:

> The world must know and understand: From this hour, from this day, from this hall, we step forth with a new sense of purpose, a new sense of possibilities. We stand together, prepared to swim upstream, to march uphill, to tackle the tough challenges as they come—not only as the United Nations, but as the nations of the world united. . . . The United Nations is now fulfilling its promise as the world's parliament of peace. I congratulate you. I support you. And I wish you Godspeed in the challenges ahead.[26]

In fact, by invading Kuwait in August of 1990, Saddam Hussein had provided a dramatic and unexpected impetus to the further improvement of relations between the United States and the United Nations and to the reemergence of the UN as a factor to be reckoned with in the conduct of world affairs.

Iraq: Catalyst for US-UN Rapprochement

When Saddam Hussein decided on a military solution to his dispute with Kuwait, it seems certain that he did not anticipate that his actions would lead to the mobilization of an enormous multinational military force in

Saudi Arabia and to the war that drove him from what was to be the newest Iraqi province. Nor did he anticipate that the United Nations Security Council would adopt, one after another, some of the strongest resolutions in its forty-five-year history, culminating on November 29, 1990, in Resolution 678, authorizing the use of "all necessary means" (i.e., force) if he did not promptly comply with those other resolutions.[27]

Iraq would, of course, have considered the possibility that its invasion and annexation of Kuwait would lead to some kind of international response. It must have anticipated a negative reaction in many quarters; a move for condemnation by the United Nations was probable, considering Charter support for the principles of sovereignty and nonaggression. But Iraq seemed to believe that its own claims against Kuwait and justifications for its action would override any sentimental concern for a nouveau riche oil sheikdom, and it certainly did not believe that opposition to its invasion and annexation would be much more than pro forma. It would, in other words, confront the world with a fait accompli and ride out any resulting diplomatic unpleasantness without great difficulty.

Saddam Hussein could be forgiven for miscalculating the severity of the response to his invasion and annexation of Kuwait. The United Nations had mounted only one military enforcement action under Article 42 of the Charter in its entire history, and that, of course, had occurred during the fortuitous absence of the Soviet Union from the Security Council at the beginning of the Korean War. For all practical purposes, collective security had become a dead letter. There had, to be sure, been another instance in which the UN had imposed sanctions,[28] but it involved a pariah regime in Southern Rhodesia, a case that was easily distinguishable from one involving a member in good standing of the Non-Aligned Movement and the Group of 77, not to mention a respected regional power that had only recently enjoyed relatively broad international support in its war with Iran. The doctrine of collective security had had no deterrent value in the years since the drafting of the UN Charter; it had none in the summer of 1992.

Moreover, as William Kincade has observed, "there were many signs that might have been read as favoring the conclusion that no nation strong enough to protect Kuwait was deeply committed to its security."[29] Kincade has taken Richard Ned Lebow's thesis that brinkmanship crises[30] are a function of both need and opportunity and applied it to Iraq's behavior in the Gulf crisis. Saddam's frustration with "the desperate circumstances Iraq faced and the absence of thanks and compensation for its years of sacrifice"[31] may have been sufficient to cause him to seize Kuwait, even in the face of evidence of a persuasive commitment to that country's defense. But his calculus was simplified by the fact that his need was matched by what he must have perceived as an attractive opportunity.

The politico-military environment for seizing Kuwait must have seemed very auspicious to those driven by perceived necessity and a predisposition to violent methods. Much of Syria's army was tied down in Lebanon; Jordan was not a factor; Saudi Arabia was too weak to defend Kuwait and might prefer to seek safety in its 1989 nonaggression pact with Iraq so as to avoid losing its vulnerable northeastern territory; Iran was highly unlikely and probably unable to protect Kuwait; and Egypt and Turkey were poorly positioned to assist it, even assuming that they were willing.

The U.S. and Israel were capable of exacting military penalties for aggression, but also ill-positioned to do so quickly and effectively and suffered other liabilities, as well. Israel would expose itself to action from Iraq and other Arab states and had no interest in aiding Kuwait. The U.S. was hampered by a dearth of security arrangements with the Gulf states and by long lines of supply and communication. There was no precedent at all for an international coalition as broad and effective as the one Iraq came to face, so Saddam might plausibly think his army could withstand, wear down, or break up a smaller, less cohesive force.[32]

Of perhaps even greater significance in Saddam's calculations were the signals emanating from Washington. While the United States was undoubtedly displeased with Iraq's human rights performance, it continued right up until the moment of Iraq's invasion of Kuwait to provide reassurances of US support for essentially normal relations. Thus as late as July 1990 the administration was resisting congressional efforts to end commodity credit guarantees, close out a line of credit from the US Export-Import Bank, and require the government to oppose future loans to Iraq from multilateral banks. The reassuring messages conveyed by a group of US senators in April of that year and by Ambassador April Glaspie a week before the invasion have been extensively reported and commented upon. It is clear that neither the senators nor the ambassador meant to give Saddam a green light for his invasion of Kuwait, but it is equally clear that what they said and what they did not say had the effect of reinforcing Baghdad's conviction that the risk of war with the United States was indeed very small.[33]

Although it may be interesting to speculate as to the probable evolution of the Gulf crisis and US-UN relations had the United States taken a different approach to Iraq in the spring and summer 1990 and demonstrated an unequivocal commitment to Kuwait's integrity, that was the road not taken. Driven by a combination of perceived need and perceived opportunity, Saddam did invade Kuwait on August 2 and was almost immediately confronted by an unexpected demonstration of US and UN resolve.

Diplomacy in the Security Council

The UN Security Council, meeting in emergency session on the very first day of the Iraqi invasion of Kuwait, adopted the first of what would become a series of strong resolutions on the Gulf crisis. Resolution 660 condemned the invasion and demanded the immediate and unconditional withdrawal of Iraqi troops from Kuwait.[34] While this resolution echoed the position taken that same day by the Bush administration, it was a sponta- neous and broadly based response to an egregious violation of the UN Charter and in no way reflected pressure from Washington. The vote was fourteen to zero, with Yemen not participating. Although it was not clear at the outset of the crisis how far the Security Council would go in invok- ing the enforcement measures in Chapter 7, it was immediately apparent that the paralyzing hand of the Cold War had been lifted. Perhaps the most important event of this opening round of the crisis was the joint statement issued on August 3 by Soviet Foreign Minister Eduard Shevardnadze and US Secretary of State James Baker calling for the unconditional with- drawal of Iraqi troops and urging all states to cease arms deliveries to Iraq. This statement was nothing less than an announcement that the Cold War was over and that the UN might now be able to play a significant role in crises heretofore beyond the effective reach of the global body. Without that message, the United States would almost certainly have been stymied in its subsequent efforts to obtain UN endorsement for enforcement mea- sures against Iraq. With it, the response to Iraqi aggression could move forward on parallel tracks—the coalition rapidly being assembled by the United States and the broader international community represented in the UN Security Council.

Most of the analyses of the crisis in the Gulf have focused on deci- sionmaking within the US government, on the buildup in Saudi Arabia of coalition forces in Operation Desert Shield, and on the decision reached in Washington to abandon sanctions in favor of war in the form of Operation Desert Storm.[35] The United Nations is a minor player in most of these analyses, and the implication is clear: The real story unfolded in Washing- ton, not in New York, and involved President Bush, Secretary of Defense Richard Cheney, Chairman of the Joint Chiefs of Staff Colin Powell, Na- tional Security Advisor Brent Scowcroft, General Norman Schwarzkopf, and assorted other US officials, most of them members of the military. Even Secretary of State Baker plays a secondary role in much of the post- crisis literature, underscoring the conventional wisdom that the decision for war was made early (and unilaterally) and that diplomatic activity was largely an irrelevant sideshow. The corollary, of course, is that the United Nations was part of that sideshow—that what happened in the Security Council was of secondary importance.

This view of the crisis is understandable, given President Bush's early assertion that Iraq's occupation of Kuwait "will not stand," his subsequent comparison of Saddam with Hitler, the shift from a defensive to an offen- sive force posture in early November, and the transparent unwillingness of the United States to negotiate with Iraq as the January 15 deadline for withdrawal from Kuwait approached. Students of the crisis seem to be in agreement: President Bush decided at some point in early autumn 1990 that Iraq's withdrawal from Kuwait was not enough, that Saddam also had to be humiliated. Inasmuch as humiliation was the outcome Saddam most wanted to avoid, war became inevitable.[36]

But this view of the crisis should not be allowed to obscure the diplomatic activity that was taking place concurrently. President Bush may have decided for war, or at least for a crisis strategy and tactics that made war a virtual certainty, but he wanted—some would say he needed—UN support. And while that support was unequivocal in Resolution 660 and relatively easy to muster in most of the other resolutions adopted by the Council during the first three months of the crisis, the United States paid the UN the compliment of serious attention during those months. It assiduously worked the diplomatic channels both in New York and in capitals, seeking to maximize Security Council support for resolutions designed to tighten the screws on Iraq and compel compliance with Resolution 660.

Later, after "American objectives appeared to escalate from getting Saddam Hussein out of Kuwait to eliminating Saddam Hussein as a threat to stability in the Gulf region,"[37] the task confronting US diplomats from Ambassador Thomas Pickering to the president himself became considerably more challenging. The UN had agreed in August that Iraq must get out of Kuwait and had adopted sanctions with the objective of making its continuing occupation of that country so painful that it would feel compelled to comply. A coalition of twenty-nine states had contributed to a military buildup in Saudi Arabia that was intended to be a deterrent to further adventurism by Saddam and would demonstrate the seriousness of the international community's commitment to Kuwait and to the principle of nonaggression. But the ground rules shifted for both coalitions—the military one in the Gulf and the diplomatic one at the United Nations. As a trenchant study of leadership and followership in the Gulf conflict put it, "what had begun as a relatively minor and painless contribution to a multilateral effort to impose sanctions to coerce Iraq into withdrawing from Kuwait and to deter an Iraqi attack on Saudi Arabia was transformed at least five times by war's end, always at American instigation or by unilateral decision."[38] Although the authors of this essay are doubtless correct in their conclusion that "the freedom of maneuver for coalition members fell dramatically the moment they signed on in August 1990,"[39] it is also clear that coalition members became less and less enthusiastic about following Washington's lead as the United States became increasingly committed to a military solution to the problem posed by Saddam Hussein. That loss of enthusiasm was also evident in the Security Council, where members were confronted with a difficult choice: Continuation of the embargo, which had achieved a remarkably high level of compliance, or authorization of the use of force, which would effectively shift control of the Gulf crisis to the United States.

During this critical phase of the crisis, the Bush administration at one and the same time resisted the efforts of other states to broker a political settlement with Iraq and pursued with rare diplomatic vigor support for a Council resolution that would legitimize the use of force by the coalition. The United States had what amounted to a fall-back position: It could invoke Article 51 of the Charter to justify military action against Iraq. Article 51 provides that states may assist one another in resisting aggression and requires no authorization by the Security Council for its implementation. The Kuwaiti government was presumably willing to agree to the use of force by the United States to expel the occupying Iraqis. But Article 51 was, as Bush's people well knew, a very poor alternative—useful perhaps for purposes of leverage to achieve their real objective but not an effective vehicle for sustaining broad coalition support and almost certainly a poor basis for mobilizing domestic support, especially in the Congress. What the government needed, both for international and domestic purposes, was strong Security Council endorsement of US-led military action. In other words, the United States needed the United Nations.

For a period of roughly a month prior to adoption of Resolution 678, President Bush, Secretary of State Baker, and Ambassador Pickering were engaged in truly hyperactive diplomacy. Baker was especially busy, traveling the globe in an effort to generate support for the necessary Security Council authorization. As one detailed review of this diplomatic offensive assesses the task facing US officials, "They had to secure support for a resolution worded so as to convince Iraq that force would be used unless it complied with existing UN resolutions requiring its unconditional withdrawal from Kuwait. But the wording had to be such as, at a minimum, to avoid a veto by any of the five permanent members of the Security Council."[40] This was no easy task. Of the Council's other permanent members, only the United Kingdom posed no problem for Washington. And the United States needed the support of most, if not all, of the nonpermanent members; a mere nine votes (the minimum required for passage of a Council resolution) would hardly constitute an impressive demonstration of international unity.

The final vote for Resolution 678 was twelve in favor, two opposed (Cuba and Yemen), and one abstention (China). But that result came at the end of several weeks of intensive negotiations, important compromises on language, and at least one important side payment.

The Cold War may have ended, but the Soviet Union could not be counted as an automatic "yes" vote. Gorbachev had to contend with conservatives at home who were not prepared for a de facto alliance with the country's long-standing principal enemy, and he and his colleagues were sensitive about the Soviet Union's reduced role in world affairs. Yevgeny Primakov, a Soviet envoy actively seeking a face-saving way out of the crisis for Saddam Hussein, said, "we should gather up all the things that have been said in the United Nations and the Arab League about negotiating Iraq's dispute with Kuwait and settling the Palestinian problem and give them to him in one big face-saving package."[41] The Bush administration, not surprisingly, rejected this idea, insisting that Saddam could not be rewarded for his aggression. The United States found it necessary, however, to accommodate Soviet reluctance to support a resolution specifically mentioning force (hence the alternative phrase, "all necessary means," proposed by Baker and accepted by Shevardnadze). And even more importantly, it had to accept Gorbachev's insistence that the resolution provide an opportunity for further negotiation—what the Soviet president (and Resolution 678) termed a "pause of goodwill." If there was to be a pause, there would need to be a deadline, and here, too, the United States had to compromise. The date set was January 15, 1992.

China proved to be less of a problem for the United States than the Soviet Union was. It indicated early in the discussions regarding a Council resolution authorizing use of force that it did not expect to cast a veto. But in spite of its need to use the crisis to regain favor in Washington and other Western capitals, Beijing remained something of an enigma throughout the negotiations. It obviously wanted a quid pro quo for support of a US-sponsored resolution, and sought one by pressing for Baker to visit China, "a high diplomatic price [for the United States to pay,] given the prohibition on official exchanges imposed by the US after the Tiananmen Square massacre in 1989."[42] Although that invitation was not accepted, the United States did invite the Chinese foreign minister to visit Washington after the vote in the Council, a move generally regarded as diplomatic payment for China's abstention on the key resolution.[43]

French support for the resolution can best be described as pragmatic acceptance, rather than enthusiastic support. Indeed, as Cooper, Higgott, and Nossal claim in their essay on leadership and followership in the Gulf crisis, "With the one exception of Britain, no other state that joined the anti-Iraq coalition showed much zest for the increasingly military nature of the enterprise as it was being worked out by Washington over the crisis."[44] Although France had made clear its support "in principle" for the resolution sought by the United States, and would later participate in Operation Desert Storm, it would not announce its support for the resolution in advance of Council debate; subsequently, the Mitterrand government put some distance between itself and the United States as the January 15 deadline approached, resurrecting the idea of linkage to the Palestinian question and otherwise seeking to revive the possibility of a diplomatic solution even after it was clear that the decision had been made for war.

The task of obtaining the support of the nonpermanent members of the Council, none of whom could be described as enthusiastic about the military option, was simplified by the Council's composition. The United States held little hope of persuading either Cuba or Yemen to support a resolution endorsing use of force, although Baker went the extra mile, paying a rare visit by a senior US official to the Yemeni capital and meeting with the Cuban foreign minister. These diplomatic efforts did not pay off,[45] but they are testimony to the effort mounted by the US government as it sought international legitimacy for its Gulf policy. But except for these two states, no other nonpermanent member of the Council was either a friend of Iraq's or reflexively anti-American.

A case can be made that the United States was lucky, especially in the fact that the African states on the Council were, as one US official put it to the author, "good Africans, not ringleaders of knee-jerk, Third World anti-US posturing." Neither Zaire nor Côte d'Ivoire posed a problem for US diplomacy, and even Ethiopia, with its memory of the League of Nations' failure to save it from Mussolini's aggression in the 1930s, was "hawkish on the Gulf issue from the start."[46] Nor did any of the other elected members appear to pose a special dilemma for US diplomacy; in the case of each of the regions represented on the Council, it is possible to imagine those seats occupied by more difficult, intransigent states (from the point of view of Washington). Colombia and Malaysia, both nonaligned but moderate, at one point joined Cuba and Yemen in appealing for a peaceful resolution of the crisis, but in the end succumbed to Baker's and Pickering's entreaties and to the bandwagon effect.

On November 29, 1990, the Security Council met, debated, voted on, and adopted Resolution 678, ending weeks of intensive diplomacy and behind-the-scenes negotiations. Throughout much of that time the United States had not even formally acknowledged that it was seeking a UN resolution, preferring instead to "engineer a 'rolling consensus'—a continual, cumulative and intentionally visible process intended to give those not yet persuaded the impression of inexorable momentum."[47] The US government succeeded in this endeavor, and the margin by which it succeeded and the absence of any demurrer when Baker declared that the words "all necessary means" constituted an authorization for the use of force make it difficult to argue that Operation Desert Storm lacked the support of the United Nations. The Bush administration had sought and obtained a critically important UN vote of confidence in its leadership of the international community's effort to dislodge Iraq from Kuwait.

The Road to War

The story of Baker's (and Bush's) personal diplomacy during autumn 1990 tends, of course, to make the point that the United States was simply using the UN as an instrument of its own foreign policy, and that it managed to overwhelm the members of the Security Council with a combination of high-pressure salesmanship and something akin to bribes. Resolution 678 would not have been adopted had the United States not worked hard for its approval; nevertheless, there is an element of condescension in the argument that the members of the Security Council allowed themselves to be manipulated by the United States. Eleven resolutions specifically concerning the situation in the Gulf had been adopted before Resolution 678 was approved. Only three votes were cast against all of those resolutions, two in the case of Resolution 666 on September 13, 1990, and one in the case of Resolution 670 on September 26. Cuba and Yemen opposed Council guidelines for delivery of foodstuffs and medical supplies in the first case, and Cuba opposed expanding the embargo to include air traffic in the second.[48] No other state either opposed or abstained on any of these resolutions, and the cumulative record suggests that Council members were genuinely outraged at Iraq's aggression against Kuwait and did not need the United States to tell them how to respond to it.

A bumper sticker seen on US highways asserted that there would have been no hue and cry, much less an Operation Desert Storm, had Kuwait's principal export been broccoli—obviously a product of anti-Bush sentiment. There is almost certainly some truth in its message, as evidenced by subsequent reluctance to confront Serbia over its assault on Bosnia, a state whose only defense against aggression is its sovereignty (rather than its sovereignty plus its strategic importance or its value as a source of scarce and critical resources). But the alacrity with which the Security Council challenged Saddam Hussein and ratcheted up its challenge to his annexation of Kuwait still suggests a strong commitment to fundamental Charter principles, and a willingness to go well beyond rhetorical creed protection.

The reservations of some Council members regarding the resort to military force are understandable, in view of the fact that economic sanctions had been in effect for only a few short months and that, in the absence of the means spelled out in Chapter 7 of the Charter, the Council would necessarily have to "sign away to interested powers the operational responsibility for applying military force."[49] But the members were able to overcome those reservations, aided by Saddam's behavior during the crisis—an "in your face" performance that could hardly have encouraged those who hoped for a peaceful settlement. They did have their "pause of goodwill," however, which gave Saddam an opportunity to make a conciliatory move before the January 15 deadline.

As for the manifest discrepancy between the Charter prescription for enforcement measures and the ersatz version before the Council on November 29, the members knew that they were abdicating control. Yemen's foreign minister was quite correct when he called it "a classic example of authority without responsibility."[50] As Bruce Russett and James Sutterlin have pointed out, "The major danger [of such an abdication of control by the Council] is that the entire undertaking will be identified with the country or countries actually involved in military action rather than with the United Nations."[51] And this is exactly what has happened, in the view of many critics of the Gulf crisis and war. But the tools for enforcement envisioned by the Charter's framers were simply not available to the Security Council during the Gulf crisis, having been among the many casualties of the Cold War; nor was there any prospect that these tools could be forged in the heat of the crisis or brought to bear, untested, against a country allegedly possessing the world's fourth largest army and a singularly truculent leader. If in Kuwait "the UN was less the world's policeman than its sheriff deputizing a posse,"[52] it nonetheless was prepared to demonstrate a commitment to the spirit of collective security. If the Council could not itself conduct a military operation if one became necessary, it was prepared to entrust that mission to a broadly based coalition, led by the only state in a position to assume that role. In effect, the members of the Council seemed to be responding, however reluctantly, to the questions, "If not here, where? If not now, when?"

On the day following the adoption of Resolution 678, the Bush administration proposed direct negotiations between Secretary of State Baker and Iraq's Foreign Minister, Tariq Aziz. Thus opened what was for most observers the most frustrating phase of the crisis, the pause for negotiations that the Soviet Union had insisted upon and most Council members hoped would produce progress toward settlement—a pause during which Iraq and the United States argued over the date of a Baker-Aziz meeting, the Congress debated and authorized the president to use US armed forces against Iraq, and absolutely no negotiations took place between Washington and Baghdad. Indeed, the Bush administration never intended to negotiate, as that word is customarily understood. It made clear that it would make no concessions, that Iraq would have to comply fully with all Security Council resolutions and would have to do so by January 15. As Linda Brady observed, "The offer to negotiate was merely the political price the administration had to pay to ensure the passage of the United Nations resolution."[53] It also enhanced Bush's credibility by suggesting that he preferred a peaceful solution to the crisis, helped hold the coalition together, and strengthened his hand with domestic critics, especially in the Congress.

Reasonable people may disagree as to whether Operation Desert Storm was necessary, or whether it was necessary when it was launched on January 16. A very sizable minority in both houses of Congress believed that the resort to force was premature, and it seems clear that many members of the international community, including much of the Security Council's membership, became resigned to the use of force rather than enthusiastic about it. Soviet reticence is well documented. France, on the very day of the January deadline, made a last ditch effort to head off war and proposed that the Council agree on an international conference to deal with the Palestinian question if Iraq would agree to withdraw from Kuwait. Germany and Japan, both indisputably major powers with an interest in Middle Eastern oil, but neither a member of the Council and hence precluded from participating in the drafting of Resolution 678, were conspicuously not eager for a military solution of the crisis.

> Many Germans, for example, having had just-war rhetoric rebound on them in the past, proved highly skeptical of the kind of justifications for the use of force against Iraq that surfaced during the crisis. Likewise, in Japan, there is a deep commitment to non-military solutions to international affairs, and the Gulf crisis with its obvious military demands on all allies caused not only a kind of policy paralysis in Tokyo, but a governmental crisis. In short, Americans may be convinced that the failure of Germany and Japan to contribute to the Gulf War was free ridership; it can be persuasively argued that their reluctance was due to a failure of U.S. leadership, a failure to secure followership from these states. Put bluntly, the United States failed to provide a sufficiently convincing argument that the big idea was also a good idea.[54]

This author is inclined to the view that the military operation that began on January 16 was overly determined, and that William Kincade is correct in his assessment that "no combination of rational interests or strategic imperatives compelled Saddam Hussein to invade Kuwait *or George Bush to drive him out.*"[55] (Emphasis added.)

The reluctance of so many to abandon diplomacy and sanctions in favor of military action does not alter the fact that the United Nations did nothing to undermine or qualify its approval of the use of force. However much the members may have preferred a peaceful settlement, no resolution was introduced to rescind or extend the deadline. The Council seemed cognizant of the risks in appearing to equivocate on its commitment to full compliance with the twelve resolutions.

The handling by the United States of the negotiations over whether and when to negotiate certainly tended to confirm the judgment that the Bush administration viewed "the possibility of a negotiated settlement and a peaceful withdrawal (the 'nightmare scenario') with fear, not relief."[56] The United States refused to treat Saddam's announcement that he would release all hostages as a positive signal, in spite of the fact that this had been one of President Bush's conditions. Even more significantly, the United States rejected Saddam's invitation to Baker to come to Baghdad on January 12 for talks, even though that date fell within the time frame Bush had announced on November 30. As James Bennet observed, Iraq had to regard this effort on Bush's part to dictate the date on which the

Iraqi president should receive Baker as a humiliating and unacceptable bait-and-switch.[57]

At the UN it was well understood that the pause of goodwill had degenerated into a charade in which "the process, rather than the underlying objectives, became the issue"[58] while Iraq and the coalition moved inexorably toward a military showdown. But the Council adopted no further resolutions until President Bush had called a halt to the carnage in the desert. The paradox of general acquiescence in a war that most states would have preferred to avoid has been perceptively analyzed in a recent study of the relationship during the crisis between the United States and the international community.

> It is not that the government in Washington did not continue to act within a multilateral framework throughout the conflict. On the contrary, the Bush administration has clearly been one of the most multilaterally-minded administrations in the postwar period. Both the president and his secretary of state worked assiduously at channelling the conflict through the United Nations; at keeping in touch, often personally, with other leaders; and at widening the support for the anti-Iraq line. The real problem was that leadership turned into headship, where decisions for the group are arrived at unilaterally by a leader whose overweening power ensures that subordinates will have few other options than to comply. . . . The leader's preferences quickly become the group's by default, not by consensus. For no member of the coalition was in any position to resist the overwhelming inertial force of Washington's decision-making once it started to roll.[59]

This analysis is focused more on the military coalition than on the diplomatic coalition, and it arguably overstates the case in its claim that the Bush administration has been one of the most multilaterally minded; however, it nonetheless makes an important point about the US-UN relationship in the Gulf crisis. After many years during which the United Nations had played a marginal role in US foreign policy—years during which US leadership there had been exercised largely for purposes of damage limitation—the United States was confronted with a situation in which the UN was vitally important and in which US leadership of the global organization was required. It is possible to conclude that the reassertion of US leadership at the UN had three negative characteristics:

1. It was excessive, constituting little less than coercion of the Security Council into endorsing Washington's policies.
2. It was cynical, displaying a highly selective concern for the principles of nonviolence and the rule of law.
3. It was even abusive, manipulating the Council into an unconscionable abandonment of its obligation to seek the peaceful settlement of disputes.

It is not possible, however, to ignore the fact that the United States was once again taking the United Nations seriously and acting as if the global body had a major role to play in the conduct of US foreign policy. In that sense, there had been a dramatic about-face in the US-UN relationship.

President Bush was able to draw upon that newly enhanced relationship in dealing with the Congress. During the 1980s the administration had, in the words of one career official involved in UN affairs, incited a riot that quickly spread to Capitol Hill and to an orgy of UN-bashing by the Congress. When Reagan, and later Bush, sought to return US-UN relations to normal (read proper, not enthusiastic), the Congress was slow to respond. After all, the perception in Washington was not that the UN was suddenly doing something positive, which made it once again an appropriate venue for US foreign policy initiatives, but rather that it had merely ceased to be as much of a problem for the United States. But when Iraq invaded Kuwait, the Congress as well as the administration was treated to the sight of the international community expressing its outrage through the United Nations. Instead of the posturing and indecisiveness and deference to Communist states and Third World radicals that the United States had found so objectionable in the past, the Security Council had moved quickly and emphatically to align itself with US policy.

As a result, when the Congress finally got around to debating the issue, both the administration and congressional supporters of a joint resolution authorizing the use of US military force in the Gulf crisis were able to invoke Security Council Resolution 678 as a principal rationale for their position. We cannot know with certainty what the outcome of this debate would have been had there been no UN resolution authorizing "all necessary means" to obtain Iraq's unconditional withdrawal from Kuwait. But it is reasonable to assume that an Article 51 defense of the use of US military force would have been much more problematic; indeed, there is a good likelihood that the president would not have gone to war (and that the Congress would never have had its debate or adopted its "use of force" resolution) in the absence of Resolution 678 or something very much like it. As it was, the margin for the president was slim in the Senate (fifty-two to forty-seven).[60]

Other factors played an important part in the debate and the vote, including the sensitivity of the Congress regarding its role in making war (the Vietnam experience had not been forgotten), partisanship (congressional Republicans were solidly behind their president, whereas a majority of Democrats favored continuation of international economic pressure), and, of course, personal assessments of the wisdom of the president's switch to an offensive strategy in November and of the probable success of a sanctions-first policy.

But those who favored authorizing the use of US military force were able to wrap themselves in the UN flag. Typical are the remarks of Rep. Bill Green (R-N.Y.):

> UN Resolution 678, with its predecessors, is the first effort of the United Nations to function on behalf of collective security since the end of the Cold War. If Congress now undercuts 678, it will likely destroy this initiative to reconstitute the United Nations as it was originally conceived—the vehicle by which the nations of the world work together for collective security.[61]

A similar sentiment was voiced by Rep. Paul Henry (R-Mich.), who argued that

> the US Congress ought not to put itself at odds against the United Nations or question the considered opinion and actions of the Security Council. Turning against the United Nations in this instance would strike a blow against the struggle to refine and strengthen international peacekeeping institutions that will be so important in the post–cold war era.[62]

Senator Slade Gorton (R-Wash.) sounded an even more apocalyptic note, claiming that failure to authorize the use of force upon the expiration of the Council's deadline could result in "the United Nations suffering the fate of the League of Nations."[63]

The Joint Congressional Resolution adopted on January 12, 1991, makes no fewer than five references to the United Nations, and twice links the resolution to Security Council Resolution 678. Those who favored the sanctions and opposed an open-ended authorization of the use of force actually included more of the UN's strongest supporters on Capitol Hill than could be found on the other side. But they were reduced to arguing that Resolution 678 did not reflect the true interests of the international community. Senator Joseph Biden (D-Del.) put it this way: "What model, of any future utility, would be established by a process whereby the United Nations imposes sanctions briefly after which the United States undertakes massive and unilateral action with a veil of UN approval?"[64] Biden may have been correct, but his was the more difficult case to make.

War's Aftermath

Operation Desert Storm began on January 16, 1991, with the first of what were to become almost continuous air strikes against military targets in Iraq. It ended forty-three days later, after more than 100,000 air sorties had been flown and four days of ground war had decimated Iraqi forces. The announcement that the "liberation of Kuwait" had begun was made by White House spokesman Marlin Fitzwater, not by the office of the Secretary-General of the United Nations, reflecting the fact that the United States, not the UN, was giving the orders. When President Bush went on television two hours later, however, he managed both to place the military assault firmly within the UN mandate and to make of the war a patriotic US mission.[65]

Six weeks later, on February 27, the president was able to announce that "Kuwait is liberated" and that he was calling for a suspension of offensive combat operations because "our military objectives are met."[66] The war had been decidedly (and for many surprisingly) one-sided. On television sets in living rooms in the United States, the war sometimes resembled a video game rather than a violent conflict in which thousands of Iraqis were being killed. It generated a tremendous surge of national pride in the United States. The president was able to say, only a few days after the war had ended, "By God, we've kicked the Vietnam syndrome once and for all."[67] The sense that the liberation of Kuwait had been a product of US-UN cooperation—that is, that the role of the Security Council in mobilizing international condemnation of Iraq and legitimizing the military action that drove it from Kuwait was critical to the whole enterprise— had largely been lost sight of in the smoke of battle and in the victory parades after the war. In his address announcing the liberation of Kuwait, President Bush did say that "this is a victory for the United Nations, for all mankind, for the rule of law, and for what is right."[68] He could hardly have said less. But once the shooting started, the United Nations faded from the picture, not to reappear until the adoption by the Security Council of the first important postwar resolutions, 686 on March 2 and 687 on April 3, 1991.[69]

Early in February, after more than three weeks of intensive bombing of Iraqi targets, Soviet President Gorbachev expressed his concern that the military operations threatened to exceed the Security Council's mandate; on the eve of the land war, and after talks between the Soviet and Iraqi foreign ministers, Gorbachev put forward a peace proposal that would have had the effect of repealing the Security Council's resolutions in return for Iraq's prompt and unconditional withdrawal from Kuwait.[70] But this maneuver was viewed in Washington as an attempt on Moscow's part to guarantee Saddam's survival and preserve its own influence in the region. The Bush administration, now confident of a decisive military victory and openly promoting the overthrow of Saddam, was not about to cede control of events in the Gulf to anyone else. Nothing came of the Gorbachev initiative, and General Schwarzkopf's tanks rolled according to plan on February 24.

The Gulf War suggests that Russett and Sutterlin were quite right to be concerned that, in the absence of Security Council control, military action taken in the name of the United Nations will be associated with the states providing the planes and the troops rather than with the UN.[71] That was certainly the case with most of the US public and the media, and even the government scarcely paid lip service to the UN's role once the war began or its role in the decision to end it. Moreover, the Bush administration had obviously come to the conclusion that the demands made upon Iraq in Security Council resolutions 660 through 678 were insufficient. Although it repeatedly invoked those resolutions and insisted that Saddam comply promptly and unconditionally with all of them, it also began the process of ratcheting up its own expectations as to the postwar situation in Iraq. At no time did President Bush unilaterally make new demands upon Iraq, but he made no secret of the fact that he wanted Saddam to be deposed and the threat posed by Iraq's weapons of mass destruction, especially those of an "unconventional" character, eliminated. The potential for a rift between the United States and the United Nations was very much present during the war.

The wisdom of the decision to end the war before the complete destruction of the Iraqi military and without a sweep to Baghdad has been much debated. The tenacity with which Saddam retained power, the roadblocks he placed in the way of efforts to achieve the objectives of Security Council Resolution 687, and the brutal way in which he suppressed dissident populations in the country inevitably led to second-guessing of the president's decision to end the war when he did. But that decision was entirely consistent with the Council resolutions under which the war was fought, and a failure to halt the slaughter when it was clear that the objective of liberating Kuwait had been achieved would almost certainly have provoked a split between the United States and the United Nations.[72]

With the war won, however, the Bush administration had no desire to establish a US imperium in the Gulf region. It had no wish to see the disintegration of Iraq, an event it believed would be destabilizing for the entire region. And it certainly did not want to create a situation in which "US forces would become bogged down in Iraqi politics," the liberators turning into "an unwanted army of occupation."[73] The White House continued to entertain the hope that Saddam would be overthrown, but its primary concern after the war was that Iraq would not again be able to threaten its neighbors. Thus, although the United States may have pressed reluctant Security Council members into acceptance of a military solution of the problem posed by Iraq, conducted the war on its own terms without further consultation with Council members, and treated Operation Desert Storm as a glorious triumph for US arms, it did not sever or seriously jeopardize the UN connection. When it came time for the Council to establish a formal cease-fire and define Iraq's postwar obligations, the United States found that the broad consensus that had existed within the United Nations during the previous summer and fall had survived the war.

The United States sought and received strong Security Council endorsement for a resolution that made unprecedented demands on Iraq. Far from taking the position that with Kuwait liberated the international community could forgive and forget, Resolution 687, which has been referred to as "the mother of all resolutions," presented the most ambitious, far-reaching challenge to the prerogatives of a sovereign state ever adopted by the Council. This resolution may, of course, be viewed simply as the Council's attempt to close the book on the collective security exercise begun almost eight months to the day earlier with Resolution 660. But Resolution 687 does much more than merely tidy up the loose ends of this first post–Cold War application of Chapter 7. By April 1991 there was no longer an act of aggression or a breach of the peace to contend with. Saddam Hussein's forces had been expelled from Kuwait. What remained, in the judgment of twelve of the Council's members (Cuba opposed 687 as it had 678, and Yemen and Ecuador abstained), was the threat to the peace posed by Iraq's residual military capability, especially in view of the continued presence in Baghdad of a regime that could not be trusted to respect the rights of neighboring states.

The Council was, in effect, saying that once Chapter 7 has been invoked, it constitutes a hunting license, which does not expire once an act of aggression has been undone. Or, to put it somewhat differently, the UN may act intrusively with respect to a state's sovereignty not only to compel that state to give up its ill-gotten gains and renounce the policies the international community has found offensive, but also to make sure that that state does not maintain or acquire the capability to pose such a threat again. Whether this is viewed as punishment for past offenses or as a form of prior restraint, it certainly presents a vigorous challenge to the prerogatives of the sovereign state, as Iraq was quick to point out.

Iraq may not, as Baghdad has argued, have been reduced by Resolution 687 to some kind of international trusteeship, but it was placed under Council orders to do some things (and not to do others) that lie well within areas in which sovereign states have traditionally brooked no outside interference. Specifically, Iraq was required:

- To agree to the destruction or removal of all of its chemical and biological weapons and all ballistic missiles of a certain range
- To allow a UN commission to inventory its chemical and biological weapons and ballistic missile sites and oversee destruction of its missile systems and launchers and take charge of all chemical and biological weapons and sites

- To submit to the Secretary-General a list of its nuclear weapons or weapons-usable material and related facilities, and to place all of its nuclear weapons–usable material under the control of the International Atomic Energy Agency for custody and removal
- To open itself to on-site inspection of its nuclear weapons capabilities so that the Secretary-General may develop a plan for their destruction
- To declare that it will not acquire or develop chemical, biological, or nuclear weapons or ballistic missiles in the future, and submit to ongoing monitoring and verification of its compliance

Resolution 687 also enlarged upon the original Council objective of making Kuwait whole by initiating an embargo on conventional armaments, weapons of mass destruction, missiles, licensing and technology transfer, and personnel or materials for training, technical support, and maintenance. In effect, the Security Council was determining the nature of Iraq's military capabilities, at least in the negative sense of stipulating that certain weapons would not be part of its arsenal. Finally, Resolution 687 asserted Council control over decisions affecting the economic life of the state by decreeing that a percentage of Iraq's oil revenues were to go into a fund to compensate for losses and damages for which it was deemed liable.

Both the ends and the means outlined in Resolution 687 were unprecedentedly intrusive, and went well beyond the agenda of enforcement spelled out in resolutions 660 through 678. To be sure, Resolution 678 did authorize the use of "all necessary means to uphold and implement Security Council Resolution 660 and all subsequent relevant resolutions *and to restore international peace and security in the area*" (emphasis added). It is possible to argue that just as these words contemplated the use of force, so did they contemplate the dismantling of Iraq's offensive military capability if that was the only way to ensure a restoration of peace and security in the area. But although the measures stipulated in 687, taken together, may have been a logical (and most would say a necessary) next step, considering Iraq's defiance of Charter principles and Council resolutions and its reckless performance during the crisis, they still constitute a remarkable challenge to the prerogatives of a sovereign state. That this path-breaking resolution was adopted with a minimum of acrimony seems to suggest that the Council members were seized with the historic importance of the situation—that they were determined that the United Nations should regain control of the crisis and demonstrate both its willingness and its capacity to play a pivotal role in the maintenance of what President Bush had referred to as a new world order. The alternative, after all, was that that new world order would turn out to be nothing more than Pax Americana.

Resolution 687 thus reflected a convergence of US and UN interests. Neither wanted a return to the status quo ante. The United States wanted a militarily declawed Iraq, but was not prepared to undertake the task itself. The United Nations, or at least the overwhelming majority of the members of the Security Council, were desirous of resassuming the initiative, which had passed to the United States during the winter months. The so-called Big Five, in spite of their differences, had worked reasonably well together during the crisis and had discovered the satisfactions of shared power and influence during that crisis; the postwar situation in Iraq provided an opportunity for a continuation of that role. And although all UN members, and especially those in the Third World, were understandably uneasy about compromising the principle of nonintervention contained in Article 2 (7), it was not difficult to make the case that the measures contained in Resolution 687 were part of a continuum, begun with Resolution 660 and necessitated by the challenge Iraq had posed to the equally basic Charter principle found in Article 2 (4).

If the Gulf crisis is broken down into three phases—Iraq's invasion of Kuwait until the launching of Operation Desert Storm, the war itself, and postwar efforts to bring the crisis to satisfactory closure—it is the third phase that has been the most frustrating for both the United States and the United Nations. The problem has not been that there has been a serious falling out between the United States and the other members of the Security Council, although there have inevitably been some tense diplomatic moments; the principal difficulty has been that Iraq has proved to be a most recalcitrant adversary, even in defeat. Saddam Hussein has both challenged the patience of the international community *and* appealed to its humanitarian instincts, confident that neither the United States nor the Security Council has any stomach for resuming military action. He has seemed convinced that anxiety about UN encroachment upon matters "essentially within the domestic jurisdiction" of the state, together with latent frustration with Washington's double standard in the region, would in time lead to a reassessment of the crisis and a less judgmental view of Iraq's policies.

The postwar period has been characterized by repeated efforts by Iraq to frustrate UN officials in the discharge of their duties under Resolution 687. The UN's Special Commission tasked with overseeing elimination of Iraq's weapons of mass destruction had first to identify and locate those weapons and the facilities for producing them, and the Iraqi government did what it could to make that mission as difficult as possible. It was this phase of the Special Commission's work that produced the early and much publicized detention of UN inspectors in possession of secret nuclear documents in a Baghdad parking lot and the subsequent refusal to permit their access to the Ministry of Agriculture. Since that time, Saddam has repeatedly tested the will of the Security Council. He has challenged its agents in their work of destroying or removing the weapons and the facilities for building and using them, and he has fought its efforts to establish the controls necessary to ensure verification of his compliance with Resolution 687. The United States invariably took the lead in insisting that sanctions be kept in place until the objectives of Resolution 687 were fully satisfied. When asked how the Special Commission would know when that goal has been reached, its head, Rolf Ekeus, testified to the nature of the problem:

> When those weapons are eliminated or removed from Iraq and there is a solid control system in place to ensure that Iraq will not acquire new weapons, then the time is right for considering lifting the sanctions. . . . Our task is to do a lot of deductive work and see if we can put the jigsaw puzzle together or whether there are pieces missing. We might calculate by educated guessing, some outside help, and our own overviews of the precise number and kind of missing pieces, and then we have to go after that. If we don't find it, we have to notify the Council.[74]

But it is the United States that has the final say. With its veto, it is in a position to block any attempt to modify the conditions laid down in Resolution 687—and hence any attempt to remove sanctions before the US government is satisfied that Iraq has been stripped of its capacity to produce nuclear, biological, and chemical weapons.

The situation that produced the most serious problem for the United States in the war's immediate aftermath, however, was the failed rebellion of the Kurds in the north of Iraq. The Bush administration wanted Saddam overthrown, but it did not want the disintegration of the state.[75] Unfortunately for US policy, the forces that rose up against Saddam in the chaos that accompanied the end of the war were separatist forces—the Shiites in the southern part of the country and the Kurds in the north. The revolts of the Shiites and the Kurds reflected deep-seated resentment of the Baath establishment and were a reminder that Iraq was not a nation. Moreover, the rhetoric emanating from Washington had almost certainly encouraged those revolts; what else were these peoples, with their history of grievances against Saddam and his regime, to make of Bush's obvious desire that the Iraqis rid themselves of the scourge of Baghdad?

Saddam's military had been badly mauled in the war, but it was still quite capable of crushing rebellion, especially if those in revolt were denied the air cover that the United States, with or without its coalition partners, could provide—as they were initially. But the United States was not interested in redrawing the map of the Middle East; indeed, its approach to the opportunities presented by this remarkable demonstration of collective security in action was in the main a very cautious one, suggesting how limited was Bush's concept of a new world order.

The consequences of the brutal suppression of the popular uprisings, and especially that of the Kurdish minority in the north, was soon on display in the United States on television screens and in the press, and it quickly became apparent that President Bush had a public relations problem on his hands. There may not have been strong sentiment for establishment of a state of Kurdistan (indeed, few in the United States knew anything about the great complexities of that issue), but it was obvious that a terrible humanitarian crisis was unfolding in the north of Iraq along the Turkish border and that the United States had helped to create the conditions for that crisis and was able, with all of the manpower and hardware available in the region, to do something about it. Finally, and with a reluctance borne of anxiety that it might be setting off down a very slippery slope, the US government undertook to airlift supplies to the several hundred thousand Kurds who had fled into the mountains between Iraq and Turkey.[76] This was the beginning of Operation Provide Comfort.

It was also impossible for the Security Council to ignore the situation resulting from the failed revolt of the Shiites and the Kurds. The humanitarian efforts of two UN agencies—the UN Coordinator for Disaster Relief (UNDRO) and the UN High Commissioner for Refugees (UNHCR)—were seriously complicated by postwar civil strife and by the Iraqi government's repression of the two dissident populations. On the same day that President Bush announced the US relief effort, the UN Council addressed the subject of the repression of the Iraqi civilian population in a resolution even more controversial than resolutions 678 or 687.[77]

Resolution 688 reflected the concern of UN members with the humanitarian crisis and the Iraqi government's responsibility for some of its worst features *and* with the implications of UN action for the cherished principles of sovereignty, territorial integrity, and political independence. This resolution produced the fewest number of affirmative votes of any of the Council's many resolutions dealing with the Gulf crisis, as four developing countries and China, deeply troubled at the prospect of UN interference with efforts by a sovereign state to control dissident populations in a multinational or multi-sectarian society, either cast negative votes or abstained (Cuba, Yemen, and Zimbabwe opposed the resolution, whereas India and China abstained). Nor were these states alone in their concern for this dangerous precedent; Iraq may have been in the international doghouse, but it was still distinguishable from a state such as South Africa in the minds of much of the UN membership.[78] It was clear that the Council had gone about as far as it could go; there was general agreement that stronger measures risked vetoes from either China or the Soviet Union or both.

The language of Resolution 688 constitutes a fascinating balancing act, at one and the same time affirming the UN's obligation to provide humanitarian relief, castigating the policies of the Iraqi government, and reminding the world that Article 2 (7) of the Charter, with its prohibition of UN interference in matters within the domestic jurisdiction of states, was still operative. The resolution condemned the repression of its civilian population by the Iraqi government (especially in Kurdish populated areas), demanded that it end that repression, and insisted that it allow access by international humanitarian organizations. No reference was made to Iraq's aggression against Kuwait or to any of the Council's antecedent resolutions, but Resolution 688 did invoke the magic words "threat to international peace and security," thereby providing justification for a resolution that otherwise would presumably have violated the Charter.

The Bush administration and the members of the Security Council were, at this point, treading very carefully. Both felt compelled to do something about "the magnitude of the human suffering"[79] in Iraq, but both felt that they were at or near the limit of what they could do. Secretary of State Baker's remarks upon his arrival in Turkey on April 7, 1991, illustrate the dilemma.

> Once again, the world finds it necessary to respond to Saddam Hussein's savage and indecent use of force. Only this time, the victim is not a neighboring country. This time, Iraq's forces are killing, threatening, and committing crimes against the Iraqi people. . . . We are not prepared to go down the slippery slope of being sucked into a civil war. We cannot police what goes on inside Iraq, and we cannot be the arbiters of who shall govern Iraq. As the President has made repeatedly clear—our objective was the liberation of Kuwait. It never extended to remaking Iraq. We repeatedly said that could only be done by the Iraqi people. . . . However, we cannot be indifferent to atrocities and human suffering in Iraq . . . we will not tolerate any interference with this humanitarian relief effort.[80]

Within less than two weeks of the April 5 decision to provide humanitarian relief to the Kurdish refugees, President Bush found it necessary to send military helicopters and US troops into northern Iraq to construct refugee camps and provide security so that the Kurds, fearful of reprisals by Saddam's forces, might safely return to Iraq and eventually to their homes.[81] As the heading of a *New York Times* news analysis piece phrased it, this was perceived as "A Risky Undertaking," one that took "Bush to the Edge of the Tangle He Has Tried to Avoid."[82] Not only did it demonstrate the political and military dimensions of what had been described as a humanitarian operation; it also generated tensions between the United States and the United Nations, arguably the most serious since Iraq's invasion of Kuwait.

The United States, with British and French cooperation, proposed to construct camps, set up supply lines, establish aircraft landing strips, and begin the process of moving in food, medicine, tents, blankets, and other needed supplies. It had hoped to turn the entire endeavor over to the United Nations as quickly as possible. Both the US action and the proposed substitution of UN police for US and other Western troops as guarantors of the Kurds' security provoked immediate controversy.

Secretary-General Perez de Cuellar, who was already deeply involved in the problems of postwar Iraq as a result of mandates contained in Security Council resolutions 687 and 688, was quick to question Washington's authority to implement its plan without Iraq's agreement and the consent of the Security Council.[83] One UN official was quoted as saying that the United States and the United Nations were on a collision course. But the United States and its allies were not willing to give Saddam a veto over the establishment of a relief zone in northern Iraq, and they were quite certain that either China or the Soviet Union, if not both, would block Council authorization of the plan. The safe-haven zone quickly became a fait accompli, and the debate shifted to a quest for a formula that would enable the United Nations to take over for the US and allied forces.

At this point, US and UN purposes once again converged. The Secretary General's special refugee envoy, Prince Sadruddin Aga Khan, had negotiated an agreement with the government in Baghdad that authorized the UN to take over refugee assistance operations in Iraq.[84] But the problem of the security of the refugee camps remained; without some convincing guarantee that they would not be attacked by government troops, most of the Kurds could not be persuaded to come down from their mountain refuge. To resolve this dilemma, Prime Minister John Major of the United Kingdom proposed—and the United States quickly endorsed the idea— that a UN police force be established to take over from the United States and its allies the job of securing the camps. The rationale was that UN police, unlike UN peacekeepers, would be civilians, not soldiers; would carry only sidearms, not automatic weapons; and would in other respects not appear as the challenge to Iraqi sovereignty that a full-fledged peacekeeping force would. In effect, they would provide only symbolic security for the camps, but in light of the agreement reached by Prince Sadruddin, that would presumably be enough. The proposal had the advantage, it was argued, that no additional Council resolution was required, a police force being a logical extension of that agreement.

Saddam Hussein initially rejected this plan, thereby frustrating US efforts to disengage from Iraq and creating a situation in which US policymakers began to make use of "the Q word" (quagmire).[85] But UN officials persisted in their efforts to achieve a compromise that would obviate the necessity of seeking Security Council approval; these efforts led first to the UN assuming administrative control of a key refugee camp, a step Prince Sadruddin called "a confidence-building exercise that I hope will ultimately bring people home."[86] In due course, and under admittedly heavy US pressure, the United Nations and Iraq signed an agreement to allow some 500 UN security guards to move into northern Iraq.[87] This arrangement was not wholly satisfactory, inasmuch as the security it provided the Kurds was more symbolic than real. But the decision to leave an allied contingency force in southern Turkey to intervene as required to protect the Kurds, together with the appearance of progress in negotiations between the Iraqi government and Kurdish rebel leaders, made it possible for US and other Western troops to withdraw from northern Iraq in July.[88]

In the months following the conclusion of Operation Desert Storm, there was always the danger that US-UN cooperation in the Gulf would break down. Once the Council had legitimized the use of force, the United States had not needed the UN to wage war. But to create a stable peace, the overarching US objective after war's end, the United States did need an effective UN presence in Iraq. However, the behavior of Saddam Hussein's government not only made it extremely difficult for the UN to carry out its postwar mandates, it also pushed the United States, however reluctantly, to take steps (and consider others) that threatened the always fragile consensus within the Security Council. This was particularly evident in the case of Saddam's campaign against the Kurds and against the Shiites in the marshes of Southern Iraq. Even when the humanitarian rationale for intervention was compelling and came in the wake of a popular enforcement action against an unpopular regime, the principle of state sovereignty still commanded powerful support in a world in which ethnonationalism poses either an active or a latent challenge to many UN member states.

The United States, in the name of the coalition and always in cooperation with its principal allies—the United Kingdom and France—established no-fly zones north of the 36th parallel (to protect the Kurds) and south of the 32nd parallel (to protect the Shiites).[89] Neither zone was the product of a Security Council resolution, although Washington held to the view that the prohibition against Iraqi military flights over substantial portions of that country's own territory was consistent with the logic and spirit of Council Resolution 688, which had condemned Iraq's repression of its own citizens as a "threat to the international peace and security."[90] Saddam never accepted the legality of the no-fly zones as he had, albeit reluctantly, UN weapons inspection activities under Resolution 687. Although he displayed great caution in testing the coalition's determination to enforce the no-fly zones, he was certainly cognizant that they constituted a potential wedge between the United States and the United Nations. It was not until late fall and winter 1992–1993, however—nearly two years after the launching of Operation Desert Storm and during the US presidential transition—that Saddam sharply escalated his challenge to the no-fly zones. The United States responded militarily, shooting down Iraqi war planes and attacking ground-to-air missiles and radar sites in the southern air-exclusion zone. This pattern of challenges by Iraq and measured military responses by the United States not only cast a shadow over the political transition in Washington; it also demonstrated, if demonstration were still needed, that the crisis that began with Iraq's invasion of Kuwait had not ended, and that it was too soon to make a final assessment of the impact of that crisis on the US-UN relationship.

But in our analysis of US-UN rapprochement during the Gulf crisis, the most important point is not that Washington experienced difficulty preserving UN support, which it occasionally did, but that it wanted that support, worked diligently to cultivate it, was willing to compromise to preserve it, and studiously avoided forcing issues when the result would presumably have been to lose it. Many have criticized the Bush administration for "using" the United Nations, but the fact remains that during the Gulf crisis the UN was once again useful to the United States. The government rediscovered the importance of multilateral diplomacy (although much of what took place was bilateral diplomacy in a multilateral framework) for purposes other than damage limitation.

Not everyone was pleased with the UN's performance. Hard-core US critics were unimpressed. After making the condescending observation that "the Gulf war showed what the United Nations can do if skillfully handled," Brian Crozier, for example, went on to dismiss the global body. "The aftermath of the battle showed what the UN can't do, and the time is ripe for a fundamental change. Such as putting something in its place. . . . The old UN would be consigned to where it has long belonged: that mythical place that Khrushchev and other Communists used to call the garbage heap of history."[91]

But the US Congress, as a body, displayed none of the animus toward the United Nations that had characterized its performance throughout much of the 1980s. Many eloquent voices were raised in opposition to President Bush's decision to go to war,[92] but almost uniformly they declined to include the United Nations in their indictment. Perhaps the most commonly voiced complaint about US policy, and particularly about the US-UN relationship, was that the administration was guilty of a hypocritical double standard—eager to rally the UN against Iraq's occupation of Kuwait but not against Israel's occupation of the West Bank, quick to seek UN condemnation of Saddam Hussein's invasion of a small neighbor but dismissive of UN condemnation of its own invasion of Panama.

But although opinion may have been divided regarding US policy during the Gulf crisis, there can be no denying that the UN figured more prominently and more positively in that policy than it had in many years. There had clearly been an about-face from the UN bashing that had been the hallmark of US policy toward the global organization in the 1980s.

Financial Crisis Versus Gulf Crisis

The context in which the Gulf crisis unfolded was, of course, very different from that in which the financial crisis took place. As noted earlier in this chapter, the end of the Cold War (if not yet of the Soviet Union) and the change in the dramatis personae both in Washington and on the world stage had created conditions in which it was much easier for the United States to work cooperatively with the UN in meeting the challenge posed by Saddam Hussein. But any comparison of the way in which the US government approached the UN in the two crises must also take note of several distinguishing features of the crises themselves.

The first is that at the time of the financial crisis, the problem, from the US point of view, was diffuse, whereas the problem in the case of the Gulf crisis was concrete and focused. In the 1980s, the Reagan administration and many in the Congress were generally disenchanted with the UN, not because of any one failure or shortcoming but as a result of a variety of grievances that had been festering for quite some time. At the time of the financial crisis, virtually all of the US expectations for the United Nations outlined in Chapter II had met with disappointment, including, of course, the expectation that the UN would conduct itself in an efficient and frugal manner. The US response to its grievances was to withhold funds, focusing attention on the UN budget and management. But the crisis was about much more than money. Withholding was simply the weapon of choice of those who wished to express their displeasure with the UN and provide incentive for reform.

In the Gulf crisis, the problem was very specific and easily comprehended by all: Iraq had invaded and occupied its neighbor, Kuwait. All of the conditions customarily associated with the definition of a crisis were met when Iraqi troops crossed the border on August 2, 1990: Decision-makers were taken by surprise, they were confronted with what they perceived to be a major threat, they believed that they had a finite period of time in which to respond, and military hostilities had suddenly become a distinct possibility.[93] The grievances that had been festering in Washington and had precipitated the first crisis were largely beside the point in the wake of Iraq's aggression. President Bush's felt need to mobilize international support for action against Iraq transcended any residual frustration with the UN. And fortunately that frustration was by the summer of 1990 more residual than rampant.

A second distinguishing feature is that the financial crisis was a crisis only for the United Nations, whereas the Gulf crisis was a crisis for both the UN and the United States. Iraq created the latter, precipitating crisis decision behavior in both Washington and New York. But the United

States created the earlier of the two crises; as a result, in the mid-1980s the UN soon found itself in crisis mode (except, of course, that there was no danger of war), whereas decisionmaking in the United States remained largely routine (if somewhat chaotic).

The two crises are also distinguishable by the way in which they engaged the US political process. The Gulf crisis involved relatively few high-level decisionmakers, all of them in the executive branch (the fact that hearings were held by the Senate Armed Services Committee and that the two houses of the Congress ultimately debated and adopted a Joint Resolution authorizing the use of military force does not alter the fact that this crisis was largely handled, as crises typically are, *in camera* by the president and a few close advisors). US involvement in the financial crisis, on the other hand, entailed participation at all stages of the process by far more people, in both the executive and legislative branches—a characteristic of noncrisis decisionmaking.

Finally, there is the matter of money. Although the financial crisis was not exclusively and perhaps not even primarily a result of US concern with UN costs, the debate within the United States was very much about what the US should pay to the UN and when, and this inevitably made the Congress a powerful player in the crisis. Conversely, although the cost of the Gulf crisis and war was incomparably greater than the US contribution to the UN for a comparable period of time, the burden on the US treasury was virtually nil. Thus money never became a major issue in the domestic debate, and the Congress was denied a major source of leverage in the decisionmaking process. It would be interesting to speculate as to whether and how US decisionmaking in the crisis would have been different had the administration been unable to persuade Japan, Germany, and other countries to pay for Desert Shield and Desert Storm.

In these and other respects, the two crises present something of an apples and oranges problem for those who would use them to explore changes in the relationship between the United States and the United Nations. But if one makes allowances for these differences, the two crises still emerge as significant milestones in that relationship. The first appears as the low point, even in a generally negative trend line, whereas the latter appears as a sudden and quite dramatic up-turn in the US-UN relationship. Whether the rediscovery of the importance of the UN by the United States is a temporary, situationally specific phenomenon, or the harbinger of a new era in which the UN plays a significant role in US foreign policy, remains to be seen.

Notes

1. Thomas G. Weiss and Meryl A. Kessler, "Moscow's U.N. Policy," *Foreign Policy* 79, Summer 1990, pp. 94–95.

2. See ibid. for a review of these initiatives and the role of Gorbachev and especially Soviet former Deputy Foreign Minister Vladimir Petrovsky in drafting and demonstrating that the Soviet Union meant business. Petrovsky has since become the UN Undersecretary-General for Political Affairs.

3. SC Res. 622, October 31, 1988.

4. ONUC (United Nations Operation in the Congo); UNFICYP (United Nations Force in Cyprus); UNIFIL (United Nations Force in Lebanon).

5. John Q. Blodgett, "The Future of UN Peacekeeping," *Washington Quarterly*, Winter 1991, p. 210.

6. United Nations Angola Verification Mission (UNAVEM). SC Res. 626, December 20, 1988.

7. United Nations Transition Assistance Group (UNTAG). SC Res. 435, September 29, 1978, and SC Res. 626, February 16, 1989.

8. United Nations Operation in Central America (ONUCA). SC Res. 644, November 7, 1989.

9. United Nations Observer Mission to Verify the Electoral Process in Nicaragua (ONUVEN). The Secretary-General created ONUVEN pursuant to GA Res. 43/24, November 15, 1988.

10. United Nations Observer Mission to Verify the Electoral Process in Haiti (ONUVEH). GA Res. 45/2, October 10, 1990.

11. United Nations Transitional Authority in Cambodia (UNTAC), SC Res. 745, February 28, 1992; United Nations Mission for the Referendum in Western Sahara (MINURSO), SC Res. 690, April 29, 1991; United Nations Operation in El Salvador (ONUSAL), SC Res. 693, May 20, 1991, and SC Res. 729, January 14, 1992.

12. Weiss and Kessler, "Moscow's U.N. Policy," p. 99.

13. David P. Forsythe, "The United States, the United Nations, and Human Rights," in Margaret P. Karns and Karen A. Mingst, eds., *The United States and Multilateral Institutions,* Boston: Unwin, Hyman, 1990, pp. 283–284.

14. *New York Times,* November 21, 1991, p. A31.

15. John Tessitore and Susan Woolfson, eds., *Issues Before the 44th General Assembly of the United Nations,* Lexington, Mass: D. C. Heath and Company, 1990, pp. 210–211.

16. GA Res. 43/48, November 30, 1988.

17. The Esquipulas II Agreement was negotiated by the presidents of Costa Rica, El Salvador, Guatemala, Honduras, and Nicaragua, and was designed, inter alia, to bring about the cessation of aid to insurrectionist forces and the use of territory of one state for attacks on others.

18. See GA Res. 41/31, June 27, 1986. The vote was ninety-four to three, with forty-seven abstentions.

19. See, for example, Charles Maechling, Jr., "Washington's Illegal Invasion," *Foreign Policy* 79 (Summer 1990), pp. 113–131.

20. GA Res. 44/240, December 29, 1989.

21. See Noam Chomsky, "The Use (and Abuse) of the United Nations," in Micah L. Sifry and Christopher Cerf, eds., *The Gulf War Reader: History, Documents, Opinions,* New York: Random House, 1991, pp. 307–310.

22. See GA Res. 44/42, December 6, 1989, and GA Res. 44/43, December 7, 1989.

23. *Department of State Bulletin,* May 1988, p. 69.

24. *Washington Weekly Report,* published by UNA-USA, is invaluable for tracking the vicissitudes of this process.

25. *US Department of State Dispatch,* October 8, 1990, p. 151.

26. Ibid., p. 153.

27. Security Council (SC) Res. 678, November 28, 1990.

28. Thomas G. Weiss and Jarat Chopra correctly call the Southern Rhodesia case "the clearest instance of the United Nations using force to uphold its decisions under Chapter VII of the Charter." They explain this now largely forgotten action in *United Nations Peacekeeping: An ACUNS Teaching Text,* Academic Council on the United Nations System, Reports and Papers, 1992–1, pp. 24–26.

29. William H. Kincade, "On the Brink in the Gulf: Part 1, Onset of the 'Classic' 1990 Crisis," *Security Studies* 2, 2 (Winter 1992), p. 181.

30. For a definition and analysis of brinkmanship crises, see Richard Ned Lebow, *Between Peace and War,* Baltimore, Md.: The Johns Hopkins University Press, 1981, pp. 57–97.

31. Kincade, "On the Brink in the Gulf: Part 1," p. 173.

32. Ibid., p. 181.

33. By summer 1992, two years after the Iraqi invasion of Kuwait, congressional concerns over the Bush administration's alleged "coddling" of Iraq prior to the crisis and subsequent cover-up of that relationship had produced multipronged investigations by the Congress. See *New York Times,* August 9, 1992, p. A18, for a review of the allegations.

34. SC Res. 660, August 2, 1990.

35. See, for example, Bob Woodward, *The Commanders,* New York: Simon and Schuster, 1991.

36. William H. Kincade, "On the Brink in the Gulf: Part 2, The Route to War," *Security Studies* 2, 4 (Fall 1993).

37. Linda P. Brady, "Negotiation and War: The Role of Diplomacy in the Gulf Crisis," paper presented at the annual meeting of the International Studies Association, Atlanta, Ga., March 31–April 4, 1992, p. 11.

38. Andrew F. Cooper, Richard Higgott, and Kim Richard Nossal, "Bound to Follow? Leadership and Followership in the Gulf Conflict," *Political Science Quarterly* 106, 3 (Fall 1991), pp. 401–402.

39. Ibid., p. 402.

40. Martin Staniland, *Getting to No: The Diplomacy of the Gulf Conflict, August 2, 1990–January 15, 1991: Part 3: The Making of Resolution 678* (Pew Case Studies in International Affairs, No. 449), Washington: Institute for the Study of Diplomacy, Georgetown University, 1992, p. 3.

41. Ibid., p. 11.

42. Ibid., p. 7.

43. *New York Times*, November 28, 1990.

44. Cooper, Higgott, and Nossal, "Bound to Follow?" p. 403.

45. The meeting with the Cuban foreign minister was apparently intended, in part, to persuade Cuba not to persist in seeking to place a motion on sending a peacekeeping force ahead of the US-sponsored resolution (678). See Staniland, *Getting to No,* p. 15.

46. Staniland, *Getting to No,* p. 6.

47. Ibid.

48. SC Res. 666, September 13, 1990; SC Res. 670, September 26, 1990.

49. Jeffrey Laurenti, *The Common Defense: Peace and Security in a Changing World,* New York: UNA-USA, 1992, p. 11.

50. Frederick K. Lister, "Thoughts on the Use of Military Force in the Gulf Crisis" (Occasional Papers No. VII), New York: The Ralph Bunche Institute on the United Nations, City University of New York, 1991, p. 2.

51. Bruce Russett and James S. Sutterlin, "The U.N. in a New World Order," *Foreign Affairs* 70, 2 (Spring 1991), p. 76.

52. Laurenti, *The Common Defense,* p. 6.

53. Brady, "Negotiation and War," p. 18.

54. Cooper, Higgott, and Nossal, "Bound to Follow?" pp. 404–405.

55. Kincade, "On the Brink in the Gulf: Part 2."

56. James Bennet, "Sand Trap. U.S. Diplomacy Did Work: It Got Us Into War," *Washington Monthly,* April 1991, p. 27.

57. Ibid.

58. Ibid., p. 28.

59. Cooper, Higgott, and Nossal, "Bound to Follow?" p. 407.

60. In the House of Representative, the Joint Resolution was adopted by a more comfortable margin of 250 to 183.

61. Quoted in *Washington Weekly Report,* UNA-USA, XVII-2, January 18, 1991.

62. Ibid.

63. Ibid.

64. Ibid.

65. President Bush's speech of January 16, 1991, is reprinted in Sifry and Cerf, *The Gulf War Reader,* pp. 311–314.

66. This address is contained in Sifry and Cerf, *The Gulf War Reader,* pp. 449–451.

67. Katherine Boo, "Wham Bam, Thanks Saddam," *Washington Quarterly,* April 1991, p. 19.

68. Sifry and Cerf, *The Gulf War Reader,* p. 449.

69. SC Res. 686, March 2, 1991, and SC Res. 687, April 3, 1991.

70. The essential elements of the Soviet peace proposal are reprinted in Sifry and Cerf, *The Gulf War Reader,* p. 345.

71. Russett and Sutterlin, "The U.N. in a New World Order."

72. Was the coalition acting within the spirit of Resolution 678 and even more importantly of Chapter 7 of the Charter when, from the beginning, it made Iraq the target of bombing rather than prosecuting the war on Kuwaiti soil? Thomas G. Weiss and Jarat Chopra argued that "it should have been enormously controversial for military forces to cross the border into Iraq, just as it had been for UN forces to cross the 38th parallel in Korea." See Weiss and Chopra, *United Nations Peacekeeping,* p. 29.

73. Martin Indyk, "Watershed in the Middle East," *Foreign Affairs* 71, 1 (America and the World 1991/2), p. 73.

74. *The Interdependent* 18, 1 (January–February 1992), p. 6.

75. Richard Haass, President Bush's special advisor on Middle Eastern matters, in *New York Times,* May 10, 1991, p. A10.

76. President Bush's statement of April 5, 1991, is contained in *US Department of State Dispatch,* April 8, 1991, p. 233.

77. SC Res. 688, April 5, 1991.

78. The great majority of the UN's members had long since ceased to accept the Article 2 (7) defense of apartheid put forth by the government of South Africa, treating that country's ethnic and racial policies as an exception to the rule of non-interference.

79. See the preambular paragraph of SC Res. 688, which notes that the Council is "deeply disturbed by the magnitude of the human suffering involved."

80. *US Department of State Dispatch,* April 15, 1991, p. 271.

81. *New York Times,* April 18, 1991, pp. A1, 16.

82. Ibid., p. A1.

83. Ibid., p. A16.

84. *New York Times,* April 30, 1991, p. A1.

85. *New York Times,* May 10, 1991, p. A1.

86. *New York Times,* May 14, 1991, p. A10.

87. *New York Times,* May 24, 1991, p. A8.

88. See *New York Times,* June 22, p. 12, and *New York Times,* July 13, p. 13.

89. The no-fly zone in the north was established in April 1991, concurrent with Security Council Resolution 688. The no-fly zone in the south was not established until August 1992, after it had become apparent that Saddam's campaign against the Shiites was a major problem, as was his treatment of the Kurds in the north.

90. Resolution 688 contained no reference to enforcement, nor was it authorized under the provisions of the Charter explicitly authorizing military action.

91. Brian Crozier, "Closing Time for the U.N.?" *National Review,* May 13, 1991, pp. 44–45.

92. Among the more eloquent of these were Lewis Lapham, "Onward Christian Soldiers," and Robert Scheer, "What a Wonderful War," both in Sifry and Cerf, *The Gulf War Reader,* pp. 452–460 and 492–497, respectively. See also essays under the general heading of "What We Lost in the Desert," *Washington Monthly,* April 1991.

93. For definitions of crisis, see Charles Hermann, *International Crises,* New York: The Free Press, 1972; and Lebow, *Between Peace and War.*

Chapter VI

Back to the Future?

The Gulf crisis occurred at roughly the halfway point between George Bush's overwhelming victory in the 1988 presidential campaign and the 1992 presidential election. When he called a halt to Operation Desert Storm on February 27, 1991, President Bush's popularity with the US public was so great that most Democratic leaders of stature decided that it would be futile to mount a challenge for the presidency the following year. Although his decision to abandon sanctions and wage war had had its critics, the president's performance in mobilizing an impressive coalition in support of US policy both at the United Nations and on the battlefield was widely regarded as masterful. The quick and decisive triumph of US arms only served to heighten the esteem in which he was held by the US public.

If Bush was the winner, so apparently was the United Nations. The president's invocation of a New World Order had reflected the view that the United Nations would assume a more important role, not only in US foreign policy, but in global management generally. The Gulf crisis strengthened that presumption, as John Newhouse noted:

> Among the great expectations aroused by the rout of Communism was a role for the United Nations that would match its lofty purpose. With the Cold War over, threats to peace and stability could at last be managed as they ought to be managed. The performance of the UN's Security Council during the past two years—especially its resolutions authorizing sanctions and more against Iraq—seemed to confirm the arrival of what was called grandly, if unwisely, the new world order.[1]

President Bush returned to this theme in his "victory" address to a joint session of the Congress at the end of the Gulf War.

> Until now, the world we've known has been a world divided, a world of barbed wire and concrete block, conflict and cold war. And now we can see

135

a new world coming into view. A world in which there is a very real prospect of a new world order. . . . A world where the United Nations, freed from cold war stalemate, is poised to fulfill the historic vision of its founders.[2]

This address was very probably the high water mark of the Bush presidency. Within a matter of months, the president was on the defensive at home, his credentials in the field of foreign policy of little help in stemming the erosion of his popularity. The national euphoria that had greeted military success in the Gulf had dissipated at an alarming rate, partly as a result of Saddam Hussein's retention of power and the messy aftermath of the war, but even more as a consequence of economic recession and political paralysis at home. The stunning victory of Democrat Harris Wofford over prominent Bush cabinet member Dick Thornburgh in the race for a Pennsylvania Senate seat effectively ended any pretense that the 1992 presidential election would be about creating a new world order.

On November 3, 1992, the US public elected Bill Clinton as president of the United States. George Bush, who had enjoyed a remarkable 90 percent approval rating at the conclusion of the Gulf War, was sent packing with less than 40 percent of the popular vote. In a strange three-cornered race, he had been bested by the governor of a small state who had virtually no national name recognition as recently as a year before the election, no foreign policy experience, and a single-minded approach to the campaign, summed up succinctly by the poster on the wall of his headquarters: "The economy, stupid!"

With the Cold War over, it was as if the world beyond the nation's shores no longer mattered. Foreign policy had disappeared, almost without a trace, throughout both the primaries and the general election and seemed destined for benign neglect after election day. Although neither the public nor the politicians (Pat Buchanan was an exception) were actively promoting either US nativism or isolationism as it had been practiced between World Wars I and II, there was clearly a turning inward to address the country's economic problems. Most critics welcomed this rearrangement of priorities, both because of the sheer magnitude of the nation's budget deficit and in order that the United States could play the dominant role in a post–Cold War world in which economic strength and competitiveness seemed likely to be more important indices of power than military might.

But in spite of a consensus that domestic issues should be the first order of national business, it is nonetheless striking that, in a matter of only a little less than two years after the rout of Saddam Hussein's armies by the US-led coalition, the excitement generated by Operation Desert Storm had vanished and with it the vocation for leadership on behalf of a new world order. The "increasingly pessimistic, inward and nationalistic"[3] mood in the United States not only ended talk of a new world order, it also effectively shifted the further cultivation of US-UN relations to the back burner. The relationship between the United States and the United Nations did not again become adversarial as the US national mood turned sour and the 1992 presidential election began to heat up. But interest in the UN and its place in US foreign policy inevitably became a casualty of the decline of interest in foreign policy (except for such issues as Japan's economic challenge and the North American Free Trade Agreement, issues which do not involve the UN).

But in December 1992, barely a month after the election, George Bush, now a lame duck president, put foreign policy and the US-UN relationship back on the front page and high on the president-elect's agenda by announcing that he would put some 28,000 US troops into Somalia to provide security for relief efforts in that fractured and rudderless country. It was a dramatic and unexpected step, and not only because of its timing. With the Cold War over, the United States had no strategic interest in that region, and there was no precedent for US military intervention so far from home for humanitarian purposes.

Bush's offer of troops for Somalia, promptly and unanimously accepted by the UN Security Council, has important implications for the balance between foreign and domestic policy issues in the Clinton administration; it has equally important implications for the role of the UN in US foreign policy. Nor is it only Somalia that has refocused attention on the US-UN relationship. Events in what used to be Yugoslavia and in a militarily defeated but unchastened Iraq, together with the response to those events by George Bush in his last weeks in office and by Bill Clinton during the first months of his presidency, have served as further reminders that US policy is critical for the United Nations and that the US-UN relationship, however much improved since the 1980s, is not without its problems.

The question of whether the rapprochement between the United States and the United Nations during the Gulf crisis is likely to be sustained can perhaps best be addressed by reexamining the set of US assumptions or expectations regarding the UN identified in Chapter II of this volume. We noted that the United States had been disappointed throughout the years in most of those expectations. At the end of the century, with the Cold War over and the UN responding to US leadership in the wake of Saddam Hussein's ill-considered assault on Kuwait, are these expectations now being met? Have some of them been abandoned as unrealistic or anachronistic, or simply as no longer important impediments to the realization of a strong and durable US commitment to the United Nations? And finally, have new problems arisen that have not been part of the historic equation—problems that threaten (or have the capacity to threaten) the recently improved relationship between the UN and the only remaining superpower?

The United Nations in a Changing International System

Before revisiting the set of US expectations regarding the United Nations to see whether and how they may have been transformed in the last few years, it will be useful to review briefly those characteristics of the UN and those features of the international system that, by their interaction, contributed so significantly to US frustration with the global body.

The five most salient characteristics of the United Nations described in Chapter III have remained essentially unchanged. The Charter has inevitably undergone some modest reinterpretation at the margin, but it is still very much the document that emerged from the San Francisco Conference in 1945. The Charter has to date been formally amended only for the purpose of enlarging the Security Council and the Economic and Social Council, and those changes occurred long ago. All other changes, including some of such importance that they amount to de facto amendments of the Charter, have been the result of precedential decisions, which have been accepted over time and become established practice. But the fundamental characteristics of the organization are still intact, meaning that the United Nations is still formally essentially the same institution it was nearly half a century ago.

The broad mandate remains in place, although the end of the Cold War has had as one of its consequences a refocusing of attention on the UN's primary mission, peace and security. This development seems, at least temporarily, to have pushed other elements of the broad mandate somewhat further into the background. Decisions in the General Assembly and in all subsidiary organs except the Security Council are still formally made according to a formula in which each state has one vote, with a majority (simple or two-thirds) of states present and voting deciding the issue. In practice, consensus is frequently substituted for voting (this is an important qualification of majority rule on budget matters, as noted in Chapter IV), but there is no binding obligation to seek consensus, and the egalitarian/majoritarian decision rules remain one of the UN's most important features. The corollary of this principle has been the UN's limited authority. That characteristic of the organization has also survived, in the absence of a formal Charter amendment, although it has been challenged with increasing vigor, especially in the human rights field. The fence erected by Article 2 (7) has been battered and even breached in a place or two, but the UN remains a body with largely recommendatory, not binding, authority.

The Security Council is now, as it was in the beginning, a major exception to the egalitarian/majoritarian and limited authority principles. It is in that forum that the great powers still possess greater privileges as well as greater responsibilities. But it is here also that events have most conspicuously overtaken Charter prescription. The five states that were made permanent members of the Council and granted a veto were supposedly the five principal powers at the end of World War II (although the privileged position given to China hardly accorded with the facts). By the 1990s no one was prepared to argue that France and the United Kingdom were more powerful than Germany and Japan, and the UN had to resolve a potentially sticky constitutional problem by treating Russia as the successor state to the now-defunct Soviet Union. Nonetheless, great power responsibility and privilege remained one of the UN's fundamental characteristics, even as problems arose as to which states should be entitled to great-power status.

The fifth of the fundamental characteristics of the UN, universal membership, had not changed by the 1990s, and it had come even closer to being a description without need of qualification.[4] The dissolution of the Soviet Union and Yugoslavia contributed most significantly to the late surge in UN membership, but other states, such as the two Koreas—long on the outside due either to their own choice or the vicissitudes of global politics—joined the organization, and even Switzerland was reported to be considering doing so.

The United Nations was a much different organization in the 1990s than it had been in 1945, but its constitutional framework was essentially the same as the one drafted in the closing months of World War II. What made the UN so different was the systemic context in which it functioned. Just as the systemic context that prevailed throughout most of the long years of US disenchantment with the UN was not the one envisioned by the framers, so is the systemic context of the early 1990s not the one that shaped UN purposes and policies throughout most of the previous several decades.

The most important systemic change by far is the end of the Cold War. The easing of Cold War tensions more than anything else created the conditions in which Security Council agreement on the response to Iraq's invasion of Kuwait was possible. But although the Berlin Wall had been torn down and communist regimes had crumbled throughout Eastern Europe before the Gulf crisis erupted, the Soviet Union was still in existence and many in Washington were worried that forces of reaction would overthrow Gorbachev and reinstitute a hard line. Not until after the aborted coup by the military and the KGB in August 1991 and the subsequent collapse of both the Communist party and the Soviet Union itself was it possible to say with certainty that the decades-long bipolar confrontation between East and West was truly at an end.

With the demise of the Soviet Union and the overwhelming evidence that Russia not only has no interest in challenging the United States, but desperately needs help from the only remaining superpower, the prospect is that the United Nations will be much less likely to resemble an ideological war zone. Russia is far less likely to exercise the veto to frustrate US and other Western initiatives in the Security Council; it is far less likely either to lead or to follow the UN's majority of what have been called Third World states into confrontation with the United States and the West in the General Assembly; and it is far less likely to treat the Secretariat as cynically as it did throughout so much of the UN's history. In brief, Russia seems likely to look at the United Nations more or less as other states, particularly large and important states, do—as a place to pursue its interests rather than as a place to mount a relentless ideological campaign. The result will be that issues that come before the global body will no longer automatically acquire a Cold War dimension. This is no guarantee that Russia will regularly side with the United States or that debate in the various UN organs will be free of rancor and end amicably with the adoption of broadly backed resolutions. But the systemic feature of the postwar era, which more than any other paralyzed the UN and made it an unattractive venue for the conduct of US foreign policy, has been removed, opening up possibilities heretofore foreclosed for the UN and improving the prospects for enhanced US-UN cooperation.

The other principal axis of interstate conflict that has made itself felt at the United Nations—the one that, in fact, came into being and was sustained in considerable part because the UN facilitated it—is the one between North and South. Like the East-West conflict, the North-South conflict had abated somewhat by the time of the Gulf crisis; it was neither dead nor dying, but only in remission. The present prognosis is uncertain. On the one hand, the so-called Third World—the South in the North-South conflict—no longer exists in the original sense of the term. It was a function of the East-West conflict, and consisted of states that, at least in the beginning, wished to distance themselves from both Moscow and Washington. Even before the collapse of the communist bloc and the end of the Cold War, however, the Non-Aligned Movement had become badly frayed, its radical and moderate wings chronically at odds regarding the strategy and even the meaning of nonalignment. With colonialism largely a thing of the past, the glue that held Third World states together at the UN was largely a shared belief in their common status as developing countries and a conviction that most of them could not "hope to cope with their international vulnerability except by challenging principles, norms, and rules preferred by industrialized countries."[5] But even this conviction was shallow. The unity of the Group of 77, the Third World's economic coalition at the UN, could be sustained only by sticking to generalities and preserving the myth that the South's agenda constituted a coherent package.

In spite of the diversity of the Third World, however, and the ultimate futility of its efforts to achieve a new economic order based on authoritative rather than market allocation, the UN's developing country majority has managed to keep the North-South conflict alive in UN forums. Unlike the East-West conflict, which ended when the East collapsed and in a sense sued for peace, the North-South conflict survives because the problems at its core remain unaddressed and the states that mounted the attack on the liberal international economic order remain unappeased. Although this conflict has been carried on in less strident terms in recent years than it was during the 1970s and early 1980s, it remains an important feature of the systemic context in which the UN functions. This fact was illustrated dramatically by the United Nations Conference on Environment and Development (UNCED) at Rio de Janeiro in June 1992.

Ironically, the end of the Cold War seems temporarily to have made attention to the problems of developing countries of the South by the industrialized countries of the North less, rather than more, likely. But that lack of responsiveness can—some would say that it already has—become part of the problem, increasing frustration and potentially generating another cycle of confrontation at the United Nations.

The revolution in technology, which has been another of the important characteristics of the international system impinging on the UN, continues unabated, largely unaffected by shifts in the distribution of power in the state system. The Gulf War provided impressive evidence of advances in weapons technology. One expert, William J. Perry, assessed the situation this way:

> In Operation Desert Storm the United States employed for the first time a new class of military systems that gave American forces a revolutionary advance in military capability. Key to this capability is a new generation of military support systems—intelligence sensors, defense suppression systems and precision guidance sub-systems—that serve as "force multipliers" by increasing the effectiveness of US weapons systems. An army with such technology has an overwhelming advantage over an army without it, much as an army equipped with tanks would overwhelm an army with horse cavalry.[6]

While the technological advantage now lies with the United States, Perry acknowledges that other countries will seek to emulate the technical systems that produced US success in the Gulf and that, "even if Washington tried, it could not control this technology."[7]

Nor is this the only area in which the revolution in technology is affecting the climate in which the UN functions. Some of the issues on the agenda at UNCED were the product of scientific and technological progress and its corollary, threats to the global ecosystem. The issue that stimulated the most heated controversy at the Law of the Sea Conference and ultimately persuaded the United States not to sign the treaty is traceable to the development of technology for mining on the ocean floor.[8] Walter Wriston has recently spoken to the issue of rapid and consequential technological change, offering a catalogue of developments that led him to the conclusion that policymakers "are driven by technologies which they may only dimly understand."[9] He noted, for example, that photographs taken by a privately owned French satellite compelled Moscow to admit the seriousness of the Chernobyl disaster, and he reminds us that in the realm of finance, "the entire globe is linked electronically" with consequences that are "more draconian than the gold exchange standard and a great deal faster in coming."[10]

The revolution in technology directly affects the fourth of the systemic factors noted above, the phenomenon of the sovereign state under siege. It gives every evidence of continuing to weaken some states by giving adversaries more means with which to challenge them and to weaken all states by facilitating penetration of the polity, the economy, and the culture. But the most dramatic evidence of the weakened condition of the state is the recent disintegration of the Soviet Union and Yugoslavia, where even the tradition of centralized authoritarian rule was unable to prevent the triumph of long-suppressed but still potent ethnonationalism.

Lawrence Freedman has characterized this development as "the culmination of the decolonization process"[11] as well as a manifestation of the end of the Cold War. Like earlier phases of decolonization, it has resulted in the creation of new sovereign states. But it is clear that the concept of self-determination of peoples has taken a new turn, and that the centrifugal forces at work in Europe (and elsewhere) pose a different kind of threat to regional and perhaps even global stability than did the breakup of the colonial empires in the decades after World War II. Many of the new states that emerged in Africa and Asia during that period were multinational, frequently as the result of the artificiality of borders, which was colonialism's legacy. But few of the conflicts that followed posed threats to other states, and most of the groups that sought autonomy or independence were denied international support.[12] Self-determination was widely construed as a right of peoples living under colonial rule, but not as a right of disaffected minorities within sovereign states.

In the post–Cold War era, that distinction has been vigorously and successfully contested. Sovereign states have been breaking up, and the circumstances in which their disintegration is taking place make this one of the most important features of the systemic context in which the UN functions today. For years, the acquisition of nuclear weapons by nonnuclear states was a major concern, and its prevention was the rationale for the Non-Proliferation Treaty. Now the international community is confronted with a situation in which the former Soviet Union's nuclear weapons stockpile is shared by three of the successor states. Many of the new states that were until recently part of the Soviet Union and Yugoslavia contain large ethnic minorities, which guarantee turbulence, generate pressures for further fragmentation, and invite outside intervention. The result is a highly volatile situation in Europe, which until recently had been one of the world's most stable regions for many years. Sovereign states in other regions are also in trouble, but it is Europe, the core area of the Westphalian system, where the problem appears to be most acute and most dangerous.

A case can be made that the overriding attribute of the international system in which the UN must function at the close of the twentieth century is the crisis of statehood. This crisis, so conspicuously on display in places as diverse as Somalia and Bosnia, already occupies a prominent place on the UN's agenda. In the absence of the stabilizing influence that the Cold War is alleged to have brought to international politics for much of the period since World War II,[13] the corrosive social and political forces that are weakening so many states confront the United Nations with a challenge that seems certain to test its capacity to manage the "new world order."

US Expectations About the UN Revisited

As we have argued in Chapter II, the US-UN relationship was shaped from the beginning by a set of US assumptions about the United Nations—about what kind of organization it should be and about what it should do. These assumptions created expectations, and, as we have seen, those expectations were frequently disappointed in the decades after the San Francisco conference. Indeed, the UN's performance was, from the perspective of Washington, so disappointing and even so irritating that by the time the global organization celebrated its fortieth birthday the United States was either treating it with contempt or coercing it to change through resort to tactics of dubious legality.

The two case studies presented here—the financial crisis and the Gulf crisis—constitute the nadir and the zenith of US-UN relations. This relatively sudden reversal in the US perception of the UN and of its utility for US foreign policy invite a reexamination of those expectations the United States brought to its relationship with the global body. We shall find that some have changed very little and that some have become moot. We shall find that the UN comes much closer to satisfying US expectations in some instances but seems still to pose a problem, real or latent, for the United States in others.

Hegemony

A major reason for the dramatic improvement in the US view of the United Nations during and after the Gulf crisis was that the UN accepted

US leadership of the effort to expel Iraq from Kuwait. For the first time in a long time, the United States assumed the mantle of hegemon (or something very much like it) at the UN and found the membership deferential. The need to badger Japan and Germany into covering the costs of the war took some of the luster off this exercise of hegemonic power, but the US performance provided a reasonable facsimile of hegemony and led to talk about a New World Order in which the United States was clearly cast in the role of hegemon. Nothing like it had happened since the UN's formative years, and even then the United Nations was at the periphery of US interests and efforts.

Charles Krauthammer, surveying the state of the world at the end of the Cold War and on the eve of Operation Desert Storm, referred to it as "the unipolar moment."[14] According to conventional wisdom, there had been but two superpowers, states "characterized by possession of a nuclear arsenal, by which each . . . rendered the other vulnerable, and by the claim each made to represent a model of the future of mankind."[15] Now there was but one state that met this test: The United States had won the Cold War and was unquestionably preeminent. The New World Order would be made in the United States.

But this view of the post–Cold War and post–Gulf War world is, as the many critics of the Krauthammer thesis are quick to tell us, badly flawed. The United States may be militarily dominant, although its military power is not everywhere fungible, but to confer upon it the label "hegemon" and expect its performance to measure up to Haas's definition of hegemony[16] smacks of either naiveté or misplaced arrogance. State power rests on economic as well as military capabilities. Krauthammer seeks to refute this proposition, claiming that "the notion that economic power inevitably translates into geopolitical influence is a materialist illusion."[17] But Nye is much closer to the truth with his layer-cake analogy:

> No single hierarchy describes adequately a world politics with multiple structures. The distribution of power in world politics has become like a layer cake. The top military layer is largely unipolar, for there is no other military power comparable to the United States. The economic layer is tripolar and has been for two decades. The bottom layer of transnational interdependence shows a diffusion of power. . . . But military prowess is a poor predictor of outcomes in the economic and transnational layers of current world politics. The United States is better placed with a more diversified portfolio of power resources than any other country, but the new world order will not be a era of American hegemony.[18]

Comparisons of Japan's and Germany's economic power with that of the United States certainly tend to weaken the latter's pretensions to hegemony, although the results are less obvious at the United Nations than in other contexts. But even if one dismisses the Japanese and German challenges as irrelevant to an assessment of the US claim to hegemony, the economic problems that plague the United States cannot be dismissed. Hegemons are presumed to be willing and able to bear disproportionate costs to sustain their vision of a desirable world order. Quite aside from the fact that the United States has no clear vision of its preferred post–Cold War world order, the would-be hegemon is not willing and arguably not even able to bear such costs. The response to Iraq is widely regarded as a one-time event, and even it had to be financed by Japan and Germany and the oil-rich Gulf states. The United States is still in arrears in its payment of UN assessments, and is talking about reducing its share of the cost of UN peacekeeping operations to a level considerably below its capacity to pay. John Bolton, former assistant secretary of state for international organization affairs, recently told a House committee that the US share "does seem excessive," and that "we will fight to ensure that the US share of UN peacekeeping is kept at an absolute minimum."[19] This position may well be prudent politically, but it is not exactly hegemonic.

Only time will tell whether the deference paid the United States by the Security Council during the Gulf crisis will survive and transfer to other issues (and other UN forums). But the United States must first decide whether it wishes to remain actively and constructively engaged at the United Nations. George Bush repeatedly said that the United States does not intend to become the world's policeman, and there is no evidence that President Clinton disagrees; but it is not yet clear, short of that, whether the United States aspires to a leadership role on the important issues now before the international community.

Congruence

For the United Nations to meet US expectations regarding congruence, the decisions it reaches and the manner in which it reaches them would need to be consonant with US values and generally in accord with US preferences. Moreover, those decisions would not adversely affect US power or enhance the power of other states at the expense of the United States. Although the UN cannot be said ever to have diminished US power (although it often helped to demonstrate the limitations of that power), it produced a pattern of decisions on a variety of issues that was conspicuously incompatible with US preferences and in some cases at variance with US values. In other words, the UN became incongruent from Washington's perspective.

During the Gulf crisis, congruence was reestablished. The Security Council shared the US view that Iraq's invasion was intolerable and "would not stand," and it proceeded through a series of resolutions both before and after the war to adopt positions that reflected and endorsed US preferences. It was this compatibility between US policies and UN positions during the gulf crisis that gave birth to the belief that the UN would occupy a prominent place in the new world order that President Bush was touting.

Inevitably there will be occasions when the relationship between the United States and the majority of UN members turns incongruent again. It happened at UNCED, and no amount of last-minute compromises on language could mask the differences. But the test is not whether US preferences are regularly and uniformly endorsed by the United Nations, but whether congruence is the norm. On the whole, early indications are encouraging. The UN budget continues to be approved by means of consensus, reflecting deference to the US position. The worst of the excesses of the Cold War years have been exorcised, including the notorious resolution equating Zionism with racism. It is worth noting that this bitterly debated subject, which had done so much to alienate the United States, was quietly laid to rest in a simple one-line resolution in which the General Assembly simply decided "to revoke the determination contained in its resolution 3370 of 10 November 1975."[20] The vote was not close (111 to 25, with 13 abstentions), which augurs well for the further improvement of US-UN relations.

But there are any number of latent threats to congruence. One is the newfound preeminence of the Security Council, reflecting the fact that peace and security issues, long hostage to the Cold War, are now once again the UN's most important responsibility. The corollary of this trend has been the relative decline of the General Assembly, a fact that diminishes the influence of that vast coalition of developing, Third World states that dominated UN politics for so many years. It would be surprising if efforts are not made to reverse this trend and reinvest nonsecurity issues with a new sense of urgency. If that happens, congruence may again become a casualty.

The Status Quo

The United States had wanted the UN to be among those institutions that would embody and defend the new post–World War II status quo of which it was the principal architect. The UN might be an instrument of change in some instances, but they would be changes within an agreed framework and in accordance with principles and norms to which the United States had given its assent during the so-called second try at world order. However, several characteristics of the organization actually facilitated a challenge to the status quo when a combination of Communist bloc states and newly independent developing countries, which had not been present at the creation, banded together and sought to use the UN to legitimize new principles and norms for international governance. The resulting assault on the status quo had the United States on the defensive at the UN for many years and contributed significantly to US disenchantment with the organization.

Recent developments have deflated much of that campaign to alter the status quo. The collapse of the Soviet Union and the disintegration of its empire, the resurgence of democratic forces where authoritarian and even totalitarian governments had ruled for decades, the failure of Communism and the worldwide rush to embrace capitalism, the abandonment as lost causes of issues that had long energized the global majority—all of these developments have seemed to vindicate the principles on which the postwar order was built. And so they have, up to a point. But the global order confronting the United States at the end of the century is demonstrably not the one it created at mid-century. If the UN is to be an agent for preserving the status quo, it will be a very different status quo from the one the Communist bloc and the UN's Third World majority spent so many years attacking.

Even its most enduring features have been transformed until they scarcely resemble their prototypes. States are still the principal actors in the system; the UN has been among the factors encouraging their proliferation. But today 180 of them belong to the United Nations, most only nominally sovereign and all penetrated by a variety of forces only dimly imagined in 1945. The very number of these states, their enormous diversity, and the fragility (and in some cases nonviability) of many of them distinguish the present order from the one originally envisioned by the United States. Capitalism may have triumphed over socialism, but in a form so different from that envisioned by the United States at the time of the Bretton Woods and San Francisco conferences as to make it virtually a new phenomenon. Production has been globalized; financial markets have been internationalized. There will clearly be no going back to the future.

The United States will presumably want to relish its victory in the Cold War and enlist the United Nations in its efforts to solidify and expand the triumph of capitalism and democracy, that is, to preserve what George Bush called the new world order. Although that concept remains somewhat fuzzy, it seems reasonable to assume that its principal tenets are "liberalism and free markets, the rule of international law and an era of peace and prosperity."[21] Unfortunately, these are turbulent times. As John Lewis Gaddis has argued, the end of the Cold War "brings not an end to threats, but rather a diffusion of them."[22] General principles of the kind that make up Bush's new world order concept are an inadequate guide for dealing with these threats.

The United States has yet to determine its agenda for a post–Cold War world. The old one will not do.

> The three principles that have guided its [US] foreign policy—American exceptionalism, anticommunism and world economic liberalism—are of

little help, because others are less receptive, or because "victory" has made anticommunism irrelevant, or because the market itself is the problem (as in U.S.-Japanese relations) or provides no answers (as in ecological matters).[23]

This assessment by Stanley Hoffmann of the US dilemma points to a problem for US-UN relations. Until the United States develops more specific goals for the postwar era and strategies for achieving them, US leadership at the UN is likely to remain ad hoc, as it was in the Gulf crisis and subsequent international crises, or largely rhetorical and ineffective. The US assumption that the United Nations would be an agent for preservation of the status quo has lost much of its meaning in the absence of a coherent post–Cold War foreign policy agenda. The 1992 presidential election campaign and early signals from the Clinton administration suggest that formulation of that foreign policy agenda still lies somewhere in the future.

The Unit Veto

The United States protected itself and its interests in the Security Council with the veto provision in Article 2 (7). Of equal importance was the right to opt out of compliance with decisions of other UN organs when it disagreed with them. The unit veto is available to other states as well, but the fact that the United States cannot be bound by majority decisions without its consent has been far more important to it than the UN's inability to compel other states to act as the United States wishes they would. This principle is so basic in a world of sovereign states and decentralized authority that it is usually taken for granted; it is the exceptions that command attention. But the unit veto was vitally important to the United States during the many sessions of the General Assembly when it was part of a small minority on what it considered important issues.

With the end of the Cold War and the truce in the more virulent forms of the North-South confrontation, the principle that states cannot be bound without their consent would appear once again to be taken for granted rather than contested by large, revisionist majorities. If anything, the US position is even stronger with the de facto requirement that the UN budget, previously determined by a two-thirds majority in the General Assembly, is now subject to a unit veto.

Struggle between the principles of consent and majority rule can, of course, resurface at any time. The modest erosion of the protection of the principle of state sovereignty in the fields of human rights and humanitarian intervention, stated in Article 2 (7), is instructive in this regard. The boundaries of permissible UN intervention are still being explored; the response to US enforcement of the no-fly zones in Iraq makes it clear that the subject is highly controversial. What seems certain is that the principle of consent will not yield quickly or easily, even to a reconstituted and more representative UN majority. Too many states have a stake in preserving that principle. The United States, of course, will be quite able to exercise the unit veto should it need to. The more important question for the future of US-UN relations is whether and how often it will need to do so.

Functional Specificity

As we have noted, one of the assumptions that shaped US expectations regarding the United Nations was that the UN system would be characterized by a division of labor and that technical agencies and their agendas would not be politicized. A corollary of this assumption was that, however broad its mandate, the UN would not presume to instruct the specialized agencies in their areas of competence. Events demonstrated that neither assumption was warranted. Many of the specialized agencies became infected by the political virus, and the UN General Assembly (and subsidiary organs such as UNCTAD) espoused policies that directly challenged those being pursued by the more conservative international financial institutions.

Politicization is obviously in the eye of the beholder, and the beholder of politicization is typically in the minority when the votes are cast. During those years when it frequently found itself in a minority on matters it deemed to be important, the United States was quick to raise the charge of politicization. The tactics and the resolutions that have given rise to this charge have been associated with the Communist bloc and with the Non-Aligned Movement and, to a lesser degree, with the Group of 77. The demise of Communism and the Soviet Union, the marginalization of the Non-Aligned Movement in a post–Cold War world, and the more realistic assessment of its agenda and its prospects by the Group of 77 have made the politicization issue largely moot. This is one US expectation for the United Nations that seems to be fulfilled, at least in the near future.

However, it should be remembered that the original US preference for functionally specific agencies was rooted in the belief that fundamental principles had already been determined and that the task of the agencies would be largely technical. But at the end of the twentieth century, the principles on which the liberal international economic order was based are not so firmly in place as the United States once believed or as the collapse of challenges from the East and the South might suggest. The emerging conflict among the major economic powers promises to be about principles as well as market shares. Indeed, as Miles Kahler argued, the goal of a liberal world economy is now being openly questioned; protectionism and industrial policy are on the rise, and "the infallible wisdom of markets . . . is less likely to be taken for granted in the future."[24] Functional specificity among international institutions will be much harder to maintain in a world of intensive economic warfare.

The Market

Shintaro Ishihara's prediction that the twenty-first century will be a century of economic warfare constitutes a sobering if perhaps overly alarmist antidote to the widespread belief that the death of Communism in the Soviet Union and Eastern Europe seals the triumph of capitalism.[25] One of the more important US assumptions about the postwar world was that market forces should have free rein and that international institutions would exist, not to regulate the international economy but to help to create conditions that would result in minimizing government intervention and maximizing free trade. This assumption was challenged throughout much of the UN's history by the Soviet bloc, which rejected capitalism on principle and as part of its broad gauged challenge to the West, and by the UN's developing country majority, which pursued a metapower strategy and advocated authoritative allocation of resources as a way to compensate for economic and political weakness.[26]

It is difficult to quarrel with the conclusion that Communism has failed. Whether capitalism has triumphed is not so obvious, although it is unquestionably in much better health at the end of the century than its long-time rival. Russia is trying to recreate itself as a market economy state, as are other states in Eastern Europe and the former Soviet Union. Elsewhere, states that had looked to the Soviet Union as a patron and model are struggling to come to terms with a world in which there is no Soviet Union and in which heavily interventionist government policies are no longer economically or politically correct. The situation in Africa is typical. "For those countries that had put state-directed economies at the center of their political program—the self-described 'African socialists' like Ghana, Kenya, Mali, and Tanzania, and the 'Marxist-Leninists' like Angola, Benin, Congo, Mozambique, and Somalia—the loss of legitimacy was profound."[27] Centrally planned and controlled economies are out, privatization and competition are in, from Moscow to Accra.

Lawrence Freedman has argued that the unipolar model of the post–Cold War world is dubious because "it mistakes the implosion of the Soviet Union for the rise of the United States."[28] A corollary of this argument might be that we risk mistaking the collapse of Communism for the triumph of capitalism. There are at least three reasons why this is so and why it may be premature to assume that US-UN relations will continue to be smoother because the anticapitalist bias has been exorcised.

The first is that Russia and any number of other former Communist states face enormous difficulties effecting the transition to capitalism. By any yardstick, Russia's agenda is, as Michael Mandelbaum claimed, one of staggering proportions, without any close historical parallel.[29] At best it will take a long time, and "along the way the temptation will be considerable to stop, to retreat, to adopt populist remedies for economic hardship, and above all to cast aside governments responsible for the hardship."[30] Failure of this great experiment will have negative consequences not only for Russia but for capitalism, for the Western capitalist states that were unable to provide sufficient and timely assistance, and conceivably for international security.

The second prospective problem with declaring capitalism triumphant is that a great many states in the former Third World are mired in endemic poverty and saddled with demographic, resource, and political problems that make them unpromising candidates even for the most creative infusions of free market principles. Moreover, whereas Russia is assured of at least some Western help with its transition, much of the South, and Africa in particular, seems destined for years of benign neglect. In the words of a French diplomat, "Economically speaking, if the entire black Africa, with the exception of South Africa, were to disappear in a flood, the global cataclysm will be approximately nonexistent."[31] It is inconceivable that these problems will not reappear on the UN agenda and that the discourse will not again become heated. UNCED is an early warning signal that the North-South conflict has not been removed from the UN agenda, and that not everyone is convinced that market allocation is the answer to the problems of the overwhelming majority of the UN membership.

Finally, there is the troublesome fact that the victor in the Cold War and the state that has been the principal model and advocate of free market principles is itself beset with serious economic problems. At the very time that Operation Desert Storm was demonstrating US military prowess, the United States was struggling to cope with an unpleasant fact with important international political and economic consequences: It had become the world's largest debtor nation. Not only does the magnitude of the US debt and its domestic economic malaise deprive Washington of leverage in world affairs. It also tarnishes the victory of capitalism by demonstrating the weakness of its principal model.

By the 1990s, deprecation of market allocation in UN forums had largely been silenced, and for that the United States could be grateful. But it was by no means certain that the old debate would not resurface.

Pluralism

The United States has assumed that pluralism and democracy are intrinsically desirable. It expected the United Nations to reflect that conviction, inasmuch as its primary mission was the preservation of peace, and democratic societies were the least likely to be instigators of violence against their neighbors. But for much of its history, the UN membership was top-heavy with states that were conspicuously undemocratic. Single party rule was common. The private sector was stunted where it was not nonexistent. Mediating structures between the government and the people were typically few and subject to harassment and worse by the government. Not surprisingly, except for support for the principle of self-determination of peoples living under colonial rule, military occupation, and apartheid, these states displayed little interest in democratic principles when confronted with issues that gave them an opportunity to declare themselves.

The situation at the United Nations in the 1990s is, both objectively and from the US point of view, dramatically better. Democracy, like capitalism, is gaining ground. Russia's experiment with democracy after centuries of totalitarian and authoritarian rule has attracted the most attention, but efforts to open up previously closed political systems are under way in many countries on several continents. In addition to the transition from Communist rule in Eastern Europe, the situation has improved in Latin America, where "for the first time in history, elected civilian governments rule every country in Latin America, save one: Cuba,"[32] and in Africa, where "nearly three-fourths of 47 countries south of the Sahara are in various stages of political liberalization."[33]

The trend is impressive, but the soil in which democracy is trying to take root is shallow. As Rosenberg observed, "Latins can now vote in democratic elections every few years, but most still deal with undemocratic courts, police, bureaucracies, and militaries every day."[34] In Africa, in addition to the problem posed by weak and untested political parties, the growth of democratic regimes is handicapped by "the absence of a political culture supportive of effective democracy."[35] This observation about Africa applies also to Russia and other states of the former Soviet Union, which lack the "fertile soil for the cultivation of democracy: tolerance, the willingness to compromise, respect for differing opinions."[36] And the failure of democracy to succeed in Russia can have incomparably greater consequences for the United States and the United Nations.

Nonetheless, the fact that more countries are now becoming more pluralistic and democratic, together with the UN's greater "willingness to put more teeth into some of the human rights norms and standards it has promulgated over the years,"[37] has substantially improved the prospects for improved US-UN relations. The importance of China and Cuba on the UN scene lies in the fact that they seem to represent a rear-guard action against democracy (and capitalism), rather than the wave of the future. The success of the democracy movement is not assured, but the trend is an encouraging one.

Reform, Not Revolution

Another of the US assumptions that affected its view of the United Nations was that the UN would "say no" to radicalism. The United States was not opposed to change per se, and was supportive from the beginning of the UN era to such change-oriented principles as self-determination, but it sought orderly change. The UN would be an agent for reform, both at the state and at the systemic levels, not an advocate of revolution. Here, too, the United States was frequently disappointed in the United Nations, where radical rhetoric, advocating what Washington perceived as radical means to achieve radical ends, was commonplace. This had long been a problem from the US perspective, but it became especially acute in the 1970s and early 1980s; it was not coincidence that the United States lost patience with the global body in the years that followed.

There is much less evidence of the radical impulse at the UN in the 1990s. A softening of rhetoric and the greater willingness to pursue negotiated settlement of difficult and frustrating issues is attributable to many factors: The end of the Cold War; Russia's switch from a policy of confrontation to one of accommodation; movement, however glacial, toward dialogue on the Palestinian and South African issues; marginalization of the more radical "Third World" states in the post–Cold War climate; and a generally more pragmatic approach by more states to more problems after years of heated rhetoric and failed policies.

The United States has itself contributed to the change. For example, President Bush insisted that Israel not intervene in the Gulf War when attacked by Iraqi missiles, orchestrated direct negotiations between Israel and its Arab neighbors, criticized Israel's frequent resort to force in dealing with Palestinian unrest, and—perhaps most significantly—demonstrated his opposition to Israel's policy of building settlements in the occupied territories by withholding for a time $10 billion in loan guarantees. These positions seemed to demonstrate a more even-handed approach to the problems of the Middle East (some have argued that they constituted an anti-Israel policy), and they helped to defuse an issue that had produced some of the angriest debate and, from Washington's point of view, some of the UN's most extreme and unacceptable resolutions.

President Bush had also set a different tone at the UN early in his administration with his selection of Thomas Pickering to serve as the US ambassador there. Vernon Walters had been a welcome change from Jeane Kirkpatrick, whose tenure had been characterized by confrontation and whose manner many had found abrasive. Pickering was an even greater success, a man "viewed by many diplomats and international civil servants as probably the most successful of the 19 people who have represented the

United States at the United Nations since 1946."[38] His relatively quiet, highly professional style had much to do both with the realization of US objectives and the moderation of some of the extreme positions the United States had found so offensive. He has summarized that style, saying that "Our approach has been to ask others, 'Do you want to make a futile gesture, or do you want to look for a compromise that will avoid a veto?' . . . Invariably we've been able to persuade others to work out a resolution we can live with."[39] As with capitalism and democracy, recent trends could easily be reversed. But the 1990s have begun with the UN more interested in reform than in revolution and the United States more interested in the UN as a result.

Preemptive Imperialism

The United States, from the onset of the Cold War, sought to enlist the United Nations in support of its resistance to Soviet expansionism and the spread of international communism. It was modestly successful in the organization's first years, in spite of the Soviet veto, inasmuch as the Soviet Union at the time commanded only a small handful of votes and the concept of nonalignment had not yet been introduced into the political calculus of the General Assembly. But increasingly the membership demonstrated an unwillingness to accept the US assessment of the Soviet threat. To make matters worse, when the United States unilaterally pursued foreign policies designed to counter that threat, the UN was more likely to condemn Washington than Moscow. Preemptive imperialism had no significant constituency at the United Nations.

The end of the Cold War has removed these points of friction. UN observers and peacekeeping forces have been dispatched to virtually every continent to monitor ceasefires, verify troop withdrawal, disarm insurgents, observe elections, and otherwise preserve order and assist the transition to a post–Cold War world. A decade ago, such missions would in most cases have been impossible. There is a temptation to claim that with Soviet imperialism (or what the United States labeled Soviet imperialism) dead, US preemptive imperialism, lacking a raison d'être, is also dead. The possibility remains, however, that some US administration will feel compelled—as the Bush administration did in the case of Panama—to intervene militarily and without the approval of the United Nations in Central America or the Caribbean for reasons unrelated to the communist threat. But for the time being, this is another of the sources of tension that has been rendered moot by systemic developments.

Efficiency, Frugality

There are probably quite a few members of the Congress and even a few officials in the Bureau of International Organization Affairs in the State

Department who would be tempted to agree with the speech given by one of the characters in David Hare's play *A Map of the World*.

> Words! Meaningless words! Reports! So many reports that they boast from New York alone there flow annually United Nations documents, which, laid end to end at the Equator, would stretch four times around the world! Yes! Half a billion pages! And this . . . this week one of the year's seven thousand major UN meetings. With working papers, proposals, counter-proposals, records, summaries. A bureaucracy drowning in its own words and suffocating in its own documents. The wastepaper basket the only instrument of sanity in an otherwise insane organization.[40]

Hare has resorted to hyperbole, but the mood in Washington, and especially on Capitol Hill, has often reflected some of the same frustration. The confrontation with the UN in the 1980s may have had mixed motives, but if there was one lesson most members learned from it, it was that the UN was a poorly managed place. That view persists, even as Washington acknowledges reform, congratulates the UN on its role in the Gulf crisis, and pays arrearages.

The UN's budget is now adopted by consensus, the result of the US pressure that produced General Assembly Resolution 41/213; this means that the United States has a de facto veto over that important document. It exercised that veto in General Assembly consideration of the UN budget for the 1992–1993 biennium. When a budget with 0.9 percent positive real growth was proposed, former Ambassador Pickering insisted that that was not good enough. He argued that such a budget "does not reflect the need to move the organization in new directions. Too much of it appears to be business as usual, maintaining too many of the outdated programs and ineffective secretariat structures of the past."[41] The United States prevailed; the budget ultimately adopted by the General Assembly met the US demand for no growth.

But the US interest in improved management at the UN runs deeper than a cap on budget growth, as Pickering's statement makes clear. As a report in the *Washington Post* on Secretary-General Boutros-Ghali's efforts to streamline the UN secretariat reminds us, "For more than a decade, US administrations have demanded a wholesale cleanup of what they call the United Nations' profligate mismanagement and pork-barrel dispensing of jobs and benefits to the Third World countries that dominate the membership."[42] In the 1980s, a major concern in Washington, especially among conservative members of the Congress, had been Soviet abuse of the international secretariat. By the early 1990s, with a new Secretary-General at the helm, that concern extended to the bureaucracy as a whole and to the need for reform of the personnel system if the UN were to become the lean and efficient organization the United States was determined it should be.

To make sure that the streamlining of the UN Secretariat would not be derailed, President Bush selected his former attorney-general and ex-governor of Pennsylvania, Dick Thornburgh, to serve as the highest-ranking US national in the UN Secretariat in the post of undersecretary-general for administration and management. Thornburgh's appointment, a controversial one,[43] meant that the United States was insistent on occupying the top management post at the UN, when it could have held some other, more political, portfolio. Shortly after assuming his new post, Thornburgh provided a succinct summary of the US position: "It doesn't mean more infusions of huge amounts of financial support," he said, "but doing more with less, stretching resources and enhancing the credibility of the UN so people are more willing to pay arrears."[44]

Insofar as the UN is more frugal and efficient, the change for the better is largely attributable to sustained US pressure rather than to systemic factors. But UN reform is an old issue that has historically produced more ideas and reports than it has significant action, and Washington is far from satisfied. On the other hand, efforts to improve management threaten to reduce opportunities for many of the UN membership to assume positions of influence and prestige in the Secretariat, and the possibility of a revolt by Third World states over the "management issue" cannot be discounted. Efficiency has its costs, as the United States may be reminded in the years ahead.

Elements of National Character

It was suggested in Chapter II that certain elements of the US national character—a tendency to premillennialism, optimism regarding progress, naiveté, and impatience—have influenced the way in which the United States has viewed the United Nations. If the US public sees international relations as a contest between the forces of good and evil, the UN will suffer if it appears to embrace the doctrine of moral equivalence. If they are basically optimistic about progress, the UN will be a source of frustration if it acquires a reputation as an institution that serves as a dumping ground for problems that do not get solved. If the US public is insular and somewhat naive in this understanding of the world, the UN will be both a puzzle and an irritant because it is an assemblage of unfamiliar peoples, driven by widely divergent experiences and needs. If the US public is impatient, the UN will often appear to be a place where talk substitutes for action and where time and energy must too often be invested in what appears to be the unproductive work of multilateral diplomacy.

The US view of the United Nations has been colored by all of these attributes of national character. As with some of the expectations the United States brought to its relationship with the UN, however, time and events have effected some changes.

With the demise of the Soviet Union and the lifting of the threat of Communism, the premillennial struggle between good and evil, which came to be called the Cold War, was over, the forces of evil having been defeated. It is possible that other evils will emerge and rekindle the premillennial impulse, but it is not likely. Saddam Hussein played that role briefly, but he hardly qualifies as a surrogate for the Soviet Union. Neither does Japan; it may be the principal adversary of the United States in the years immediately ahead, but its challenge, although serious, is not ideological and certainly not in a league with that of international Communism.

If the United States displays a certain naiveté about the world beyond its shores, the consequences will presumably be less serious if, with the end of the Cold War, the world is a less dangerous place. The 1992 presidential election campaign suggests that the US public and their political parties were making exactly that assumption, turning away from foreign affairs and focusing their attention on the condition of their own country. That the post–Cold War era will be more benign may, of course, be a mistaken assumption, in which case "the phenomenon of its deaf ear"[45] may again become a problem for the United States. It was certainly a problem in the period prior to the Gulf crisis, when the US government, first in the case of Iran and then in the case of Iraq, displayed its failure to understand the forces at work in the turbulent Gulf region. In the unsettled circumstances of this transitional era, issues are bound to arise and crises to erupt involving states and peoples with which the United States has little familiarity. These issues and crises will find their way to the UN agenda, where US policymakers will be expected to take positions, even as the United States turns inward to address its own problems.

US impatience, so often in evidence with respect to the United Nations, is still an important element of the national character, as George Bush could attest. His approval rating was unprecedentedly high following Operation Desert Storm, but it plummeted sharply in a matter of months, demonstrating the durability of the "what have you done for me lately?" phenomenon. If US impatience with its own president could materialize so quickly after the impressive demonstration of his diplomatic skills and the dramatic triumph of US arms, it seems unlikely that the surge in US support for the UN is secure. In 1990, a Gallup poll found that 54 percent of the US public believed that the United Nations was doing a good job, an impressive 16 percent increase over the previous year.[46] But 1991 and 1992 were less good years for the UN than was 1990. The crisis in what had been Yugoslavia showed the UN once again as indecisive, its words more cautious than they had been in the Gulf crisis, its actions tentative and far short of what was needed to bring a halt to Serbia's mauling of Bosnia. Although there are important differences between Kuwait and Bosnia, and there may be good reason for UN caution, the United Nations, like George Bush, loses some of its luster for those who are impatient for results.

Optimism regarding progress—the notion that change and development are easy and that all good things go together—might seem to be vindicated by the worldwide trend toward market allocation, pluralism, and democracy, not to mention the UN role in the Gulf crisis. But there is considerable evidence that native optimism is becoming a casualty of poor economic performance and chronic political paralysis at home. The 1992 presidential election campaign gave evidence of widespread disillusionment with "the system" and with politics, and barring some dramatic development not now foreseeable, that more pessimistic mood could persist for some time.

Paradoxically, if the UN relationship suffered in the eyes of the US public when the country was optimistic about progress and UN accomplishments were few and far between, it is even more likely to suffer as the national mood turns sour. Optimism creates expectation, which the UN has typically not been able to match; pessimism is likely to be confirmed by what happens (or does not happen) at the United Nations, and in any event tends to promote indifference rather than engagement.

The US-UN Relationship: Four Large Problems

US disenchantment with the United Nations had been eased considerably by the time President Clinton moved into the White House. Many of the sources of US frustration had either disappeared or gone into remission. But four large problems remained. Two of these problems—the frustrated majority and management—are, in effect, current versions of old expectations, alluded to previously but in need of further comment. The third, the issue of intervention, is new, or at least newly salient, and it may well pose the largest challenge to the future of the US-UN relationship. And the fourth, money, is a legacy of the era of UN-bashing by the United States in the 1980s, compounded by the problem of the US budget deficit and efforts to bring it under control.

The Issue of the Frustrated Majority

Historically, one of the principal complaints the United States levied against the United Nations was that it labored under the tyranny of the majority. And after the UN's first few years, the United States was all too often not a member, much less the architect, of that majority. The UN was not congruent with US interests and values.

Recent events would seem to have changed all that. Renewed emphasis on peacekeeping and enforcement in the aftermath of the Cold War has meant the ascendancy of the Security Council, a development much to Washington's liking. The United Nations is once again concentrating on what the United States regards as its primary mission, the maintenance of peace and security. The Security Council is a relatively congenial forum in which the United States can more effectively lead and shape outcomes. And the General Assembly, where incongruence has been most pronounced, has been marginalized.

But the view from Washington is not the view from many of the world's other capitals. The events that have propelled the Security Council to center stage and moved the General Assembly to the wings have had the effect of reducing the great majority of the UN membership to the role of spectators in an organization that is arguably more important to them than it is to the United States. Most of the 180 members of the UN are necessarily excluded from participation in the Council's deliberations; moreover, those deliberations have been dominated by five states, each with a permanent seat and a veto—a state of affairs that strikes many UN members as an anachronism.

The UN's Third World majority seeks increased representation on the Council and revision of the Charter's veto provision, although it is inconceivable that the United States (or the other powers) will countenance significant reform along these lines. But the real problem, from the point of view of the South, is the marginalization of the General Assembly. For these states, the General Assembly is the UN's most important forum, the place where all states participate with equal voice and vote and where issues of primary importance to them, especially those having to do with development, are addressed. The Non-Aligned Movement, meeting in Jakarta in September 1992, issued a call for a more authoritative General Assembly.[47] Although prospects for major reform of the General Assembly may be even less promising than they are for the Security Council, the United States can expect to be confronted there by a testy majority unwilling to quietly accept a diminished role in a UN run like a club by the powers.

The United Nations Conference on Environment and Development, as noted earlier, is illustrative of the problems that persist for the US-UN relationship when the focus shifts to the Third World's agenda and the forum is plenary. Whether the scientific case had been made for the various environmental initiatives on the agenda at UNCED, whether the linkage between measures to protect the environment and at the same time to promote development was in every case persuasive, whether the demands upon the United States (and other developed countries) were balanced and reasonable—the fact remains that the United States found itself the villain of the conference. From the perspective of a great majority of those participating in negotiation of the major UNCED documents,[48] the United States did not display the requisite political will to advance the cause of environmental protection *and* sustainable development.

For the developing countries, UNCED must have invoked a sense of deja vu. They would have been reminded of the dismissive way in which the United States treated efforts to launch a New International Economic Order, refusing to be drawn into what champions of the NIEO liked to refer to as "global bargaining" and effectively gutting such major proposals of the Group of 77 as the Common Fund for Commodities.[49] Or they would have seen a parallel in President Reagan's rejection of the Law of the Sea Treaty, citing its provisions regarding seabed mining, a decision particularly galling to Third World countries because of the constructive role US diplomats had played in negotiating those provisions. The message seemed to be clear: the United States might be the only country capable of driving Saddam Hussein out of Kuwait, but it was not prepared to assume a leadership role on environmental issues and it remained unresponsive to the agenda of developing countries.

UNCED reminds us that the United Nations is about many issues other than peace and security (as traditionally defined), and that what the global majority wants may not in many cases be what the United States is prepared to accept. Ironically, its new-found position of dominance at the UN may portend trouble for the United States. Efforts by a frustrated majority of the UN's 180 members to regain control of the organization and its agenda have the potential to undermine US willingness to work cooperatively with the global organization. UNCED may yet be a more important harbinger of things to come than was Operation Desert Storm.

The Issue of Management

Washington's expectation that the UN be run efficiently and frugally was never more than one of many expectations, and not the most important one, at that. The US concern with what it regarded as fiscal irresponsibility by the United Nations had always been as much of a commentary on UN politics and policies as it had on UN administration. But the exercise of major withholding in the 1980s seems to have produced a much intensified preoccupation with the issue of UN management. A conviction has grown that the United Nations is out of control, that it has become, in Brian Urquhart's words, "an enormous ramshackle structure."[50]

As a result, the US government (with the Congress scrutinizing the results very closely) has zeroed in on the UN bureaucracy, criticizing its size, its composition, its work habits, and its accountability. Charges of mismanagement have focused attention on the office of the Secretary-General, where responsibility for effecting the reforms demanded by the United States resides. Both Boutros-Ghali and his predecessor, Perez de Cuellar, have been under unrelenting pressure by Washington to be what UN Secretaries-General have never been—tough administrators, willing to say "no" to the many vested interests in a multinational secretariat.

Although some progress has been made, the prevailing view is that *much* more needs to be done. In September of 1992, the *Washington Post,* a generally liberal paper not known for animus toward the United Nations, published a series of four feature articles that mounted a scathing critique of mismanagement and even corruption at the UN.[51] It is no secret that the United States, and the Congress in particular, will not be satisfied with a few fewer undersecretaries-general and assistant secretaries-general, a hiring freeze, or the termination of a handful of programs (and their staffs), which have long since outlived their usefulness.

Reform of the magnitude sought by the United States is inevitably extremely unpopular, and will be resisted by an entrenched staff and by governments that view the US position on reform as an attempt to reduce Third World access and influence. Moreover, US expectations in this area and the difficulties certain to be encountered in satisfying them are very likely to place a strain on the relationship between the United States and the Secretary-General.[52] It is no exaggeration to say that the prospects for an amicable US-UN relationship would seem to depend heavily on the outcome of the struggle over management of the global body.

The Issue of Intervention

Iraq's invasion of Kuwait provided the occasion for a dramatic demonstration of what the United Nations could do with US leadership and what the United States could do with UN support. Subsequent events, including those within Iraq since the conclusion of Operation Desert Storm, the human tragedy in Somalia, and most particularly the violent collapse of Yugoslavia, tell a rather different story. For those who believed that the Gulf crisis and its handling by the UN and the US-led coalition heralded the dawn of a new post–Cold War international order, the difficulties encountered in these subsequent crises have led to sober second thoughts.

For all of their differences, these crises have had two common threads. In the first place, in none of them has the United States been convinced that its vital interests are at stake, at least not to the degree that they were (or were alleged to be) when Saddam Hussein invaded Kuwait. The result is that US leadership has been less assured. In the second, all of these crises have unfolded, in whole or in part, within rather than between states. This has meant more than a little ambivalence at the United Nations, given the domestic jurisdiction barrier of Article 2 (7) and the general reluctance to set precedents for military intervention in the affairs of sovereign states. The fact that in all three cases the UN Security Council has authorized intervention, albeit cautiously and in deliberately limited ways, and that the United States has ultimately and without enthusiasm assumed leadership responsibilities, does not alter the fact that both the United Nations and the United States have set out with some anxiety across unfamiliar terrain. Not surprisingly, in each of these cases there has been at least the hint of trouble in the US-UN relationship.

As noted in Chapter V, US intervention in northern Iraq to provide security for the Kurds was undertaken reluctantly, and UN support for that intervention was equally reluctant and tentative. The members of the Security Council were well aware that there was a significant qualitative difference between authorizing enforcement against an aggressor state and restricting the state's freedom of action against segments of its own population. The ambivalence surrounding intervention in Iraq, as well as the latent tensions between the United Nations and the United States over that issue, surfaced again in the waning days of the Bush administration when the United States launched air attacks on Iraq in enforcement of no-fly zones designed to protect Kurds and Shiites against the Baghdad regime. Although the United States claimed that its position was consistent with and in defense of Security Council resolutions, the no-fly zones had never been authorized by the Council and several of its members had serious reservations about the US actions. Although US-UN cooperation did not break down over this issue, it was clear that the Council was having second thoughts about allowing the United States to interpret its resolutions as it saw fit, especially in so sensitive an area as humanitarian intervention.

Somalia provided another test case of the US-UN relationship, and once again the issue was humanitarian intervention. That tortured country had turned into something of a public relations disaster for the UN, and the Secretary-General was arguing vigorously for intervention on a scale that would ensure the delivery of food to a starving population. Eventually the United States, presumably driven by photographic evidence of the human tragedy in Somalia and President Bush's desire to leave office on a positive note, did intervene militarily.

The result was one the UN wanted (the Security Council promptly endorsed the US action),[53] but the form it took made many members uncomfortable. Once again, as with Operation Desert Storm, the UN had turned control of a UN-authorized military mission over to the United States. The US government was no more willing in Somalia than it had been in Iraq to place its troops under a UN command. Almost immediately after the launching of Operation Restore Hope, the US government and the Secretary-General became embroiled in controversy over responsibility for disarming Somalia gangs and the conditions that would justify a US decision to withdraw troops and turn the task of providing security over to UN peacekeepers.

Although the UN decision for humanitarian intervention in Somalia was simplified somewhat by the fact that there was no effective central government in Mogadishu, it was still a difficult and precedent-setting one. The Council's resolution marked the first time the UN had intervened in the internal affairs of a sovereign state with a mandate to use force other than in self-defense. Whereas this constituted a welcome expansion of UN authority for some, it looked very much like a slippery slope to others. Either way, it constituted a major test of the capacity of the United Nations and the United States to work cooperatively together.

Bosnia has proved to be an even more difficult case than either Iraq or Somalia. When fighting originally broke out in Yugoslavia, UN members, the United States included, saw no reason to intervene. It was, after all, civil strife, and too many states had their own problems with ethnic groups desirous of autonomy or independence. Moreover, it was widely understood that the deep-seated animosities among the ethnic groups and the inhospitable terrain would make intervention a costly and precarious proposition. The situation was transformed when the United Nations recognized Slovenia, Croatia, and Bosnia. As of that date, the UN was confronted not only with civil war but with aggression by Serbia in support of ethnic Serbs in sovereign states now members of the United Nations.

But intervention still looked like a hazardous undertaking to the Security Council, in considerable measure because that is the way it looked to both the United States and the European Community. The measures that were adopted by the UN failed either to end the fighting or to arrest the spread of Serbian nationalism at the expanse of Croatians and Muslims. The arms embargo imposed by the Council in September 1991 actually benefited the Serbs;[54] the peacekeeping mission to Croatia, approved in February 1992, had the effect of acknowledging Serb gains in the war;[55] and the UN relief effort in Bosnia, buffeted by the battle raging around Sarajevo, was unable to relieve the misery of that city's Muslim defenders.

By the winter of 1992–1993 it was apparent that the UN was failing even in its limited mission. Bosnian Muslims were still being raped, slaughtered, and forcibly driven from their homes and villages by Serbs. The policy of "ethnic cleansing" had largely succeeded; the state of Bosnia-Herzegovina bore little resemblance to the Yugoslav republic that had so recently declared its independence. The UN presence in the region not only had almost no bearing on the progress of the war; it had become a major argument against enforcement of the Council-mandated no-fly zones, the British and French fearing that their troops would become targets of Serbian retaliation.

In spite of differences with its allies and other key members of the Security Council throughout the crisis, the United States was at no point more eager to become embroiled militarily in the region than they were. Unlike Somalia, Bosnia did not appear to be "doable." Late in his administration, President Bush did launch a brief diplomatic offensive aimed at obtaining broad international support for the use of air power in support of relief efforts; but nothing came of it, and within a matter of weeks the

Clinton administration was reluctantly pursuing a diplomatic settlement not vastly different from the one put forward by Cyrus Vance (for the UN) and David Owen (for the EC),[56] a settlement that essentially accepted the triumph of Serbian arms as a regrettable fait accompli.

The crisis in Yugoslavia, already a sobering reminder of the constraints under which the United Nations will work in the post–Cold War world, has the capacity to become considerably worse, especially if the conflict spreads to Kosovo or Macedonia. The prospect of a wider Balkan war, conceivably involving Bulgaria, Turkey, and Greece, is a major concern in both Washington and New York, and is probably the one event that could generate support for major military intervention on the ground. In the meanwhile, President Clinton for the first time was seriously considering US air strikes against Serb positions.

Whatever the final outcome, the UN involvement in the Balkan crisis, together with its role in the crises in Somalia and Iraq, has already demonstrated the problems and uncertainties that lie ahead for the US-UN relationship in the disorderly post–Cold War world. The credibility of the UN's newfound but still very tentative vocation for humanitarian intervention within sovereign states, and indeed the credibility of the UN itself, has become hostage to events in Iraq, Somalia, and Bosnia. The success of those interventions has, in turn, become heavily dependent on US policy. And there is every reason to believe that these crises are but the forerunners of others that will further challenge both the capacity and the will of the United Nations and the United States to deal with them in a forceful and timely manner. It takes no great stretch of the imagination to recognize that therein lies a potential minefield for the US-UN relationship.

The Issue of Money

Each of these issues—the frustrated UN majority, United Nations management, and humanitarian intervention—has financial implications. Each raises questions that carry a price tag, and they all come at a time when the United States still has unpaid arrearages at the UN and is still running a huge deficit at home. Even if the US government did not have to worry about renewed pressures from a restless UN majority, limited and halting steps to reform UN management practices, and the dilemma posed for the UN by the human costs of ethnic and tribal conflict in an ever-growing number of states, budgetary considerations would create problems for US policy at the UN. Those issues simply exacerbate the situation.

The United States will be no more eager in the 1990s to fund UN programs it opposes than it was when it was so heavily engaged in UN-bashing in the 1980s. And it is by no means certain that the UN's disaffected majority will exercise restraint in pushing for such programs. If the

Secretary-General does not address the management issue in a manner acceptable to the United States, it is not inconceivable the UN critics in Washington will again demand the withholding of assessments. As for the interventions in conflict-ridden countries around the world, which the UN has recently undertaken and will probably be under pressure to undertake in the future, the issue of cost is an increasingly urgent one. The UN missions in Yugoslavia and Somalia, like the ones begun earlier in Cambodia and Lebanon, are relatively large, appear destined to last longer than anticipated, and cannot be assured of success. Such missions, which are already controversial, inevitably generate financial problems while they fail to solve political ones. Inasmuch as the United States pays by far the largest share of peacekeeping costs (30.29 percent under a special scale of assessments), the potential for trouble in the US-UN relationship grows in direct proportion to the US perception that the UN is overextended and its peacekeeping missions ineffectual.

Independently of the problems posed by these clouds over US-UN cooperation, the US budget deficit and the country's preoccupation with domestic problems constitute an obstacle to the resumption of vigorous US leadership at the United Nations. The United States has resumed payment of its full share of the UN budget,[57] and has been systematically reducing its arrearages in both the regular and peacekeeping accounts. But Washington is not exactly approaching the UN with an open wallet. The Congress has insisted on a full accounting from the State Department of the proposed use of US contributions, a position that reflects the perennial struggle between the two branches of government and creates the possibility of delays in payments.[58] Moreover, the United States still refuses to pay its assessments at the beginning of the calendar year, thereby contributing significantly to chronic liquidity problems at the UN. The United States rejects the Secretary-General's proposal to charge interest on unpaid assessments after sixty days, and otherwise expresses little sympathy with the argument that financial solvency is a major problem for the UN.

The constraints imposed by efforts to reduce the budget deficit and address public dissatisfaction with neglected issues on the home front have made it difficult for the government to match its words of praise for the UN with significant infusions of money. The Bush administration did seek $700 million as the US contribution to a contingency fund for peacekeeping, to be paid in two tranches in 1992 and 1993.[59] These monies would certainly help to make the UN's expanding role in this field more credible, and former Secretary of State Baker testified that it was "a good buy," arguing that the United States "should be willing to invest in 'keeping the peace' after having spent considerably greater sums to win the Cold War."[60] But congressional approval has been conspicuously reluctant, except when vital US interests are at stake, and there has been mounting pressure in the

Congress to cut the US contribution for UN peacekeeping forces back to 25 percent.[61]

It seems likely that the United States will continue to pursue a policy of low, slow, or even no growth for the UN budget. Such an approach may look prudent in Washington, but it will not win friends at the UN. For the great majority of the UN membership, the United Nations is underfunded relative to the scale and scope of their needs, and much of the problem is the lack of political will on the part of the organization's largest power. There is every likelihood that the UN's financial difficulties and the issue of US responsibility for them and leadership in resolving them will continue to complicate the US-UN relationship for the foreseeable future.

Conclusion

After forty years of frustrated expectations regarding the United Nations, the United States mounted a vigorous attack on the global organization in the 1980s. Members of the administration and of the Congress minced no words in characterizing the UN as a badly, if not fatally, flawed institution, which was not serving US interests or reflecting US values. The leverage of financial withholding available to the country paying the largest percentage of the UN budget was used to coerce the UN to "reform," but there was no guarantee that reform measures adopted by the UN would satisfy the United States or that the world's most powerful state would then be willing to resume a proactive leadership role at the UN.

Only a few years later, in the wake of Saddam Hussein's invasion and occupation of Kuwait, the United States was busily engaged in mobilizing support in the UN Security Council for a strong international response to this act of aggression. The result was a rare demonstration of UN-sanctioned enforcement action against a state found to be in violation of the Charter. It was also a remarkable reversal of the US relationship with the UN. The United States, so recently engaged in hectoring the UN when it was not dismissing it as irrelevant to the conduct of US foreign policy, was now eagerly embracing it and proclaiming its importance to an emerging new world order in which the crisis in the Gulf was the first test.

Was this about-face by the United States an aberration or was it the beginning of a new era in US-UN relations? Innate skepticism tends, of course, to discount the second and more optimistic of these views. But many of the expectations the United States had for the UN and the UN so often disappointed are now either being realized or are no longer important because of fundamental systemic changes. In effect, the UN does much better on the litmus test of US expectations today than it has in many long years, and this has to provide grounds for cautious optimism regarding the future of US-UN relations.

As we have seen, democracy and capitalism command new adherents and new respect, and that fact is beginning to have its effect at the UN. The United States need no longer worry about UN tolerance for Soviet adventurism or the spread of Communism, or about UN criticism of US efforts to contain them. The collapse of the Soviet Union and of Communism, together with progress elsewhere in dealing with heretofore intractable problems, has led to a lessening at the UN of radical rhetoric and revolutionary proposals for solving those problems. The right of the United States to opt out of compliance with UN resolutions of which it disapproves remains intact and actually has been strengthened. Politicization in the UN system is less of a problem for the United States than it has been in many years. All of this means that congruence between US preferences and UN prescriptions is today the norm in many issue areas. The United States is now acknowledged as the world's overwhelmingly dominant military power, and in that sense at least the United States can claim the role of hegemon. And although the international system is still in a state of flux after the end of the Cold War, the outlines of a crude new status quo can be ascertained, and it is one the United States finds congenial.

In all of these respects, US assumptions as to what the UN should be and what it should do are now being borne out—if not in their entirety, at least to much greater extent than was the case during much of the UN's history and particularly during the period of maximum confrontation in the early and mid-1980s. Balanced against this catalog of promising developments are a few negatives and some cautionary observations both about the United Nations and about the United States.

US hegemony is at best partial and at worst nonexistent. The world is not truly unipolar, and Japan and Germany (or Europe) are now powerful enough, especially in the absence of a Soviet threat to keep them in harness with the United States, to play increasingly independent roles on the world stage. The implications of this for the US-UN relationship are not clear and may not soon be apparent; what is clear, however, is that the United States is approaching the assumption of the hegemon's burden at the UN in a most tentative fashion.

Moreover, several of the positive signs in the US-UN relationship are based on trends that are both brief and thin. Hopes for the success of experiments with free markets and private ownership could easily be dashed in any of several places, including Russia. Most of the newly pluralistic and democratic states are fragile and vulnerable to the forces of reaction. Unfortunately, change and development are *not* easy, and all good things do *not* necessarily go together. And so it goes, through a litany of caveats regarding the prospects for a prolonged US-UN honeymoon.

The four most serious threats to the US commitment to give the United Nations a prominent place in the conduct of its foreign policy, however, are those outlined earlier in this chapter:

- The prospect that the great majority of the UN membership will feel "disenfranchised" by the marginalization of the General Assembly and the domination of the Security Council by a condominium of the powers, and that the majority will pursue policies designed to correct that condition
- The prospect that reform of the Secretariat and of UN management practices will be superficial, resulting in the perpetuation of irrelevant or redundant programs and activities that reflect vested interests in the bureaucracy and wastefully consume budget resources
- The prospect that the UN response to escalating crises and conflicts in troubled countries around the world will put the United States and the United Nations at cross purposes as to the wisdom of intervention; responsibility for such interventions as are authorized; and the nature, scale, timing, and financial underwriting of those interventions
- The prospect that the US preoccupation with domestic problems, coupled with the size of its own budget deficit, will mean that UN claims upon the US treasury will encounter stiff resistance, especially from Congress.

There are many who see the post–Cold War, post–Gulf War period as a window of opportunity. International officials, governments, nongovernmental organizations, academics, and others have been generating papers and proposals designed to take advantage of that opportunity. The Summit Meeting of the Security Council, held in January 1992, was in itself an acknowledgment that this is a singularly important moment in modern history. In a report requested of him by that summit meeting, UN Secretary-General Boutros-Ghali said:

> In these past months a conviction has grown, among nations large and small, that an opportunity has been regained to achieve the great objectives of the Charter—a United Nations capable of maintaining international peace and security, of securing justice and human rights and of promoting, in the words of the Charter, "social progress and better standards of life in larger freedom." This opportunity must not be squandered. The organization must never again be crippled as it was in the era that has now passed.[62]

Whether the opportunity is squandered and the organization crippled will depend on many factors, some of them beyond the capacity of an organization of limited authority in a turbulent world of sovereign states to manage. This author does not particularly care for the concept of "political will," a phrase that has been bandied about for many years to express the frustration of the UN majority with the failure of some state or states (often the United States) to do what the majority wants it to do. What has been castigated as a lack of political will is usually something else—a fundamental policy disagreement with the majority's agenda. But at this particular juncture in the UN's history, the exercise of a little political will by the United States is very much in order.

A window of opportunity does exist. The permanent members of the Security Council have established an unusual degree of rapport and are, in the words of Lexington in *The Economist,* "Justly proud of what they, with the Secretary-General's people, have done to help sort out the messes in Afghanistan, South Africa–Namibia–Angola–Cuba, Iraq-Iran and now Kuwait-Iraq."[63] Japan and Germany, stung by criticism of their performance in the Gulf crisis, are looking for ways to make constructive contributions to a stronger UN without shedding constraints on the use of their militaries abroad. The great majority of UN members from the South have lowered their voices and are, on the whole, approaching issues pragmatically, not ideologically. The Secretary-General has made not inconsiderable headway in the difficult task of streamlining the UN bureaucracy. Various issues that could blossom into crises or raise the temperature of debate are still over the horizon, although the disaster in the Balkans provides a troubling glimpse into the future.

The time is propitious for the United States to assume leadership, not case by case, as in the Gulf crisis and Somalia, but on a sustaining basis. It could begin by acting on legislation introduced by Senator Paul Simon (D-Ill.), which would transfer the US cost of UN peacekeeping from the international affairs segment of the federal budget to the national defense segment, that is, from the State Department's budget to the Pentagon's.[64] This would be an acknowledgment that UN endeavors in this field may now be an important contribution to the nation's defense and, given the relative size of the two budgets, it just might make it easier for the Congress to treat these UN expenses as a modest investment in national security rather than as an exorbitant claim on the treasury.

It is important that the United States rediscover the habit of leadership at the UN. It demonstrated in the Gulf crisis what can be done if it is prepared to make the effort. If its leaders are not prepared to give serious thought to the content of a new world order and to the place of the United Nations in that order, the US-UN relationship will almost certainly slide back into a rut. That relationship is unlikely to be as strained as it was in the 1980s, the rut not as deep. But it will be an opportunity missed. Moreover, the failure of US leadership could easily contribute to the realienation of the UN membership, especially if the United States is perceived as interested only in trimming the UN budget and bureaucracy without advancing a positive vision of the organization's role in world affairs.

It will not be easy to convert the recent experience of US-UN cooperation into something more ambitious and more enduring. The government still has major policy disagreements with the majority of UN member states and there are those, such as former UN ambassador Jeane Kirkpatrick, who resent Boutros-Ghali's activist interpretation of the Secretary-General's role and are once again girding for confrontation with the global body.[65] There is a concern that some problems on the UN's agenda, such as the crisis in Bosnia, are a kind of quicksand, to be approached with extreme caution. The Congress continues to be sensitive about its prerogatives, especially where appropriations are concerned, and until the US budget deficit has been brought under control, the second branch of government is likely to be hypervigilant where spending on the UN is concerned. And the national preoccupation with domestic malaise works against the development of a forward-looking approach to the United Nations.

The cooperation between the United States and the United Nations in the Gulf crisis, so widely heralded so recently, provides a foundation on which to build. It may not have been a textbook example of collective security, but it was a good example of creative problem solving under the pressure of events by both the United States and the UN Security Council. It would be unfortunate if it were allowed to become an isolated example of cooperation between the global organization and its most important member.

Notes

1. John Newhouse, "The Diplomatic Round (Change at the United Nations)," *New Yorker,* Dec. 16, 1991, p. 90.

2. *New York Times,* Mar. 7, 1991, p. A8.

3. David Gergen, "America's Missed Opportunities," *Foreign Affairs* 71, 1 (America and the World 1991/92), p. 1.

4. By the end of 1992, UN membership had reached 180.

5. Stephen D. Krasner, *Structural Conflict,* Berkeley: University of California Press, 1985, p. 1.

6. William J. Perry, "Desert Storm and Deterrence," *Foreign Affairs* 70, 4 (Fall 1991), p. 66.

7. Ibid., p. 81.

8. See provisions on deep seabed mining in United Nations Convention on the Law of the Sea, Part XI.

9. Walter Wriston, "Technology and Sovereignty," *Foreign Affairs* 67, 5, (Winter 1988/89), p. 865.

10. Ibid., pp. 70–71.

11. Lawrence Freedman, "Order and Disorder in the New World," *Foreign Affairs* 71, 1 (America and the World 1991/92), p. 25.

12. An exception occurred in East Pakistan, which broke away and became Bangladesh with India's military assistance and the rest of the world's acquiescence. Collective fear of the consequences of reopening colonial boundary issues was particularly strong among African states.

13. See, for example, John Mearsheimer, "Why We Shall Soon Miss the Cold War," *Atlantic Monthly,* August 1990, pp. 51–61.

14. Charles Krauthammer, "The Unipolar Movement," *Foreign Affairs* 70, 1 (America and the World 1990/91).

15. William Pfaff, "Redefining World Power," *Foreign Affairs* 70, 1 (America and the World 1990/91), p. 34.

16. See Chapter II, note 2.

17. Krauthammer, "The Unipolar Movement," p. 24.

18. Joseph S. Nye, Jr., "What New World Order?" *Foreign Affairs* 71, 2 (Spring 1992), p. 88.

19. Quoted in *Washington Weekly Report,* XVII-10, March 27, 1992.

20. The December 16, 1991, decision and the US reaction to it are summarized in *Washington Weekly Report,* XVII-40, December 17, 1991.

21. Freedman, "Order and Disorder in the New World," p. 21.

22. John Lewis Gaddis, "Toward the Post–Cold War World," *Foreign Affairs* 70, 2 (Spring 1991), p. 113.

23. Stanley Hoffmann, "A New World and Its Troubles," *Foreign Affairs* 69, 4 (Fall 1990), p. 118.

24. Miles Kahler, "The International Political Economy," *Foreign Affairs* 69, 4 (Fall 1990), p. 149.

25. See Yoichi Funabashi, "Japan and the New World Order," *Foreign Affairs* 70, 5 (Winter 1991/92).

26. Krasner, *Structural Conflict.*

27. Carol Lancaster, "Democracy in Africa," *Foreign Policy* 85 (Winter 1991/92), p. 152.

28. Freedman, "Order and Disorder in the New World," p. 26.

29. Michael Mandelbaum, "The End of the Soviet Union," *Foreign Affairs* 71, 1 (America and the World 1991/92), pp. 178–179.

30. Ibid., p. 178.

31. Quoted in Michael Chege, "Remembering Africa," *Foreign Affairs* 71, 1 (America and the World 1991/92), p. 148.

32. Tina Rosenberg, "Beyond Elections," *Foreign Policy* 84 (Fall 1991), p. 72. Since that article was written, Haiti's elected government was overthrown.

33. Lancaster, "Democracy in Africa," p. 148.

34. Rosenberg, "Beyond Elections," p. 72.

35. Lancaster, "Democracy in Africa," pp. 156–157.

36. Mandelbaum, "The End of the Soviet Union," p. 177.

37. John Tessitore and Susan Woolfson, eds., *A Global Agenda: Issues Before the 46th General Assembly of the United Nations,* Lanham, Md.: University Press of America, 1991, p. 171.

38. *New York Times,* November 19, 1991, p. A19.

39. Ibid.

40. David Hare, *A Map of the World,* London: Faber and Faber, 1982, p. 67.

41. Quoted in *Washington Weekly Report,* XVII-35, November 1, 1991.

42. *Washington Post,* February 12, 1992, p. A27.

43. See the comments of former UN Undersecretary General Ronald Spiers, *New York Times,* February 28, 1992, p. A15.

44. *New York Times,* March 30, 1992, p. A15.

45. Ali Mazrui, "Uncle Sam's Hearing Aid," in Sanford J. Ungar, ed., *Estrangement,* New York: Oxford University Press, 1985, pp. 179–192.

46. Jeffrey Laurenti, *American Public Opinion and the United Nations,* UNA-USA Occasional Papers, New York: UNA-USA, 1992, pp. 19–20.

47. William Branigan, "The U.N. Empire: How to Fix It? (North and South Stand Worlds Apart on Reform)," *Washington Post,* September 23, 1992, pp. A1, 32.

48. The documents that were the focus of UNCED were the framework convention on climate change; a convention on biological diversity; the so-called Rio Declaration on Environment and Development; Agenda 21 (a voluntary action plan for the twenty-first century); and a non–legally binding authoritative statement of principles for a global consensus on the management, conservation, and sustainable development of all types of forest. The United States signed the convention on climate change (in which no timetables or targets were set), but did not sign the biological diversity convention.

49. For an analysis of the Common Fund concept and negotiations, see Robert Rothstein, *Global Bargaining: UNCTAD and the Quest for the New International Economic Order,* Princeton, N.J.: Princeton University Press, 1979.

50. Quoted in William Branigan, "The U.N. Empire: Polished Image, Tarnished Reality (As U.N. Expands, So Do Its Problems)," *Washington Post,* September 20, 1992, p. A26.

51. William Branigan, "The U.N. Empire," *Washington Post,* September 20, 21, 22, and 23, 1992.

52. For perhaps the best account of the problems a Secretary-General (or any executive head) has in effecting change within the bureaucracy, see Robert W. Cox, "The Executive Head: An Essay on Leadership in International Organization," in *International Organization* 23 (Spring 1969).

53. SC Res. 794, December 3, 1992.

54. SC Res. 713, September 25, 1991.

55. SC Res. 743, February 21, 1992.

56. The Vance-Owen proposal called for ten autonomous provinces in Bosnia under a weak central government. Serbs would retain control of more than 40 percent of the land and three of the ten provinces; heavy weapons would be stored under UN supervision and 25,000 UN peacekeepers would be deployed; and ethnic cleansing would cease and human rights would be respected.

57. The United States still withholds monies from specific items in the UN's budget, such as the US share of the Law of the Sea Preparatory Commission (executive decision) and activities supportive of the PLO (legislative mandate).

58. See *Washington Weekly Report* (UNA-USA) for a running account of this struggle.

59. Ibid., XVIII-11, April 3, 1992. The first tranche of $270 million was included in the continuing appropriations resolution for foreign aid, which ended the standoff between the president and the Congress over the issue of providing Israel with $10 billion in housing loan guarantees with which to absorb new immigrants from the former Soviet Union and Eastern Europe.

60. Ibid., XVIII-7, March 6, 1992.

61. Ibid., XVIII-10, March 27, 1992. Congressmen Tom Lantos (D-Cal.) and Henry Hyde (R-Ill.) have led this move to cut the US contribution for peacekeeping forces.

62. Boutros Boutros-Ghali, *An Agenda for Peace,* Report of the Secretary-General pursuant to the statement adopted by the Summit Meeting of the Security Council on January 31, 1992, United Nations, 1992 (DPI/1247).

63. Lexington, *The Economist,* March 2, 1991, p. 32.

64. *Washington Weekly Report,* XVIII-18, June 11, 1992.

65. Jeane Kirkpatrick, "Boutros-Ghali's Power Grab," *Washington Post,* Feb. 1, 1993, p. A19.

Index

About the Book and the Author

In the wake of Iraq's occupation of Kuwait in the summer of 1990, the United States assiduously courted the support of the international community for a policy of sanctions and later of military action against Iraq. The primary venue for that successful diplomatic effort was the UN Security Council; in effect, the United States made the United Nations a critically important pillar of its foreign policy, and in the process helped to give the UN the most favorable press it had had in years.

This is a situation rich in irony, for it was but a few short years ago that the United States treated the UN with ill-disguised contempt. During the Reagan administration, US-UN relations reached a 40-year nadir, yet under George Bush, these relations were very nearly euphoric. There was a dramatic about-face in US policy.

Telling the story of this policy reversal, *About Face?* looks in depth at the period of UN bashing in the 1980s and the courtship of the UN in 1990 and analyzes the forces that produced first one and then the other of these latest phases in the tumultuous US-UN relationship. The book concludes with a critique of the thesis that, with the Cold War over and collective security rediscovered, the UN will at last assume the role envisioned for it by the founders and the United States will find in the UN a congenial vehicle for the pursuit of its foreign policy objectives.

Robert W. Gregg is professor of international relations in The American University's School of International Studies.